1993

SOCIAL POLICY

A Feminist Analysis

GILLIAN PASCALL

Tavistock Publications
LONDON AND NEW YORK

First published in 1986 by
Tavistock Publications Ltd
11 New Fetter Lane, London EC4P 4EE

Published in the USA by
Tavistock Publications
in association with Methuen, Inc.
29 West 35th Street, New York, NY 10001

© 1986 Gillian Pascall

Typeset by Rowland Phototypesetting Ltd,
Bury St Edmunds, Suffolk
and printed by
Richard Clay (The Chaucer Press),
Bungay, Suffolk

British Library Cataloguing in
Publication Data

Pascall, Gillian.
Social policy: a feminist analysis.
1. Great Britain – Social policy
I. Title
361.6'1'0941   HN390

ISBN 0-422-78660-8
ISBN 0-422-78670-5 Pbk

Library of Congress Cataloging in
Publication Data

Pascall, Gillian.
Social policy.

Bibliography: p.
Includes index.
1. Great Britain – Social policy.
2. Feminism – Great Britain.
3. Women – Great Britain – Social
conditions.   4. Welfare state.
I. Title.
HN385.5.P37   1986   361.6'1'0941
86-6021

ISBN 0-422-78660-8
ISBN 0-422-78670-5 (pbk.)

Contents

1

Social Policy –
A Feminist Critique

Women in social policy

Perhaps the most striking claim in feminist analysis of social policy is that it is impossible to understand the Welfare State without understanding how it deals with women. According to Elizabeth Wilson, 'only an analysis of the Welfare State that bases itself on a correct understanding of the position of women in modern society can reveal the full meaning of modern welfarism' (Wilson 1977: 59).

Feminist analysis is most obviously about putting women in where they have been left out, about keeping women on the stage rather than relegating them to the wings. But to do this suggests questions about the structures that have left women out; about the way academic disciplines work; about language, concepts, methods, approaches, and subject areas. Such a quest leads to a profound rethinking. What we should have at the end of such an investigation of social policy is a new understanding, not only of the way the Welfare State deals with women, but also of social policy itself. To suggest that there is such a thing as a 'feminist social policy' to put in the place of other traditions would be to claim too much. For one thing, it would do violence to the variety of perspectives held by women working and writing in this area; for another, it would suggest a completed task, and the possibility of a finished text. I propose only to claim that feminist thinking poses an important challenge to current orthodoxy, and to give some indications of its main directions.

The task of this chapter is to look (briefly) at the main traditions of social policy writing, to try to explain why these traditions neglect issues and analyses which are now commonplace in the women's movement; to ask whether approaches to welfare dominant in the 1980s are any more receptive to feminist understandings of the Welfare State than approaches developed in the 1940s. Finally, I aim to give some indication of the shift of ground and perspective that current feminist thinking involves. This will involve a brief preview of themes that will emerge throughout the book.

There is now a fairly extensive feminist literature in social policy. The first question may be to ask how far feminist writing on social policy has penetrated the mainstream. My conclusion is that it has not yet done so in a significant way. Textbooks may now have the odd remarks about women, but on the whole these amount to adding women in, rather than rethinking the nature of welfare or the nature of social policy writing. The lack is perhaps most striking in those volumes which attempt to review theoretical perspectives on welfare. None of the recent texts in this area (Room 1979; Mishra 1977; Taylor-Gooby 1981) show feminism as a distinct approach to welfare. Few social policy texts, apart from specifically feminist ones, have more than passing reference either to issues as they affect women or to the way in which feminists have analysed welfare (Ginsburg 1979 has half a chapter; Gough 1979, a few pages; Townsend 1979 has a section on mothers alone; Jones 1978 has a few references to 'sex equality'), though there is a new journal, *Critical Social Policy*, which aims to give space to feminist writing. My point in this chapter is not to carp at individuals (because we have all been subject to the same influences); it is rather to ask about the various traditions, and to ask whether they are, in fact, for various reasons, inimical to feminist thought.

The lack of a specifically feminist analysis within the main traditions is partly a matter of political history. The main period of establishment and growth for social administration departments was the post-war era. This started a particularly barren period for feminism, when sociology began to reflect a cosy view of family life and social policy concerned itself with pressing women back into its confines. Traditions of social administration that were born in this climate of the 1940s did not have a vigorous feminist movement to draw on (but, as we shall see later, there was some critical writing which they failed to notice) and feminism as a political movement did not re-emerge until the late 1960s. However, in its re-emergence feminism has taken social policy as a major part of its work. This is true in a practical context, in the refuge movement, in the political context, for example in issues about abortion and cohabitation, and in the academic context, where there is now a considerable feminist literature about women and welfare. A unifying theme of these feminist critiques of social policy has been an analysis of the Welfare State in relation to the family: as supporting relations of dependency within families; as putting women into caring roles; and as controlling the work of reproduction. This chapter will argue that this analysis presents a challenge which none of the major traditions of social administration has been able to meet at all adequately (though each fails for different reasons).

Feminist critiques and the academic disciplines

The feminist challenge extends over the range of existing academic 'disciplines'. Feminist historians and literary critics, for example, are asking what has happened to the history and writing of women, and about the approaches which have obscured them. But it seems particularly pertinent to make a feminist critique in those subject areas – like social administration and sociology – where gender hierarchy is marked. For while there are 'female' subjects from the student point of view, there are no 'female' subjects in terms of institutional hierarchies. In many departments predominantly female students confront approaches and subject areas carved out by men. The experience may well be alienating.

It is worth illustrating some of the challenges a feminist critique makes to the fabric of academic subjects in their established form, with special reference here to the social sciences. These issues are discussed at more length in *Doing Feminist Research* (Roberts 1981), *Men's Studies Modified* (Spender 1981), and *Theories of Women's Studies* (Bowles and Klein 1983). To begin with, there is language. 'The farmer wants a wife', we sing; never 'The farmer wants a husband'. The language has no way of reversing the first statement or of equalizing the partners to indicate women's agricultural work. Busily, the statisticians follow. Head of household: farmer; other members of household: wife and two children; 'economic activity' of women: nil. Ideas of women's dependency are thus built into language use, and are operationalized by those who draw the world for us.

New terminology is not necessarily an improvement. A major area of empirical study of women's lives in social administration hides under the title 'one-parent families'. The term suggests that single motherhood and single fatherhood can be lumped together. The studies cannot help showing that gender counts more than single parenthood. But the attempt to 'legitimize' single mothers under the umbrella 'families' also disguises the fact that most such 'families' are female-headed, and that an overwhelming factor in their situation is lack of a male wage. It also affects the publication of statistics and the design of research. Most work about women in social administration hides within other categories. 'Elderly' and 'disabled' people, for example, are predominantly women. This is not to imply that men who fall into such categories are unimportant; rather, that gender plays a large part in the situation of all these groups, and that the way we use language tends to obscure this.

The language of social policy is littered with words that need examining from a feminist point of view. 'Unemployment' belongs to a male working life rather than a female one (see pp. 210–11). 'Households' and 'families' are units of analysis in which women's particular interests are often submerged. The assailants of 'battered women' may be rather obviously male, but the gender of the perpetrators of 'child abuse' is not obvious; neither is the gender of the recipients of 'family therapy'.

From the most everyday language of 'the farmer and his wife' to the most elaborately worked out concepts of sociological analysis these difficulties are ingrained. Feminist concern has focused on the most commonly applied tool of sociological analysis – the occupational scale, usually taken to represent 'social class'. In numerous official statistics and social surveys households are classified according to the occupation of their male 'head'. Thus single women tend to be classified according to their own occupation, but as soon as they are married they are classified according to that of their husband. This classification may continue even into widowhood.

One effect is to make women's occupations disappear. Attempting to use the usual tools, such as the *Registrar General's Classification of Occupations* for women's jobs shows how unimportant women's occupations are deemed to be. Whereas this classification scheme grades and distinguishes men's jobs in the most detailed way, it is a very blunt instrument for typically female jobs: for example, all nurses fall into the same category, regardless of their training or position in the hierarchy.

Classification of women according to their husbands' occupations, however, and the uses to which such classifications are put, raise profound conceptual difficulties (see Delphy 1981 for a discussion of these). Where such a classification is used to indicate economic level, it disguises the fact that many households depend on two incomes rather than one (and discourages investigation of this as an important feature in itself); it disguises the fact that many women have no access to paid employment or independent income (and that this may be something important they have in common); and it implies that households are sharing institutions (i.e. that women share fully in the rewards of the occupations of their husbands). A consideration of these issues may start with the question of how to deal with women within such classification schemes; it tends to lead to a questioning of the way men's occupations are used in the social sciences.

Methodology is another area for question. While social scientists engage in a wide variety of approaches, there is an identifiable orthodoxy. Legitimate, highly regarded research is large scale, heavily funded, hierarchical. It depends on large numbers of interviews, usually by female research workers, usually under male direction. The interviews are characterized as dominated by the requirements of 'science', by the need for 'objectivity'. 'Data' is gathered by interviewers whose own opinions must be muted, for fear of bias. Feminists are unhappy with a number of features of this model – with its hierarchy, with the distance between the 'man of ideas' at the top and the 'objects' of research and the data-gathering process. Criticism has also been made of a model of interviewing which decries personal involvement. Ann Oakley argues that a feminist methodology requires:

> 'that the mythology of "hygienic" research with its accompanying mystification of the researcher and the researched as objective instruments of data production be replaced by the recognition that personal involvement is more than dangerous bias – it is the condition under which people come to know each other and to admit others into their lives.'
>
> (Oakley 1981b: 58)

In addition to language, concepts, approaches, it may be fruitful to reconsider subject and area boundaries. Hilary Graham has drawn attention to the way women's caring work is cleft by the academic disciplines. While psychology understands caring in terms of women's identity, social policy is concerned with it as women's labour. Both disciplines thus have an inadequate picture (Graham 1983). At a lesser level, within traditional subject boundaries, it is common to study the family and employment as separate contexts. An important key to women's lives, though, is an understanding of how they straddle these boundaries.

Feminist analysis is about putting women into a picture that has largely been drawn by men. But it is also about rethinking; in the end, about drawing a new picture that includes women and men. For when women have asked why women are so marginal to the concerns of major academic disciplines, they have usually concluded that marginality is not a superficial phenomenon, but rather that it is built into the foundations of academic subjects: into methodology, approaches, concepts, language, subject division, and the hierarchy of importance of academic subject areas. Thus a feminist critique does more than reinsert women into an existing framework. It poses a fundamental challenge to academic orthodoxies.

Social policy – the 'mainstream' approaches

The argument of this section is that all 'mainstream' approaches in social administration have, in practice, marginalized women; and that such marginalization is built into their fundamental premises. It should just be noted that whereas several 'traditions' are represented here as discrete entities, the reality is less clear cut and more varied.

The individualist position is here represented by Hayek. A trenchant account of the economic discipline within which his approach has its roots is provided by Eleanor Rathbone:

> 'In the work of still more recent economists, the family sank out of sight altogether. The subsistence theory of wages was superseded by theories in which wives and children appear only occasionally, together with butcher's meat and alcohol and tobacco, as part of the "comforts and decencies" which make up the British workman's standard of life and enable him to stand out against the lowering of his wage.'
>
> (Rathbone 1924/1949: 10)

An analysis which roots freedom in the play of market forces is unlikely to account for much of the space that women inhabit. While Hayek claims to recognize 'the family as a legitimate unit as much as the individual' (Hayek 1949: 31), it is the individual in the market place who fills the pages of his main works (see especially Hayek 1944/1976, Hayek 1960). Hayek's 'pre-sociological'

(Taylor-Gooby 1981: 69) approach makes sex an inappropriate category of analysis in the market place (making the individuals appear to be masculine); it also makes the family appear as an occasional appendage to the world of production. The family's specified role is to transmit traditional morality and the qualities that foster success in the market place; so that there is no justification for denying to individuals advantages 'such as being born to parents who are more intelligent or more conscientious than the average'. This applies to families or to 'other groups, such as linguistic or religious communities, which by their common efforts may succeed for long periods in preserving for their members material or moral standards different from those of the rest of the population' (Hayek 1949: 31). The intellectual heritage of this approach in social policy flows directly to Sir Keith Joseph's transmitted deprivation thesis where poor families (incompetent women) are seen as incapable of fitting their children for the labour market (Joseph 1972).

Individualist philosophy depends heavily on a notion of the traditional family, as has become very clear with the new right politics. Zaretsky points out that 'primary ties of dependence, nurturance, and mutual help are an inevitable part of the structure of any society, even one . . . ostensibly organized around individualism and independence' (Zaretsky 1982: 193). Relative independence is, in fact, a transient and fragile stage between the dependence of childhood and that of old age – and is anyway not given to everyone. This means that there are inevitable limits to individualism; these are recognized in the new right's defence of that family type in which women have the task of nurturing the dependent. Women, then, in this perspective, are neither major protagonists nor beneficiaries; on the contrary, they bear the costs of individualism. Individualists such as Hayek do not look too closely at those costs.

Among the group of 'Social Reformists' to whom I refer next, Beveridge has had much the worst press among feminists. Beveridge's misfortune in this respect has as much to do with the clarity of his statements on the subject as with fundamental differences of view among less maligned authors in this group. It also, of course, has to do with the fact that his proposals for social security were put into practice and have had direct effects on women's lives. Beveridge's most quoted words in this context are unambiguous about women's role: 'In the next thirty years housewives as mothers have vital work to do in ensuring the adequate continuance of the British race and of British ideals in the world' (Beveridge 1942: 53, para. 117). This status had practical expression in the separate insurance class given to 'housewives, that is married women of working age' (p. 10, para. 19). Most of these married women would make 'marriage their sole occupation' (p. 49, para. 108) and it was assumed that 'to most married women earnings by gainful occupation do not mean what such earnings mean to most solitary women' (p. 49, para. 106). Paid work would often be 'intermittent' (p. 50, para. 111). The married woman's benefits need not be 'on the same scale as the solitary woman because, among other things her home is provided for her' (p. 50, para 108). Married women, in general, would have 'contributions made by the husband' (p. 11, para. 20). Thus was the concept of the dependent married woman analysed with singular clarity and encased within social security practice.

Beveridge's assumptions concerning the extent of married women's employment were not wholly accurate even at the time (DHSS 1978: 92). It is arguable that Beveridge imposed an out-of-date and middle-class model of marriage and work on to women whose lives were very different (although it has to be admitted that representatives of working-class women at the time were grateful even for the crumbs offered to them as housewives under the Beveridge scheme) (Price 1979: 10–11). But Beveridge's fundamental assumption was that social security had a secondary role for married women, because of the security offered by men in marriage. While he did take some account (not followed up in the schemes) of the possibility that men's security offerings might fail on account of separation, he gave inadequate recognition to the variety of women's situations and relationships, and to the variety of possible patterns of paid work and domestic labour. Inadequate assumptions about marriage and about work both led to schemes that have treated women badly in practice.

While Beveridge was brilliantly clear in his discussion of women, marriage, and social security, he has never been taken as a major theorist of the Welfare State. One of the most influential theoretical papers of the same period was T. H. Marshall's 'Citizenship and Social Class' (Marshall 1949/1963). The theme was an understanding of the Welfare State in terms of the development of citizenship rights and a discussion of their relationship with social class. Of course, the social class theme was not one that was likely to lead Marshall into an explicit consideration of women, and the paper belongs to its period in the use of examples referring to men and children, except in relation to the vote (Marshall 1949/1963: 81).

While Marshall remarks on the importance of women's suffrage and its implementation in the twentieth century, he does not stop to analyse the development of citizenship rights from women's point of view. The historical sequence of women's 'citizenship rights' differs from the one Marshall describes for men (Stacey and Price 1981: 48); and women's relationship to these rights is problematic. Enfranchisement did not bring political participation for women in the same way as it did for men: 'The separation of political power from the home had . . . deprived all women of any such right: lower-class women had never been included' (Stacey and Price 1981: 46).

While Marshall asserts the rights of citizenship, nowhere does he analyse the problematic relationship between citizenship and dependency in the family as he does between citizenship and social class. The status of married women as dependants belongs, in terms of Marshall's analysis, to a feudal era, in that it is a status ascribed rather than achieved. Such ascribed positions are the very fabric which citizenship rights – in Marshall's analysis – are replacing. Ironically, the status of married women as dependants has often been entrenched by the very 'social rights' that are seen as the final crown of citizenship (as will be seen especially in Chapter 7 on social security). The citizenship of married women, then, remains problematic.

However, the concepts of citizenship and of social rights could be seen as theoretically open to use in analysing women's position in the Welfare State; and they can also be seen as useful in setting targets for people to achieve, or in defending existing institutions (Mishra 1977: 32). There is, of course, a distinctive liberal branch of the women's movement which finds these concepts useful in this political way. However, the notion of rights has its limitations. As Eisenstein remarks, 'Liberal rights are structured via the inequalities of man and woman' (Eisenstein 1981: 344). The problem is similar to that discussed under individualism. If women, too, claim rights as individuals (as they have often done) it offers a threat to the fabric of interdependence on which men's rights depend. It is not surprising that the rights specified in Marshall's analysis do not offer any challenge to the prevailing orthodoxies about relations between the sexes.

Titmuss has already had some attention from the point of view of feminist analysis, and I owe a lot to Hilary Rose's article (Rose 1981) both for the original idea behind this chapter, and for her work on Titmuss. Titmuss has played such a key role in the development of social administration, and the hegemony of the Timuss school was so complete (Rose 1981: 482–85) that he acts as a useful hinge for discussing the work of this social administration school more generally. There are three main points that I would make about the openness of this approach to understanding women's lives. The first is to agree with Hilary Rose that the empirical tradition and the sensitivity of Titmuss's perception do make it harder to be blind to the ways in which women's lives are lived and the effects of the Welfare State upon them. The second is that the view of the family usually assumed within this paradigm derives essentially from functionalism and is thus in practice often neglectful of power relationships and the possibilities of conflict within the family. The third is that while the strength of this approach in analysing the shortcomings of the way the Welfare State operates in practice have been repeatedly demonstrated, so has its unfortunate inability to explain these shortcomings. Thus, while the detailed accounts of the way Welfare State agencies operate in practice are useful in a feminist analysis, it is insufficient as a way of understanding why social policies offer women such short shrift.

To turn to Titmuss after searching the social policy literature of the post-war era is to see new doors opening. Women populate his pages in a way that they do not those of Marshall or Tawney (Tawney 1952: 220–21), for example, and there are accounts of the lives and deaths of women in all his publications. These include the chapter on 'Maternal Mortality' in *Poverty and Population* (Titmuss 1938: 139–56), a powerful defence of people's right to choose in matters of population and the need 'to obtain a balanced harmony between the productive, cultural and political activities of women and their function as mothers' (Titmuss and Titmuss 1942: 115), and the justly regarded account of the evacuation of the war period in *Problems of Social Policy* (Titmuss 1950). Later essays in the 1950s show some sensitivity to changes in women's lives brought about by a reduced period of child-rearing and a lengthened period of marriage, in particular the change towards greater dependence on men (Titmuss 1958: 93, 110), and the potential for women to find alternative fulfilment in paid work (Titmuss 1958: 102).

The question to raise from this is just how far the empirical method is responsible for the insights of the analysis and how far those insights can be attributed instead to the qualities of Titmuss himself as a social observer. If one examines the work of people of the Titmuss school it is possible, I think, to find some case for the first of these. A very good example can be found in Dennis Marsden's work on *Mothers Alone* (Marsden 1969), where careful interviewing and observation revealed women's painful experiences of dealing with the DHSS, especially as regards the cohabitation rule. But unfortunately it is also possible to find works where women are mentioned only in passing, if at all. Empirical investigation does not of itself guarantee that observers will see what is there to be seen: the categories of analysis can as easily exclude phenomena from vision as include them. In Titmuss's own work, the virtual exclusion of family conflict is a case in point, and the reason for this will now be addressed.

While Titmuss was suspicious of theory he was obviously not innocent of it. His eclecticism and wariness about committing himself to the higher reaches of sociological theorizing make it difficult to pin him down to any one theoretical vision, but his absorption of the main currents of contemporary thinking is nonetheless evident. It would, given Titmuss's rejection of an explicit theoretical approach to the family, be unfair to describe him in too simple terms as a 'functionalist'; but his thinking about the family was surely influenced by that body of theory, and this influence goes some way towards explaining some silences about his work.

The essay on 'Industrialization and the Family' (Titmuss 1958: 104–18) is mainly an account of the threat to family stability that comes from rapidly changing circumstances in the economic world and a plea for the need to protect the family through social welfare. One of the frameworks adopted in this essay is a homely version of the sociological account of universalistic values appropriate to the economic sphere and the particularistic values that belong in the family. He begins, 'What society expects of the individual outside the factory in attitudes, behaviour, and social relationships is in many respects markedly different from what is demanded by the culture of the factory' (Titmuss 1958: 111), and he goes on to discuss the difficulties that a state of mind encouraged by the industrial world has for family life. This concern with relations between the two spheres is entirely characteristic of functionalism and it gives a clear indication of where Titmuss's thinking about the family begins. The rest of the argument suggests tentatively that the family in Britain is accommodating to these changes in a satisfactory and democratic way (fathers are pushing prams), but that we need to 'see the social services in a variety of stabilizing, preventive and protective roles' (Titmuss 1958: 117).

Titmuss, then, follows functionalist thinking in opposing the family to the economy. Among the consequences of this approach are, first, the concentration on the form rather than the content of family life (Harris 1983: 86); second, in counterposing 'the family' and 'the economy' it is hard to see that the family itself is an economic unit; and, third, the breadwinner/dependant model of family life, connected to the economy through a family wage, is assumed to be functional to industrial society, and to be the natural object of support by social policies.

The picture of the contemporary family that emerges is ultimately a cosy one, in which the strengths and values of family life are holding out successfully against the 'gales of creative instability' (Titmuss 1958: 117) from the factories. Functionalism's assumption that the family is a 'solidary unit' where the 'communalistic principle of "to each according to his needs" prevails' (Parsons 1955: 11) underlies Titmuss's thinking. Unsurprisingly, one finds a similar blindness to that which Elizabeth Wilson describes in the empirical sociology of the 1950s: 'Where were the battered women? Where was the cultural wasteland? Where was the sexual misery hinted at in the problem pages of the women's magazines? Where was mental illness? Young and Willmott banished it to a footnote' (Wilson 1980: 69). It was the women's movement, not social administration, which much later illuminated the miseries of many housewives and the extent of family violence. The assumption that all was well within the family is a legacy which survives in social administration.

Finally I would comment on the lack of explanatory power in the Titmuss paradigm. The detailed investigation of people's lives and of the impact of state welfare has enormous strengths (and theoretical work could not have been done without it); but there is a gulf between exposures achieved in this way and the ability to explain why welfare provision so often fails. Titmuss's own explanation, in terms of the ever-increasing needs generated by technological change, bows before the evidence collected by his intellectual offspring. The Welfare State has so often been found not merely inadequate, not merely short of resources and short of vision, but often inhumane in its treatment of those to be 'helped' and unresponsive to the changes suggested by the careful arguments of its critics. Feminists would be unwise to look to this tradition to explain, for example, the response of welfare agencies to homeless women or the continued operation of the cohabitation rule.

While the traditions so far described survive, social administration is now dominated by the 'Political Economy' approach. Concerned with the Titmuss genre's lack of explanatory power, its isolation from broader theoretical perspectives, and with 'crises' in the Welfare State which existing literature seemed ill-equipped to understand, a number of writers turned to Marxism and wrestled with the attempt to bring Welfare State analyses under its umbrella. Emblem of the 1980s is *Critical Social Policy*, a journal intended 'to encourage and develop an understanding of welfare from socialist, feminist, and radical perspectives'. This rubric shows that the political economy school makes gestures in the direction of feminist writers, but there remains the question of how open the approach is in practice. Criticism of the 'sex-bind' categories of Marxism has come from Heidi Hartmann (1981a: 10–11) and Hilary Rose (1981: 501) among others, and feminist theorists are much preoccupied with the uses of Marxist analysis in understanding patriarchy in capitalist society (e.g. Hamilton 1978; Sargent 1981). The gestures of the political economists of the 1970s and 1980s could be seen as a matter of fashion as much as a matter of theory, given the intervening rise of an active women's liberation movement and radicals' unwillingness to be seen denying its existence. Or it could be argued that Marxism gives fruitful openings both for analysing women's position and explaining their oppression.

There are two areas where these openings have been used in the political economy texts: in analyses of women's place in the industrial reserve army and women's role in the reproduction of the labour force. Both Gough and Ginsburg have something to say in both these areas. Thus Ginsburg writes: 'The social security system not only reflects but strengthens the subordinate position of women as domestic workers inside the family and wage workers outside the family' (Ginsburg 1979: 26), and he characterizes the Welfare State as 'the use of state power to modify the reproduction of labour power and to maintain the non-working population in capitalist societies' (Ginsburg 1979: 44–9).

Marxist analyses of the labour market (particularly the one by Braverman 1974: 386–402), shed a lot of light on employed women's relation to capital, their use as a growing army of cheap labour, and capital's capacity to jettison them into dependent family relationships when required. The part the Welfare State plays in maintaining dependent relationships within the family can then be seen as supporting capital's exploitation of women in low paid and insecure work. This is a revealing account in so far as it locates the employment of women within larger economic trends and sets a context for their experience of paid and domestic employment. It is, however, incomplete. It does not explain why women should be such a convenient part of the industrial reserve army. It is not clearly applicable to long-run changes in the composition of the labour force, as distinct from short-term cyclical changes (see Beechey 1982/1983). And to understand the experience from women's point of view, of course, we have to look elsewhere.

The category, reproduction of labour, provides the second space in which Marxist interpretations can locate women. In Marxist terms the reproduction of labour is seen as primarily benefitting capital. Children are brought up and workers are 'serviced' in the cheapest possible way by using housewives' unpaid labour. Housewives thus have an indirect relationship to capital, but perform crucial labour which enables greater exploitation of male workers. This analysis has the merit of directing attention to the fact that housewives do significant work (though this should not be a new discovery), and it puts that work in a respectable position within an analysis of the economic system (Hartmann 1981a: 3–11). However, the economistic concern with the reproduction of labour, rather than the production of people, is unacceptable from a feminist point of view. The framework offers no explanation of why women do such an overwhelming share of domestic labour, even when they are also employed. And neither, as Hartmann points out, is the possibility that men benefit from that labour (as distinct from capitalists) given any attention (Hartmann 1981b: 377–86). However, here at least the door is opened on the realm where a large amount of women's work is done and their lives are spent; and, furthermore, on the realm in which the Welfare State's chief activities lie.

What is unsatisfactory about these accounts for some feminists is that they treat women's relationship to capital at the expense of women's relationship to men. Occasional references to 'patriarchal families' are set within a framework of class, and the families themselves are not approached directly. The political economy of

welfare makes productive relations the key to understanding;
everything else is a reflection of productive relations and therefore of secondary importance. This is shown in a very simple
way, by the relative lack of attention to reproduction, and it is also
shown in the way that political economy has been able to address
the two topics mentioned above, which involve women's relation
to capital, but has been unable to address many other areas of
concern to the women's movement.

A feminist social policy archive

If the mainstream of social policy writing has failed to appreciate
the special connection of social policy with the domestic world,
and with women's lives, this is not so of women themselves.
There is, in fact, a considerable archive of women's research and
writing, which connects social policy to the family and especially
to women's economic position in the family. Recent feminist
work is referred to throughout this book. This section focuses on
earlier work. The aim is, first, to show that feminist writing on
social policy has a long and serious history; and, second, to show
that 'mainstream' social policy writing has always had a feminist
critique available. Most of the work to which I shall refer derives
from women's politics rather than from the academic establishment: from, for example, the Women's Cooperative Guild, the
Fabian Women's Group, the National Union of Societies for Equal
Citizenship (NUSEC), and individuals active in these organizations. Women's suffrage was the prime subject of women's
political action at the beginning of this century, but women's
economic position – especially their economic position in the
family – followed close behind.

'Prior to World War I, discussion of the economic position of
married women was widespread in women's groups. . . . The
Fabian Women's Group (FWG) was founded with the main
object of discussing women's economic independence. . . .
Anna Martin, who wrote in the *Cooperative News* and suffra-
gette journals, contended that the authorities were expecting
mothers to "make bricks without straw" when they demanded
that they improved the welfare of their infants without providing any additional income. . . . One of the first major efforts to
secure a measure of economic assistance for all married women
was the Women's Cooperative Guild's campaign for maternity
benefits.'   (Lewis 1980: 166–67)

Jane Lewis's central argument is that women's groups identified the economic position of married women as the key to women's and children's health, and maternal and infant mortality. This was in contrast to the narrow official focus on women's ignorance and need for education. Political activity to enhance the economic position of married women was the prime aim of women's groups and their individual members, but along with this went a considerable literary output. As well as pamphlet and journal writing, there was analytical work, such as Eleanor Rathbone's *The Disinherited Family* (1924/1949), and detailed empirical descriptions of women's lives and domestic economy.

For political success women's groups needed evidence: evidence of the conditions of women's lives, the way they managed household budgets, the health of women and children. Thus emerged a considerable flowering of investigative social report. Some of this was based on letters, some on direct investigation, some on questionnaires. From the Women's Cooperative Guild came *Maternity: Letters from Working Women* (Llewelyn Davies 1915/1978) and *Life as We Have Known It* (Llewelyn Davies 1931/ 1977). From the Fabian Women's Group came *Round about a Pound a Week* (Pember Reeves 1913/1979). And the Women's Health Enquiry Committee (Spring Rice 1939/1981) issued *Working-Class Wives*. These works are painstaking, detailed, and highly readable accounts of women struggling against poverty. They tell of diet, household budgeting, frequent pregnancy, loss of health, miscarriages, and loss of infant life. Despite varied political sources they share an emphasis on women's poverty and the need for state economic support for maternity and child-rearing.

On the whole these works did not criticize women's identification with marriage and motherhood. They did identify and criticize women's economic dependence. And they recognized that economic dependence went with the love and care that women invested in children. Financial support for children was a common prescription, as was support for maternity through health services and financial maintenance. Thus Pember Reeves called for maintenance grants for children, national school feeding, and medical inspection (Pember Reeves 1913/1979: 228–31). The Women's Cooperative Guild wanted maternity and pregnancy sickness benefits, a women's health service of better trained health visitors (called women health officers), midwives, and nurses, proper care for delivery, milk depots, and household helps (Llewelyn Davies 1915/1978: 209–12). The Women's

Health Enquiry Committee included 'A system of Family Allowances paid to the mother' along with better maternal health services in an extensive plan (Spring Rice 1939/1981: 207–208).

These works did not offer a radical critique of the family or of women's work, but they revealed the conditions of women's lives and the effects of their economic dependence. Thus Margery Spring Rice's *Working-Class Wives* (Spring Rice, 1939/1981) describes the 'titanic job' of housework; and the misery of some women's lives cannot be missed in this painstaking and passionate investigation. While the author supports marriage, the results of bad marriages are clear to see. Spring Rice comments ironically on the women's attitudes: 'throughout their lives they have been faced with the tradition that the crown of a woman's life is to be a wife and mother . . . If for the woman herself the crown turns out to be one of thorns, that again must be Nature's inexorable way' (Spring Rice 1939: 95).

These writings emanated from divergent political groupings, from women of different social classes, but they shared an economic analysis. Sally Alexander writes about the Fabian Women's Group and speculates on their claim to speak for women in much worse circumstances than themselves:

'There was no intellectual dogmatism in the Fabian Women's Group. There were many divergent views, but the unifying theme was the fundamental acceptance of the economic basis of women's subjection. They believed they could speak for the majority of women because their analysis of sex oppression was economic. In spite of middle-class women's wider opportunities for education and training, all women were disadvantaged on the labour market compared to men. While the grossest forms of exploitation were suffered by working-class women, women in middle-class occupations were also struggling under the burden of low wages, lack of skills, and very often had other people to support as well as themselves. . . . And mothers in both classes were unable to support themselves or their children.' (Alexander 1979: xix)

If the power of the works discussed above lies in detailed description, Eleanor Rathbone's work is characterized by trenchant analysis. Her most famous work, *The Disinherited Family*, was published in 1924; a new edition, with an epilogue by Beveridge and a new title, *Family Allowances*, was published in 1949. The work consisted of an economic analysis of the family and an argument for family allowances. While some aspects of Rathbone's work are highly conservative to modern ears (e.g. her assumption that every man required a woman 'to do his cooking, washing and housekeeping' (1924/1949: 15–16), her denial of allowances to unmarried parents (p. 243), and her position on wages), there are many points that speak to feminist thinking of the 1980s. Her arguments derive from a belief in equal pay for women. They involve a critique of the idea that women should be dependants ('the very word suggests something parasitic, accessory, non-essential' – p. x); an exposure of the basis of power in relationships between men and women, which leads in a 'minority of cases' to violence and sexual exploitation as 'part of the price they (women) are expected to pay for being kept by them (husbands)' (p. 71); and a critique of legal and economic systems which set 'no price on the labour of a wife and naturally have affected the wife's sense of the value of her own time and strength' (p. 61).

Beveridge writes in the epilogue to the 1949 edition that when he read the book 'as soon as it appeared in 1924', he 'suffered instant and total conversion' (Rathbone 1924/1949: 270). However, in the same epilogue one can see how his conversion was tempered; the only justification he cites in 1949 for adopting family allowances is the concern about the relationship between earnings and benefits (p. 274). The reforms of the post-war era, then, were a very partial victory for feminists. Family allowances were paid to mothers, but went along with a reassertion of women's dependence and domestic work. And the allowances have never been enough to spell economic freedom.

Sylvie Price has written a fascinating account of women's responses to the Beveridge report in the 1940s (Price 1979), in which she shows that not all women were grateful for the benefits brought to them as housewives and dependants. The most 'developed critique' of Beveridge which she found came from the Women's Freedom League. The authors, Abbott and Bompas, describe Beveridge's 'error' as 'denying to the married woman, rich or poor, housewife or paid worker, an independent personal status. From this error springs a crop of injustices, complications and difficulties.' In criticizing the lower rate of benefits proposed for married women they wrote: 'This retrograde proposal creates (and is intended to create) the married woman as a class of pin money worker, whose work is of so little value to either the community or herself, that she need feel no responsibility for herself as a member of society towards a scheme which purports to bring national security for all citizens' (Abbott and Bompas 1943, cited in Price 1979). Thus these authors identified the way in which the state is involved in the perpetuation of dependency in the home and its connection with low pay in the labour market, an argument which has resurfaced in recent years.

Thus analyses and evidence of women's economic position in the family have long been available. Women as politicians and investigators have often taken social policy as a special subject. There has long been sufficient empirical study of women's lives to give rise to unease about a system of welfare and thinking about welfare that took the harmony and security of family life for granted. And feminist social policy thrives today, as reflected later in this book. Feminist analysis and accounts of women's lives could both have informed debates in social administration and social policy. The 'mainstream', however, remains more or less impervious.

A feminist alternative

Debates within feminism

A feminist approach should mean more than putting women in the picture. It means criticizing and renewing conceptual apparatus, and understanding social policy as part of wider social processes. Feminist theoretical analysis – which has largely focused on women's position in relation to men and to capital – is an obvious resource.

There is no single feminist social policy, partly because there is no single feminist theory. The theoretical extremes are usually characterized as radical feminism and socialist feminism. But there are dangers in ossifying such perspectives into apparently unreflexive, static positions, when the real world is much more varied and changing. There is also the danger of becoming absorbed in factionalist debates about unanswerable questions.

Characteristically, radical feminists have argued the universality of women's oppression and focused on experiences women have in common. In particular, they have generated discussion and political action around issues of reproductive biology (abortion, contraception) and of violence (rape, sexual abuse). Critics of this position have focused on its tendency of essentialism – the danger that argument for the universal oppression of women may tend to biological explanation and an inference about the consequent necessity of cultural inferiority. Blindness to differences between women is another possible hazard.

Socialist feminists have been concerned with the specific historical oppression of women under capitalism and with relations between class and gender. They are thus more open to differences between women. One major concern has been to locate domestic labour within an analysis of productive relations (the domestic labour debate). And one form of this analysis has been that the Welfare State organizes domestic life in the interests of capital. In seeking to understand the sexual division of labour – why women do the work of reproduction – socialist feminists have turned their attention to the way gender relations are reproduced under capitalism; and especially to education and other agencies of social policy as fostering the ideology and material conditions of women's oppression. Critics have been concerned at the tendency to make gender relations secondary to those of economic production; at the neglect of men's interests in the sexual division of labour (in favour of those of capital); at too close an association between the family system and the needs of capitalism; and at the tendency to an over-deterministic view of the limits that structures impose on people's lives.

The most fundamental debates between these positions concern the origins of women's subordination; who benefits from the dependence of women and the domestic division of labour; and the relationship between patriarchal domination and capitalist social relations. Such questions attempt to construct some over-arching theory. The position taken here is that there is value in pursuing lower-level questions; in analysing specific agencies of the state, even in the absence of satisfactory over-arching theory. Here I follow Carol Smart, who argues:

'To understand more adequately the specificity of women's oppression it might be useful to turn away from trying to integrate the monolithic structures of capitalism and patriarchy and instead to concentrate on concrete instances of gender domination and its interrelation with factors of race and class in specific instances.'　　　　　　　　　　　　　　　　(Smart 1984: 10)

This is not to argue that one can or should be atheoretical – rather that there is no need always to aim for the sky. The purpose of the present study is to examine relations between state social policy and the position of women, in the hope of understanding both better. No theoretical insight is barred because it falls into the 'wrong' camp.

Reproduction

This section makes a case for shifting the ground of analysis of social policy from the productive realm to the realm of reproduction. Some aspects are further developed in Chapter 2.

First the case rests on the importance of reproduction and reproductive relations in terms of material human necessity. Conceiving, giving birth, and nurturing are basic necessities for the continuance of life. There are biological processes involved, but our understanding need not be reduced to the biological. If the production of things necessary to human survival has a fundamental bearing on consciousness and on social relations, as in Marxist dialectics, a similar case can be made about the production of people. Reproductive relations and reproductive consciousness have roots in material human necessity too and, as Mary O'Brien eloquently argues, they also have historical and theoretical significance (O'Brien 1981: 20).

If reproduction is the bedrock of private life, it is also a substantial concern in public life; indeed, social policies may well be seen as state intervention in the reproductive process. The second argument for shifting the ground towards reproduction, then, is its centrality to social policy. This centrality is widely acknowledged, even by those whose main concern is to relate social policy to productive relations. For example, the new right orthodoxy of education as concerned with skills for employment is matched in this respect by Marxist notions of reproducing the labour force: both see state education in the role of developing appropriate human beings for the capitalist labour process – assisting reproduction in the interests of productive enterprise.

The difficulty in such works is that *analysis* is confined to productive relations. Thus most serious theoretical work on the Welfare State concerns relations between capital and labour and the nature of the state in a capitalist society. This applies to Marxist works of political economy as well as to critiques of those works (see Cawson 1982, for example).

Reproductive relations are subordinated to the productive process, and are not themselves analysed. One sad result is an economistic tendency to see the human results of reproduction solely as labourers in the capitalists' vineyard. Elizabeth Wilson wrote that, 'First and foremost today the Welfare State means the State controlling the way in which woman does her job in the home of servicing the worker and bringing up their children' (Wilson 1977: 40). I doubt if many of those women would relish the total submersion of their family life within the 'needs' of capitalism.

For feminists analysing social policy there is a further difficulty. State activities in the reproductive sphere do not all obviously contribute to capital's ability to exploit labour. Large areas of social policy are difficult to understand within such a framework: local authority child-care, for example, or the Invalid Care Allowance (Groves and Finch 1983). Most Marxist texts are more at home in discussions of paid employment than of unpaid employment. The relative theoretical underdevelopment of work in such areas surely has quite a lot to do with the prominence of Marxist theoretical interpretations of the Welfare State.

A feminist social policy, then, must rescue reproduction from the status of handmaiden to production. The family, the boundary between public and private life, relations between state and family – these need analysing and understanding in their own right. To do so may shed light on the many areas of darkness created by attempts to understand social policy and the reproductive sphere primarily in terms of productive relations.

This raises the question of connections between production and reproduction, productive and reproductive relations, class and gender – which have given feminists many difficulties. We have no theory which enables us fully to grasp these, despite an elaborate feminist literature. But however unsatisfactory our understanding in this sphere, to rescue reproduction from the status of subordinate activity is to escape a stranglehold.

A third reason for shifting the ground to reproduction is that reproduction is central to feminist theory, which may, therefore, be expected to shed light on those dark areas of Marxist analyses and perhaps ultimately to transform the way we think about the Welfare State.

There are several reasons for the importance of reproduction in feminist theory. One is that here lies the best hope of understanding male dominance. Another is that reproductive labour is characteristically women's labour; analyses that focused on productive relations have omitted large areas of women's work and experience; and concepts developed for the analysis of productive relations are not readily transferred to the 'private sphere'.

There are also political reasons for taking reproduction seriously: 'A widely-based women's movement cannot emerge from the devaluation of the intimate, humane, exasperating, agonizing and proud relations of women and children. The feminism of the pseudo-man is passé' (O'Brien 1981: 91). Thus argues Mary O'Brien, who puts reproduction at the heart of feminist theory: 'It is from an adequate understanding of the process of reproduction, nature's traditional and bitter trap for the suppression of women, that women can begin to understand their possibilities and their freedom' (O'Brien 1981: 8).

Feminist analysis, then, has focused on reproduction, and on the relations between production and reproduction. It is terrain that is occupied by women, in that they have major involvement in the reproduction of people, as well as in productive employment. It is also terrain occupied by the Welfare State.

Finally, the reproductive arena is one of change. If reproduction has usually been seen as static in contrast to the dynamic of productive processes, this is no longer the case. However inadequate is contraceptive technology, control over fertility has the capacity for transforming reproductive relations. The idea of 'the family' responding to the dynamic of capitalistic development can now be replaced by an understanding that reproductive relations have their own dynamic.

Two difficulties should be mentioned here. One is a problem of language and meaning. In discussing the issues raised in this chapter, feminists have used a variety of terms, mostly overlapping but not coterminous, and they have used the same terms with different meanings. Thus there is feminist work on 'the family', the 'domestic domain', 'the public and the private', and 'reproduction' and 'reproductive relations'. There is no way of legislating for one terminology rather than another, and each has its (rather different) uses. I have tended to use 'reproduction' in an attempt to link the human service work that is undertaken in the domestic arena to that which is part of public policy (and which is also largely women's work). One hazard of this particular choice is the meaning of 'reproduction', which is variously interpreted by feminists with different concerns. Most obviously, reproduction may be understood as the process of conception and birth. This meaning may be extended to the whole task of producing new generations. Other meanings have been developed by socialist feminists attempting to relate reproduction to production: labour power has to be reproduced, and thus workers have to be cared for day to day; and capitalist social relations have to be reproduced. In other words, reproduction includes physical nurturance but goes beyond, into the development of conscious human beings who are ready to take their place in the labour process. The emphasis in these latter meanings on consciousness and social relations seems to me essential. Reproductive work is human necessity but it is more than human necessity. But to see reproduction narrowly as the reproduction of labour power and capitalist social relations is to subordinate one sphere to the other. My conclusion is that reproduction is best understood as the processes of creating and sustaining human life. This includes conception, birth, and the care of children; it also includes daily maintenance (of labourers and others). The reproduction of human life also means the reproduction of social relations and human consciousness. That consciousness and those relations will certainly reflect relations in the productive realm, but not be wholly determined by them. Reproduction, then, is grounded in fundamental necessity, but it is not simply biology.

Analysis of 'the public' and 'the private', and the understanding that women have a special relationship with 'the private' also seems to me essential. Reproduction belongs primarily, but not wholly, to the private sphere; the privacy of most reproductive work is one of its dominant features; and the boundary between public and private life is of key importance in describing women's work. The use of 'public' and 'private' as tools of analysis has been criticized by feminists and does have hazards. The hazards are of seeing these spheres as distinct and unchanging; of equating public forever with male, and private forever with female, and of thus consigning women to a hidden realm. The argument in this book is that public and private life are reflected in one another. Private life is not private from social policy, and public life reflects the division of labour in the home. And the boundary between public and private is not constant. Nevertheless, the idea of public and private spheres does reflect everyday experience; it has also been used in a sensitive and revealing way (for example, Stacey and Price 1981; Graham 1985). I therefore find analysis in terms of public and private domains essential, as long as it is recognized that the division between public and private is neither unchanging nor unchangeable. These issues are discussed at length in Randall (1982), Siltanen and Stanworth (1984), and Stacey and Price (1981).

Reproduction and the Welfare State

Feminist approaches to the Welfare State have been – at least on the surface – contradictory. On the one hand, a number of writers have emphasized the aspect of control. Social policies are seen as ways in which men – or capitalists – gain control of the reproductive sphere and of women's work. Thus Elizabeth Wilson writes of the 'state organization of domestic life' (Wilson 1977: 9); Ehrenreich and English argue that the rise of the Welfare State 'expert' has subverted women's own expertise and dominated their lives (Ehrenreich and English 1978/1979); Hilary Land, in several articles, has argued that the Welfare State controls women by regarding them as dependants within nuclear families – it thus enhances the dependence of those within such families and discriminates against those outside (for example, Land 1983).

Control of reproduction may be fundamentally important to men (for a development of this argument see O'Brien 1981). It may also serve to connect reproductive work with the demands of the productive sphere, in terms of healthy and cooperative labour. In so far as it involves the protection of 'the family' it may also serve the interests of law and order.

The Welfare State, then, may be seen as public control of the private sphere, and increasing male control of female work. Most obviously, the biology of reproduction has become the property of male medicine. But the family has also lost control of significant aspects of reproductive work to the male-dominated professions of medicine, teaching, and social work. And by supporting the breadwinner/dependant form of family, with the woman at home, social policy has played a part in controlling women, keeping them in the private sphere and out of public life.

At the same time this ensures the availability of women for reproductive work. Thus women continue to care for the young, the old, and the dependant, mainly exempting men and state services from these tasks. The general failure of social policies to 'share' such caring work suggests powerful underlying forces: whatever the rhetoric, policies do not succeed if they threaten the identification of women with the private sphere or their responsibility for caring work.

Thus a number of strands in feminist thinking about the Welfare State are about the control of women and women's work. Alternatively, however, the Welfare State may be seen as supporting women, especially in their reproductive work. Some writers argue that the Welfare State redistributes income from men to women (Oren 1974: 118). It is regarded as a prize that women have wrested from the state on behalf of their reproductive work (O'Brien 1981: 166).

Developing and defending the Welfare State has also been part of feminist politics, past and present. Historically, various women's groups campaigned vigorously for financial support and for services; and they are paralleled by women's groups in the United States (Zaretsky 1982). Such groups may not have been far-sighted about the way services and money would be delivered, but they were very knowledgeable about the conditions of women's lives without them.

The argument of this book is that social policies do indeed have contradictory effects for women. They cannot be understood in one-dimensional fashion, as instruments of oppression or of liberation. Rather, the Welfare State has to be seen as articulating productive activity with reproductivity. It is argued here that the Welfare State developed in the void between factory and family, when industrial capitalism wrested major parts of production out of the domestic setting. The fracturing of public and private life, and of production and reproduction, made it difficult to ensure that dependants could be cared for. The family mitigated the insecurity of wage-dependence, and was – as Humphries points out – infinitely preferable to bureaucratic ways of caring for those who were not in the labour market (Humphries 1977: 246–48). But the inadequacy of wages, the lack of a female 'breadwinner', male control of jobs and wages – all these left those responsible for reproduction vulnerable and the work of caring for dependants inadequately done.

The 'family wage' was one 'answer' to the problem of making the resources of the productive sphere available to those responsible for reproduction. But it was a very inadequate answer: it was never large enough, it depressed women's wages, and it did not necessarily reach women and young children – as women's groups clearly showed. Thus social policy, especially in its income maintenance aspects, can be seen as redistribution towards the reproductive sphere and towards women whose lives are bound up with reproduction.

good

Intervention in reproductive work could mean financial and health support for women. But it could also mean the development of alternative institutions through which reproductive work could be more effectively controlled. Thus the control of teaching and health work – though not the bulk of the work itself – has gone into the public sphere, and into male hands.

The context within which the Welfare State articulates productivity with reproductivity is fundamentally patriarchal; but that does not mean that social policies always work against women's interests. Reproductivity is, after all, as essential to the productive sphere as is wage labour to the family. Social policies, then, often serve to enhance reproductive work to which women are often committed. If, at the same time, they undermine women's position – especially in the reproductive sphere – we should not be surprised. But a further element is that women are not merely passive victims of social policies. Women have been active in promoting and shaping the Welfare State, and are not without room to use welfare services for their own ends, in their paid labour and in their lives in general.

Again, the economic, public world to which reproductivity has to be connected is a capitalist world. And the overwhelming forces of capitalist relations reach to the heart of the private sphere. It should not be assumed, however, that the capitalist mode of production determines every aspect of private life, that profit wholly subordinates reproductive relations, moulds the family to its uses, and so on. Such a model, in which the Welfare State serves to control women and the family in the interests of capitalist enterprise, does have some currency. It does not, however, leave room for gender as such to have any independent force; and it has manifestly failed to account for many aspects of reproductive relations.

If the Welfare State articulates private to public, its role for women is ambiguous. It may involve redistribution and financial maintenance for reproductive work; it may provide a route – through the education system – for some girls to reach public life. On the other hand, it almost certainly involves loss of control over reproductive activity, a steady invasion of the private sphere, and a relegation of women to what is left of the private sphere within the family.

Dependency and social policy

It is several decades since Titmuss identified dependency and the interdependency of individuals as a key concern of social policy. Now feminists are changing the terms of this debate.

A continuing theme through feminist critiques of social policy (from Rathbone on) has been the dependent position of women within the family. Contemporary critics argue that social policy – far from alleviating this dependency – plays a large part in sustaining it. The critique in this debate is not necessarily of the family itself. It is of a particular form of family relations. And it is not necessarily of social policy sustaining families; it is of social policy sustaining particular kinds of family relations, to the exclusion of others.

One stream of women's writing about social policy has focused on the ways in which social policies have assumed and promoted the dependency of women within marriage. It has detailed the long history of social security's avoidance of paying benefits to married women in their own right, attaching instead dependants' allowances to men's benefits; the denial of benefits to women who are married or cohabiting to which they would be entitled if they were not married (for example, the Invalid Care Allowance); the encouragement of women to stay in violent homes as dependants, rather than setting up independent households. The conclusion reached is that social policy supports a particular family form with male as breadwinner and female as dependant. In doing so, social policy enhances the dependency of women in marriage as well as the difficulties of living outside such families, of forming different kinds of relationships, and of leaving particularly unhappy marriages.

However, dependent relations are not sustained only by the practices of social security and other aspects of the Welfare State. They are also sustained by women's caring work and by women's position in the labour market. Women are dependent because they care for other dependants, for children and for the sick, handicapped, and elderly. Another stream of feminist writing, then, has focused on women's caring work for other dependants. This work is well represented in a collection by Finch and Groves called *A Labour of Love* (1983). The main themes of this writing are the extent and significance of caring work in women's lives, its distribution between state and family, and its economic and emotional content.

The price of such caring work is economic dependence. Looking after people is either done for no pay, within the family, or for low pay in the public sector. Social policy's tendency to promote both these arrangements amounts to the exploitation of one kind of dependency to deal with another. On the other hand, the relations generated by these caring tasks are central to women's lives. Without them, women would not be women.

These are not 'problems' to which there are straightforward 'answers', and the search for simple one-sided solutions can be disadvantageous to women. For example, the 'solution' to women's dependence in social security which the DHSS has offered (under pressure from the EEC) is to offer women 'independence'. Women must now, in general, make their own contributions for their own benefits. The difficulty is that the arrangements give scant recognition to the fact that many women are economically dependent for substantial parts of their lives. While women do the caring work and the low-paid work they will not 'earn' equal social security.

Those policies which have recognized women's economic dependence have also largely been those which have helped to sustain it. The denial of Invalid Care Allowance to married women, for example, gives many little choice but to be dependent on husbands. On the other hand, those policies which have appeared to offer independence have often done no more than wish dependence away. Thus current arrangements for retirement pensions take little account of women's reduced earning power after child-rearing. Women's economic dependence cannot be wished away; neither can their caring relationships. The requirements of a social welfare system are that it should mitigate women's economic dependence without sustaining dependent relationships. There are ways of doing this (for example, child benefits). In asking that this should be done women are not asking for the moon.

If the dependency of women cannot be wished away, neither can the dependency of most who are cared for. The dependency of elderly and handicapped people is a more traditional theme of social policy writing than the dependency of women. However, analysis which fails to recognize the connections between the two kinds of dependency is often less than illuminating. The care of most dependants has been the province of women, has belonged to the domestic arena, and has been unpaid. It has thus made women dependent. At the same time, it is probably correct to argue, as Jane Humphries has done, that the family has generally been a more humane setting for the care of dependants than state institutions, and that the working class defended these arrangements with reason (Humphries 1977).

Feminist social policy, then, has been much concerned with dependency, with the dependency of women, and of children, of elderly and handicapped people (the majority of whom are also women). It has been concerned with just how tightly the knot has been tied between the dependency of the caring and the dependency of the cared for.

The professionalization of caring – division of caring labour

If caring work is central to women's lives, it is also central to the Welfare State. Indeed, it is often assumed that 'caring work' is what the Welfare State does. State provision of health, education, and personal services is commonly seen as the nurturing arm of the state cast lovingly around its weaker citizens. Now this, in a way, is irony. For women still do most of the caring work, and do it at home without state support; and in these circumstances the loving part may well be nearer to the truth than it is in state institutions. However much the obvious interpretation of what the Welfare State does and is may be open to question, though, it is the case that it involves the work which traditionally belongs to women.

Teaching, nursing, healing, tending, all take place under the umbrella of the 'Welfare State'. These primarily concern those who are dependent: the young, the old, the handicapped, the sick.

One conventional assessment of social policy history is that the Welfare State has thus 'taken over' functions that were once the realm of the family. The assessment of feminists working in this area is that this conventional wisdom needs rethinking. Margaret Stacey, for example, has argued that we need to look at 'human service' work as a whole, to connect the part of it that women do at home to the part that is professionalized within the Welfare State (Stacey 1981).

This illuminates the extent of what happens in the private domain, usually uncounted because private, because outside economic activity as it is conventionally defined. Most people – especially very dependent people – are cared for at home by relatives, mostly female relatives. The 'Welfare State' keeps its hands clean of most children until they are five and well able to do the basic things for themselves. Health making, as Hilary Graham (1984 and 1985) argues, is still largely women's work and largely domestically based. It is women at home rather than doctors in the NHS who take responsibility for nutrition, health education, and the restoration of the sick. Doctors diagnose, advise, prescribe; but the mother of a child with mumps or measles is likely to look after that child for twenty-four hours a day, for as long as is necessary. These points apply even more to those who are severely handicapped or very old. Few are in institutions and for the rest the services are likely only to touch the surface of daily needs. None of this is to denigrate the services that do exist. It is rather to offer a perspective on the distribution of caring work.

A perspective on caring work as a whole yields another important insight. This is that social welfare services involve a gender hierarchy. The professionalization and bureaucratization of care has made room for men at the top. This is most marked in health care, where there is intense male domination of medicine and, in turn, medical domination of other caring work (though nursing now has a hierarchy of its own with space for men). It is also apparent in teaching and academic work, where men dominate in the higher grade posts and in the decision-making authorities. Social work, too, though traditionally a female profession, has a majority of men in management posts, and an overwhelming male dominance at the top among the Directors of Social Services (see Stacey and Price 1981: 138 for a more detailed account). This does not mean that men actually do the caring work when this becomes paid work within the Welfare State. These are, in fact, areas of heavy female employment. It is the high spots that are occupied by men.

The bulk of caring work is done by low-paid women within the social services, and by unpaid women at home. A considerable amount of this work is – conventionally – uncounted and unregarded. What this means for the family and the state is not that the family has lost functions, so much as that it has lost control. The family is still the major arena for the care of dependants; but the definition and organization of health care and education belong to the state. The case may be put more strongly in terms of gender. Traditional female tasks are now organized and defined outside the family and by men.

Stacey and Price argue that this analysis can be generalized:

'throughout all the known world and in history, wherever public power has been separated from private power, women have been excluded' (Stacey and Price 1981: 27). One rather unattractive light in which to see the Welfare State, then, is as an erosion of women's power.

A postscript on legislation for 'equality'

There is not a lot, in these pages, about legislation for women's rights. 1975 saw the full implementation of the Equal Pay Act and the Sex Discrimination Act, and the establishment of the Equal Opportunities Commission. It may well be asked what is the significance of this legislation and what is its relation to the account given in these pages of a social policy much preoccupied with 'women's place'.

My answer is that equality legislation is peripheral, for two broad reasons: the restrictive application of the legislation in its own terms and the small scope of legislation around 'equality' in relation to the profound character of gender divisions. None of this is to argue the irrelevance of equality legislation; rather that the real dynamic of change lies elsewhere. (A good general perspective on equality legislation and social policy is David and Land (1983).)

These two points deserve a little development. The restrictive character of the legislation is particularly noteworthy in a book about social policy. The government of the day carefully exempted itself from the full force of the acts: the Sex Discrimination Act does not cover social security and taxation practice, and discrimination continues in these areas. The Equal Pay Act left plenty of room for (entirely legal) evasion by employers; a Department of Employment study shows how the five-year period for implementation was used to further segregate the labour force along sex lines, thus making Equal Pay cases more difficult to bring (Snell, Glucklich, and Powall 1981). Furthermore, there are difficulties for women in bringing cases, and in knowing which piece of legislation covers their case. Recent evidence indicates that real gains for women in the period after the act have since been eroded. (These issues are discussed more fully in Snell 1979; NCCL 1981, 1983.)

The second point is that legislation for equal pay and against sex discrimination makes a small ripple on a deep pool. There is no legislation about who does the housework and cares for old and young; no Act of Parliament that will put women in top jobs or give them places in the public world. Where domestic work, paid work, and political work are so profoundly gender-divided, legislation about equality can touch only that minority of situations where women's lives are like men's; it leaves out those more important areas where men's and women's lives divide.

Neither is equality legislation necessarily consistent with other significant government policy. The same period that saw these acts also saw contradictory changes. There were new disability benefits which discriminated against married and cohabiting women; and there was increasing pressure for 'community care' to fill the widening gap in the care of the elderly created by demographic change and pressure on public resources. Assessing the net effects of all these changes is complex. But my own view is that the equality legislation had little more than symbolic impact.

2

The Family and Women's Work

The family in feminist theory and social policy

'The state in its welfare aspects begins and ends with the family' (Cockburn 1977: 177) argues one feminist account of social policy. Or, more provocatively and polemically, Elizabeth Wilson remarks: 'Social welfare policies amount to no less than the state organization of domestic life' (Wilson 1977: 9).

A first aim of this chapter is to look at the family and women's position in it. This is a major undertaking, because of the substantial feminist literature on the family and the varied feminist perspectives on it. Inevitably the account is a little sparse.

However fractured are the worlds of public and private life, they are nevertheless mutually dependent on one another. A second aim, then, is to look at the way women's position in the private world of the family relates to their position in the public world. Therefore this chapter also deals with one aspect of women's public lives – paid employment. This is to leave out other aspects, in particular women's politics. However, production does have a special place, partly because of its role in Marxist and socialist feminist theory, but also because of the rapidly increasing importance of paid work in women's lives.

Thus this chapter hopes to describe 'women's place' in private and public worlds, and to look at the ways in which women are trapped between subordination in private and subordination in public.

Third, this chapter has to show the way that social policy connects to this subordination. One key way is through its 'support' for 'the family'.

Given limits of space, what follows will be largely a descriptive account, though some attempt is made to point the reader in the direction of major theoretical debates.

The family in feminist theory

The family has a special place in feminist theory. On the one hand, the family is a primary site of women's work. This gives rise to questions about the nature of that work, the social relations within which the work is carried out, and the connection of unpaid work in the family, to paid labour outside it, and to the relations under which paid labour is carried out. On the other hand, the work that women do is special kind of work. A large part is concerned with nurturing children. Therefore the family is the first place where most of us learn what it is to be male or female, what are appropriate behaviours for men and women. But some feminist writing looks beyond behaviour to the construction of identity. Nurturing children involves relationships as well as tasks. Relationships within the family have a peculiar intensity and a peculiar significance. For children, in particular, the relationships in the family may be seen as constituting elements in identity. Children become who they are through relationships with others in the family, particularly mothers. And since identity includes gender identity, the family may be seen as a core site for the transforming of sex into gender.

It should be understood at the beginning that there is no single feminist perspective on the family, and that it is impossible to do justice to the breadth and variety of feminist writing on this subject. Recent works with a social policy bias include *The Anti-Social Family* (Barrett and McIntosh 1982), as well as *The Family in the Firing Line* (Coussins and Coote 1981). Authors of the former work argue for the divisiveness of the family, oppose family responsibility to social responsibility, stress family violence, the 'tyranny of motherhood', the 'familism' which romanticizes marriage and disadvantages those outside it, and the unequal power and 'sexual asymmetry' of family relationships. The authors of *The Family in the Firing Line* are concerned to protect the interests of women and children, many of whom live in families. They add a feminist voice to the well-established 'poverty lobby', which has traditionally based its appeal on 'family poverty', the 'needs of children', and so on. This leads them to seek alliance with women whose identity lies in families. They argue that 'the elimination of family poverty and the achievement of women's equality are entirely compatible goals, rather than mutually exclusive ones' (Coussins and Coote 1981: 3).

These two sets of authors merely illustrate some of the variety of feminist perspectives on 'the family' (though they share quite a lot too). There is, in feminism, as Barrett and McIntosh remark, 'no united call for the abolition of the family' (Barrett and McIntosh 1982: 20). There have been feminists who have sought to liberate women by extricating them from domestic and reproductive roles, and feminists who have celebrated reproduction and the special values that grow from women's involvement with it. Some feminists have focused on the family as a place of work, and have attempted to connect that work to work relations in the public world; and some have focused on the family as a centre for relationships and the development of gendered personality.

While there are many feminist perspectives on the family, there is agreement on the family as a core site of women's oppression. Whether we examine the division of labour within the family or the psycho-dynamics of feminine and masculine identities, 'the family' is implicated at the very foundation of gender differentiation and power relations between the sexes. In a useful review of 'The Family in Contemporary Feminist Thought' Flax draws out some themes which are common to feminists writing from very different perspectives:

'(1) The sexual division of labor, especially women's exclusive responsibility for young children, which is a persistent feature of history, is a crucial factor in women's oppression and the analysis of it. (2) Understanding the family, its history, psychodynamics, and relation to other social structures is a central task of feminist theory. (3) The family is a complex structure composed of many elements: the sex/gender system, the varying relations to production and to other social structures, ideology, and power relations. (4) The family (at least as historically constituted) is oppressive to women and is a primary source of the maintenance and replication of both gender and identity and the pain and suffering endemic to being female. (5) The family as it is currently constituted must be changed, if not eliminated. At minimum this requires the equal involvement of men and women in the care of young children. (6) Gender is created by social relations experienced first in the family; it is not determined solely by or limited to biology. Heterosexuality is also socially, not biologically, constructed, through social relations in the family. (7) The different roles women and men play both inside and outside the family are not natural but grow out of and are the expression of a complex series of social relations; patriarchy, economic systems, legal and ideological structures, and early childhood experiences and their unconscious residues. All these relations are mutually interacting and reinforcing. . . . (8) Nothing human is unchanging or absolutely unchangeable. This includes the character of childhood, the family and human nature . . . and the variations of each of these by gender. Everything human has a social history and a social root. Even biology is mediated by, or can potentially be affected or transformed by, social relations; biology is not simply a brute fact, immediately and directly expressed in human life.'   (Flax 1983: 250)

The family and feminist social policy – supporting the family

'Supporting the family' sounds innocuous enough. It has varied uses in political discourse: it is popular among politicians of all persuasions as a campaigning slogan; it is used as part of the law and order debate; and it is used to justify reigning public expenditure on the elderly and dependent.

Concern to 'support the family', then, has been intense. From Sir William Beveridge to Sir Keith Joseph, from the 'problem families' of the 1940s and 1950s to the 'transmitted deprivation' and 'family responsibility' of the 1970s and 1980s, social policy's concern for the family has been proclaimed from the political heights. It has been argued that the post-war development of social work as a profession was built upon anxiety about the family and the apparent need to hold it together (Wilson 1977). And social policy writing in the 'reformist' tradition has taken it for granted that the key questions for social policy analysis were how well social services 'supported' the family and how they could be better made to do so (see Townsend's *The Family Life of Old People* (1957) or Moroney's *The Family and the State* (1976)). Thus, for example, Townsend wrote:

'The principle we have been developing is one of preventing old people from unnecessarily becoming wards of the State, by making it as easy as possible for them to be cared for in their own homes by their own relatives. We have seen that the most general method of putting this into effect is by means of

housing policy. The more people can be rehoused near relatives and friends, the fewer social casualties there will be. But
there are other means than prevention. The family itself needs
direct support in various ways.'   (Townsend 1957)

The assumption that the state needs to support the family, should
support the family, and can support the family, then, is widespread.

Both politicians and analysts of social policy, however, have
left a lot of questions unasked: about the 'nuclear' family as the
essential household unit, about the position of women within the
family, and about the family as an economic and political unit.
The notion of social policy 'supporting' families is – in the absence
of such analyses – an entirely uncontroversial affair.

In practice, supporting the family has rarely meant the kind of
practical support for family care which Townsend rightly advocated. The clear message, from Townsend's work through to that
now being done by the EOC, is that social services actually go to
those who do not have families; the existence of a relative,
particularly a female relative, is enough to justify the absence of
state support. And the political emphasis on family responsibility
is not reflected in the fiscal and benefit position of those with
children (Field 1985).

The real meaning of supporting the family is supporting family
responsibility, as distinct from state responsibility, for dependants young and old. State support is primarily a series of policies
for a particular family type, that in which there is a male 'breadwinner' and a female 'carer', who fortunately does not have to be
paid. These policies underlie social security practice, as well as
provision for dependants of all ages, and they are described in the
appropriate chapters.

Support for this particular family type is support for women as
dependants. It means exploiting the public/private divide in such
a way as to restrict women's place in the public world and to
deny men's responsibilities in the private. And while support
for the family appears to be neutral between various family
members, this is far from the case in practice. As Hilary Land
remarks:

'Just as the concept of "the national interest" obscures important conflicts of interest within the nation thus favouring
the superordinate in society, camouflaging the boundaries
between the State and the family and demanding only that the

State preserve and support "the family" is to the advantage of its more powerful and privileged members.'   (Land 1979: 144)

Feminist writing about social policy emerging in the 1970s had to reaffirm the centrality of the family. It had, on the one hand, to assert the significance of reproduction and the way it was organized for understanding social policy – in counterweight to the prevalent Marxist stress on production; on the other hand it had to challenge the orthodox blandness about social policy's support for the family – in opposition to more traditional writing. A critical reassertion of social policy's concern with the family is, then, one of the foundation stones of feminist social policy analysis.

A woman's place in the family and paid employment

Ideology and demography

Now you're married we wish you joy,
First a girl and then a boy;
Seven years after, son and daughter,
Pray, young couple, come kiss together.

Nursery rhymes, advertisers, and politicians seem to know what the family is. Husband (breadwinner), wife (housewife), and two dependent children is an ideal type of the modern family. This section compares this household type to the pattern of households shown in recent *General Household Surveys*. It also looks briefly at the importance of the gap between ideal type and reality from the point of view of social policy. It argues, not that the ideal is defunct, but rather that living patterns are so diversified that our ideal of the family no longer matches the way most people actually live for most of their lives.

Table 1 shows that only 29 per cent of households consist of a married couple with dependent children; some commentaries suggest that only 5 per cent of households fit every aspect of the stereotype, married men with two children and the wife not in paid work (Coussins and Coote 1981: 9). This is not because marriage is becoming less popular, or child-bearing less central to marriage. Most people still experience the two-parent and children household, both as children and as parents. But this phase of life has become shorter in relation to other phases. This is for a number of reasons: the increasing instability of individual marriages, which leads to larger numbers of one-parent families; the

Table 1 *Households, 1982*

married couple with dependent children	29%
married couple without dependent children	35%
lone parent with dependent children	4%
lone parent without dependent children	4%
1 person	23%
2 or more unrelated adults	3%
2 or more families	1%
total	100%

Source: Office of Population Censuses and Surveys, *General Household Survey* 1982: 12.

increasing number of elderly people provides part of the explanation for the numbers of one-person and two-person households; the increasing extent of cohabitation before marriage, and a possible increase in young people living independently before marriage, add to the numbers of people living outside the 'family' (for a discussion of these trends see Harris 1983: 202–22).

At any one time most people are not living in families that consist of couples with dependent children. Dependent children are present in only one-third of households; child-rearing is concentrated among a minority. Furthermore, most women are in the labour market for the majority of their adult lives before retirement; some support families single-handed and many keep their families out of poverty. These are the points to bear in mind when considering the relationship of social policy to 'the family'.

In so far as social policy relates to families rather than to individuals, it is likely to neglect certain groups – groups which are getting larger. In so far as it is modelled on a particular version of family life, it may penalize those who do not conform, and enforce a dependency which is not reflected in the choices women make for themselves. And the assumption of family support for dependants raises all kinds of questions about the small pool and shrinking size of households who care for children, and for elderly and dependent relatives.

The family economy and the domestic division of labour

The established sociological division between 'work' and the 'family' implies that all significant work goes on outside the family. Women know otherwise. Women whose whole work is in the home also know that they are not considered to 'work', and they can be appropriately militant in response. Here are some of Ann Oakley's 'housewives':

'I always say it's harder, but my husband doesn't say that at all. I think he's wrong, because I'm going all the time – when his job is finished, it's finished. . . . Sunday he can lie in bed till twelve, get up, get dressed and go for a drink, but my job never changes.' (Wife of a driver's mate)

'The husbands never look very tired do they? It's always the woman that's tired isn't it? When they've finished, they've finished. . . . Things like road digging might be harder (than housework) but there again, when they've finished, they go and have a drink and a cigarette and that's it.'

(Oakley 1974b: 45)

State policy reflects the idea that housework is not really 'work'. To qualify for 'Housewives Non-contributory Invalidity Pension' (HNCIP) women had to prove that they were both incapable of paid work and incapable of performing 'normal household duties'. The EOC found that women were frequently believed to be able to do housework even if severely disabled. They comment that, 'It is not uncommon to find women who are receiving Attendance Allowance, which in effect means that they are incapable of looking after themselves, yet who are refused HNCIP' (EOC 1981a: 11). Similarly, women's disability may be deemed sufficient to make them incapable of paid employment but capable of housework. One married woman officially retired by the Civil Service said:

'I was examined by two Civil Service doctors and my own GP, and told both verbally and have it in writing that I was unfit for clerical duties. Eventually I applied for HNCIP and was turned down for this pension – how ridiculous that I am not fit for clerical duties, but fit for heavy housework.'   (EOC 1981a: 7)

A major achievement of feminist work has been to make the invisible visible. The idea of the family as the focus of emotional ties and of recreation has obscured it as a place of work. 'The denigration and trivialization of housework is', Oakley remarks, 'a pervasive cultural theme' (Oakley 1974a: 47). Women describe themselves as 'only' housewives, are described as 'not working' or, officially, as 'economically inactive'. Yet the evidence is that women put in long hours of domestic work. Oakley's respondents – who were all mothers – averaged seventy-seven hours per week of housework and child-care, well above the standard week for people in paid employment. Children have a major impact on housework hours. A recent study finds that mothers of preschool children spend about fifty hours per week on 'basic life-support tasks' such as feeding, washing, and changing nappies (Piachaud 1984). American studies of women with and without children reviewed by Hartmann show over fifty hours a week housework as average (Hartmann 1981a: 377–78).

As a series of tasks housework has analogies to work undertaken for pay. You can wash dishes at home, in a school kitchen, or in a restaurant. The task remains the same, however different the relationship to capitalist production in each situation. All Oakley's six 'core housework tasks – cleaning, shopping, cooking, washing up, washing, and ironing' (Oakley 1974a: 49) – correspond to work undertaken for employers. The care of children and adult dependants at home is paralleled by such jobs as nursing, teaching, social work, and home help.

The economic character of housework is further illustrated by the long-run tendency for capital to make inroads into aspects of domestic production (see Braverman 1974). The interest of capitalists in 'convenience foods' – and the profits that can be made from them – indicate the arbitrariness of designating food processing in the home as non-work, not-economic-activity.

In addition to similarities there are, of course, profound differences between production for use at home and production for exchange. Women at home are not overseen or tied to a production line; neither are they paid. Family relationships may involve love as well as labour, and continuous responsibility.

Strenuous attempts have been made to connect the work of housework to the relations of capitalist production. Socialist feminists argued that women were involved in reproducing labour for capitalists. Housework might therefore be described as productive labour, contributing to capitalist profits. In practice it was difficult to fit housework into Marxist categories, but the 'domestic labour debate' which emerged as a discussion of these issues did call into question the apparently private and emotional basis of family life. It also looked towards fundamental questions about the connections between paid and unpaid labour. It is reviewed in several places, including Flax (1983).

Studies such as Oakley's have exposed the 'work' of housework. They have also shown just how much of it is done by women. In 1974, Oakley regarded 15 per cent of her sample's husbands as having a high level of participation in housework. She concluded that 'Only a minority of husbands give the kind of help that assertions of equality in modern marriage imply' (Oakley 1974b: 138). In 1984, a major Department of Employment study of women's employment questioned women and their husbands about sharing housework. Among those women 'not working' (the survey's words), 81 per cent described themselves as doing all or most of the housework, and 80 per cent of the husbands made this assessment too. By contrast, only 2 per cent of the wives and 1 per cent of the husbands of these 'not working' women regarded the husband as doing all or most of the housework (Martin and Roberts 1984: 101).

These figures relate to full-time housewives and their husbands. It might be expected that women's employment would make a difference. Where the women were 'working', 67 per cent of both husbands and wives described wives as doing all or most of the housework, and 1 per cent of both husbands and wives described husbands as doing all or most of it. The authors – on the basis of evidence from the pilot study – thought it likely that the figures understated women's share of domestic work (Martin and Roberts 1984: 100–101). When women do paid work, then, some housework is shifted to men, and hours are reduced, but the result is an unequal partnership, in which women do more. Hunt's study suggests that 'cutting domestic jobs down to size is preferred to trying to redistribute them' (Hunt 1980/1983: 112), but her study and several others show the long hours and unremitting rituals required to be paid workers and unpaid housewives. Hear, for example, some women factory workers interviewed by Sally Westwood:

'Most women spend all their time working. They work at the factory, then they do the shopping and cook and clean. I was hanging out washing before I came to work today. Mind you, I wouldn't be at home all the time; it's too lonely. When you come out to work it's more social, you meet other women and seem more alive, somehow.'

'I get up first, but not until 8.30 on a Sunday now. I get the tea on for the first lad and give him his breakfast because he has to go at 6.30 then, it's me hubby. I make the lad's bed while the tea's brewing, then it's the other two and then I get meself ready while I make our bed, cut the sandwiches and I'm off out the door. I wash about three times a week because me hubby and the lad have overalls. You have to soak them, they can't go straight in the machine, then I put them in. I do all my pressing for the whole week on Sunday afternoon and pick up all the washing for Monday. The whole house gets a clean at the weekend'. (Westwood 1984: 164, 166)

A closer look shows just how strong is women's identification with housework. Underlying responsibility for the care of house and people is rarely questioned:

'A striking aspect of these interviews was that none of the women questioned the assignment to women of the primary duty to look after home and children. This was reflected in the language they used. Housework is talked about as "my work" ("I can't sit down till I've finished *my* work"); the interior decor of the home is spoken of as the housewife's own ("I clean *my* bedroom on a Monday"; 'I wash *my* basin every day"). The home is the woman's domain. When these housewives discuss their husbands' performance of domestic tasks, they always use the word "help": "he *helps* me with the washing up in the evening"; "On Sunday he *helps* me put the children to bed". Husbands are housewives' aids. The *responsibility* for seeing that the tasks are completed rests with the housewife, not her husband; shared or interchangeable task-performance is one thing, but shared or interchangeable responsibility is quite another.' (Oakley 1974b: 159)

Housework, then, is work, and it is largely women's work. Paid work gives women the lever to lessen their identification with housework, but not to shift the burden radically. Thus, combining paid work and housework has its own costs.

The family economy and the family wage

The corollary of woman as houseworker is man as breadwinner. Women, excluded from higher paid work (see pp. 49–51) and responsible for the care of children and adult dependants, are themselves dependent on the male wage. To live without a male wage is to be at high risk of poverty. To live with one is to be dependent, upon a man and upon a marriage/cohabitation.

The idea of a 'family wage' – of a man's wage sufficient to

support two adults and their children – has a longish history as well as a contemporary currency. Nineteenth-century attempts to exclude women from industrial work, and the separation of the 'productive' from the domestic, assumed a wage that would maintain wives and children (though in practice it has never kept families out of poverty). The idea was used by trades unions in defence of men's wages, and could be seen as the most effective way for working-class families to defend their living standards (for a discussion of this issue and a historical account of the working-class interest in defending the family, see Humphries 1977).

The family wage was a major theme in debates about family allowances, focused in the 1920s by Eleanor Rathbone's *The Disinherited Family* (Rathbone 1924/1949). Rathbone argued that the wages system could not be adapted to varied family needs, and saw family allowances as the way to reconcile these needs with men's wages. Not surprisingly, trades unions suspected that family allowances would involve wages cuts, and thus argued – explicitly or implicitly – that men should earn enough to support women and children. The connection of the family wage with masculinity is nicely caught in this quotation from a leading member of the General and Municipal Workers Union in 1930:

> 'Let the men in industry take the mantle of manhood and come into the unions and fight to establish a standard of comfort that will enable them to make provision so long as work is open and they perform their service to the State through it.'
> (TUC General Council: *Report of the Annual Congress*, 1930, quoted in Land 1982: 293)

The wide variety of positions taken by women's groups and by trades unions is shown in Hilary Land's various articles (Land 1982; Hall, Land, Parker, and Webb 1975). For women, the issue is full of ambiguity. Since a high proportion of women are dependent on a male wage – either wholly as housewives, or partially as low-paid workers – the size of those wages conditions women's standard of living. Indeed, there is no other form of support available to married women at home caring for children or other dependants. Even where a wife earns, it can make sense for the man's wages to be used for regular, unavoidable expenditure, while the woman's less secure income is used for less essential items. Studies such as Pauline Hunt's have shown that this is in fact the way many such couples adapt to men's and women's different access to income (Hunt 1980/1983: 122–23).

But the other side of the coin is that family wages are actually men's wages. They thus represent a power relation of men over women. Men's greater entitlement to the family income is a theme that runs through historic documents such as *Round about a Pound a Week* (Pember Reeves, 1913/1979; Oren 1974) and recent surveys. No one knows how many women are in poverty because they never see the 'family wage'; but a sense of lack of independence, and of lack of entitlement to money to spend on themselves, appear to be widely shared. Rathbone put it in this way in 1924:

> 'The laws and customs which not only set no price on the labour of a wife, but give her no claim to any return for it except to be protected, as a dog or a cat is, from starvation or cruelty, naturally have affected the wife's sense of the value of her own time and strength. In a community where nearly all other services are measured in money, not much account is taken, at least by uneducated people, of unpaid services.'
>
> (Rathbone 1924/1949: 61)

One might remark that 'educated' people's accounts may be the more lacking. Working-class women interviewed in recent studies express themselves clearly enough. In a discussion of women who have returned to work, Hunt finds that 'financial independence is a heartfelt theme' (Hunt 1980/1983: 151). One of her interviewees put it like this:

> 'My money isn't all that, but it's my own. It comes in for holidays and things for the home, and I buy more clothes now. I decide what to spend my money on – else I wouldn't go out to work. I feel more independent now. If I want something in the home I just go out and buy it. I don't have to ask for it, you know. Whereas before I had to get round Michael, you know, how you are. Now you've got your own money in your pocket you're alright, you just go out and buy what you want. I usually go and buy something and then tell him after.'
>
> (Hunt, 1980/1983: 150)

Redundant women, interviewed by Angela Coyle, tell the same story. One of them said: 'I missed having my own money. It made me feel guilty about buying anything. Really I got a bit low that way because things that normally I would have bought, I couldn't because I wasn't earning a wage. Or if I did, I felt guilty. You definitely lose your independence' (Coyle 1984: 68).

The family wage involves the notion of men 'supporting' women and children, of women and children being dependent on men's wages. It also entails the notion of women's paid work as secondary to their domestic work, and secondary to that of men. If men's wages are 'family wages', women's wages are 'pin money'. On the surface, equal pay legislation promises equal pay for women. The reality of continuing low pay for women is justified by the underlying theme of men's 'family wage' and women's position in the family. Men are assumed to need enough earnings for the support of two adults and children; women as paid workers are assumed to be supported themselves, and to need money only for 'extras'. Women's low pay is itself discussed later in the chapter. The point here is that women's pay does not generally give independence. Low pay thus interacts with and reinforces women's economic dependence within the family.

A key theme of Rathbone's diatribe against the family wage was the impossibility of adjusting wages to varied family circumstances. The same wage was paid to a man without wife and children as to one with numerous dependants. A similar theme recurs in modern feminist writing. The instability of individual marriages, the greater variety of family forms, the increasing numbers of women supporting families alone, the numbers of women whose wages are essential to keep their families out of poverty – all these mean that the male breadwinner/female dependant model is no longer a description of the real world (see Land 1976). They also mean that to rely on the 'family wage' is to risk poverty among women and children.

Paid work

Women's paid work is intrinsic to their lives – as is their unpaid work. Now most women between the ages of sixteen and sixty are in paid work of some kind and spend a high proportion of their lives in paid work; the labour force is strongly shaped by women's presence; and there is evidence of women's commitment to themselves as paid workers. The identification of women with domestic work is still appropriate – but this goes along with a major part in paid employment.

The importance of paid work in women's lives can be illustrated by official statistics – imperfectly though they discover and measure it (MacLennan 1980; Hunt 1980) – and by recent surveys. The *General Household Survey* tells us, for example, that 69 per cent of 'non-married' (single, widowed, divorced, and separated) women, between the ages of sixteen and fifty-nine, were 'economically active' in 1982, and 61 per cent of married women. The comparable figure for men of working age was 89 per cent. A Department of Employment survey, which attempted to include less visible paid work, such as child-minding and outwork, found that only 29 per cent of women did no paid work, including some students (Martin and Roberts 1984: 9–10).

Ninety-nine per cent of married women in paid employment are also houseworkers, in the sense that they are responsible for at least half the domestic work (Martin and Roberts 1984: 97). Nearly all women maintain themselves (as distinct from having a 'housewife'); many are also responsible for husbands and houses. Women are likely to have care of children at some point in their lives, and possibly of other dependent relatives. And even women who have few of these responsibilities may be treated as if their lives will – ultimately – be moulded by them. These responsibilities profoundly shape women's experience of the labour market. Thus, women's participation in paid work varies over a lifetime. 'Not working in a paid job is associated overwhelmingly with the most intense period of child-bearing and rearing' (Martin and Roberts 1984: 19). Part-time work is one 'answer' to conflicting demands. Many jobs may be inaccessible to women – because commuting is incompatible with fetching children, for example; and women may well put the accessibility and convenience of jobs before high pay – if there are human responsibilities to be taken into account. Women's jobs may well play second string to their husband's job mobility. In all these ways women's unpaid work is reflected in their paid work. The result is a life cycle that differs markedly from men's.

It makes sense, therefore, to look at women's attachment to the labour market in terms of the changes in labour market and housework patterns over women's lifetimes. Women take paid employment – if they can find it – before the birth of their first child, and spend around seven out of the average eight years from leaving full-time education in (usually full-time) work (Martin and Roberts 1984: 125). Giving birth usually means leaving the labour market, though the period of leaving seems to be decreasing. Ninety per cent of women will have returned to

paid work of some kind for some period by the time their children are sixteen or over (Martin and Roberts 1984: 12). The study from which these figures are drawn concluded in terms of 'women's strong attachment to the labour market and increasing rates of return after child-bearing'. Women who were thirty-five or over at the time of the survey had spent around 60 per cent of their possible working lives so far in paid employment, 43 per cent in full-time work (Martin and Roberts 1984: 122).

Women's paid work is also a significant part of all paid labour. The *General Household Survey* finds that women comprise 41 per cent of the labour force (based on all economically active persons aged sixteen and over) (Office of Population Censuses and Surveys, *GHS* 1982: 118). Much of women's work is part time, and this element has been increasing. There are indications that the increasing amount of part-time work is a convenience to employers, rather than to women themselves. Part-time work is relatively poorly paid, and incurs lower commitments from employers in terms of benefits and security. While it may help to 'solve' the problem of competing demands for women, it may also create new problems. In particular, very short hours may be useful to employers in minimizing their obligations to workers, while leaving women with very low pay. Tessa Perkins, on the basis of a study in Coventry, argues that part-time work is now the typical form of work for married women, and that its extension has to do with its advantages to employers in the service industries; these depend on a low-paid and floating workforce as a permanent feature. Women's part-time work is thus a central feature of the service sector, not just a marginal one (Perkins 1983).

Another characteristic of women's work is its segregation from men's. Women work in a limited range of occupations, some hardly ever undertaken by men. 'Almost two million women worked in occupations where over 90 per cent of all employees were women: typists, secretaries, maids, nurses, canteen assistants, sewing machinists' (Hakim 1978: 1,268). More generally, the Department of Employment survey found that 57 per cent of women said that only women did the same sort of work as they did at their workplace; the equivalent figure for men was 81 per cent (Martin and Roberts 1984: 26–8). It seems that men have made inroads in previously female jobs, while men's jobs still exclude women. Segregation in different types of occupations is matched by segregation at different occupational levels.

'In manual work, the trend is towards greater segregation, with men increasingly over-represented in skilled work and women contributing an increasing share of unskilled and semi-skilled workers. These changes outweigh the gradual, but small, improvements in women's share of higher professional occupations and among employers and proprietors.'

(Hakim 1978: 1,267)

Occupational segregation of this hierarchical kind means that women are particularly likely to be subject to male authority at work. The Department of Employment survey found that 55 per cent of women had a male supervisor, where very few men had women supervisors (Martin and Roberts 1984: 28).

Finally, women's paid work connects with domestic work. Quite a lot of women's work actually takes place at home. Women as child-minders, landladies, mail-order agents, outworkers, combine paid and domestic work by working at home. Our culture thinks of work as what happens outside the home, so this kind of work has tended to be underestimated. Davidoff argues for the historical importance of a variety of ways in which women, particularly widows, gained a respectable livelihood by running schools, private apartments, and taking in apprentices and children. Further, she argues, that in neglecting these we tend to exaggerate – and treat as too natural – the distinction between public and private worlds (Davidoff 1979).

Women's public, paid work mirrors their private, unpaid work. Women work as nurses and teachers, as cleaners and servers, as helpmeets (to bosses and doctors).

Thus a lot of women's work is part time and in the service sector; it is highly segregated from men's, and generally re-stricted to a limited range of occupations; much is at low levels of skill – as skill is usually defined; some takes place at home; and most directly parallels unpaid work at home. A final, and con-nected characteristic is that it is low paid. While there is no intrinsic reason why part-time work should be paid less well than full-time, it is, in fact, concentrated in low-paying occupations (Breugel 1983: 136). The segregation of the labour-force protects employers from the Equal Pay Act – indeed the evidence is that employers have intensified segregation in order to avoid the operation of the act (Snell, Glucklich, and Powall 1981). And the identification of men's jobs with skill puts women's work down the pay hierarchy. On this last point, feminists argue that women's domestic skills and dexterity are treated as natural and undervalued in comparison with male skills. Women are disadvantaged in pay by the patriarchal definition of skill itself. The most consistent feature of women's work is its association with low pay. It appears that around the time of the Equal Pay Act, hourly rates of men's and women's pay were converging. In 1977, women's hourly pay reached 70 per cent of men's; but, by 1980, it had fallen back to 67 per cent (Breugel 1983: 137). Women's shorter hours of paid work further reduce their proportionate incomes overall. Thus, virtually all women work, caring for themselves and for others, most women work for pay for the greater part of their adult lives (retirement apart), but very few women indeed are paid an income that would make them independent.

Along with low pay and part-time work go poor conditions and unsocial hours. Part-time workers suffer particularly from the lack of benefits widely available to full-time employees. The Department of Employment study found that 77 per cent of women part-time workers were entitled to some paid holidays (though these were shorter than holidays of full-time women workers); 51 per cent were entitled to sick pay, and only 9 per cent belonged to an occupational pension scheme (Martin and Roberts 1984: 46–8). It also found that women with children – especially very young children – were quite likely to be doing evening and night work. This applies to 11 per cent of full-time women employees whose youngest child is under five, and 44 per cent of part-time women with similarly young children (Martin and Roberts 1984: 37).

Power over women

Violence in the family

The women's movement has become increasingly concerned about violence against women. Violence – in the streets and at home – is seen as expressing and enforcing male power over women.

But violence at home contradicts both sociological and commonplace stereotypes of family life: home is a place of safety and trust, a 'Haven in a Heartless World'; the family is the focus of the warmer human emotions, of love and affection; the family is a unit with common interests, even where members have different 'roles'; partnership between husband and wife exists in the 'symmetrical family', women's increasing role in public life being matched by men's increasing role in domestic activity.

Violence in families indicates that for many women the home is not a place of safety; that it is the centre of intense human emotions of all kinds – including anger and hatred as well as love; that the interests of different family members do not inevitably coincide; and that men in families assert power over women. The existence of domestic violence shows the family as a political unit as well as an economic one; the different power of its various members is something to be analysed.

Domestic violence is hard to see and impossible to count. The contradiction with images of happy families is one reason. Another is family privacy. When violence becomes murder – as it not infrequently does – then it is likely to become a public concern. Short of that, it may well be ignored – by everyone from friends and neighbours to police, courts, and academic writers. Indeed, so invisible was domestic violence in the 1950s and 1960s that the literature on the family virtually ignored its existence.

The Women's Aid movement of the 1970s had a dramatic impact (it is further discussed in Chapter 5). Women's Aid offer refuge to all women who ask. Their network of refuges for battered women spread rapidly, yet they are still overcrowded. Despite overcrowding women stay for months while awaiting safe rehousing. As a by-product of practical help, Women's Aid have lightened the darkness of sociological understanding. The use of refuges revealed widespread violence against women at home, rather than isolated, 'abnormal' instances; it showed the lengths to which women were prepared to go to escape violence; but it also suggested the difficulties of escaping brutality. Without money or accommodation of their own, women had simply lacked the material resources to escape.

Refuge accommodation was enough to give some women a route out; this was evidence of the importance of material resources – and women's lack of them – in sustaining violence against women. Many had suffered for several years; and some of the most vulnerable were women with young children (656 women interviewed had 1,465 children aged 16 or under between them) (Binney, Harkell, and Nixon 1981). These women were particularly likely to be wholly dependent on their men materially. In turn, this paints a different picture of the model family. Women's dependency goes along with men's power.

Feminists have assembled the evidence for the extent of domestic violence against women, and they have argued that it belongs to a family form in which women are dependent. 'Far from being abnormal behaviour, the violence of men towards the women they live with should rather be seen as an extreme form of normality, an exaggeration of how society expects men to behave – as the authority figure in the family' (Wilson 1983: 95). Domestic violence does not make all families scenes of misery, but it does locate ultimate power in families. This does not mean that women are without power of any kind in families – indeed, feminist writers on women's power have located the private world as the domain in which women's power is exercised, if they exercise power anywhere (Stacey and Price 1981). But the structures of the public world are reflected in the private. While male dominance is sustained in part by violence at home, it is also sustained by 'breadwinner' status in the public world. The other side of this coin is that women's experience of violence at home is conditioned by their lack of resources outside the family.

Authority at work

The evidence of studies of violence is of women's subjection in the family. Women's first experience of the public world was of exclusion, as women were excluded from public politics and from industrial labour. But, more recently, with increasing employment, women's experience is of subjection here too. The majority of women work in low-paid jobs, at the bottom of hierarchies, and under male supervision. Very few women are at the top of hierarchies, even in jobs that are predominantly female.

Sallie Westwood comments further on the detailed application of management techniques to control women's work. She describes authority relations between male management, female supervisors, and female workers; and she shows women suffering the full force of systems designed to break down work processes, speed up production, and increase management control: 'Patriarchal forms intervened in the labour process. Rules and management techniques had a special force for women workers who were more closely monitored, more highly supervised and, finally, paid less' (Westwood 1984: 43).

Sallie Westwood also argues that gender identities are forged at work as well as in the family; it is paid work that confers adulthood, and it is therefore on the shop floor that girls become women (Westwood 1984: 10–11). The subordination of women at work, then, becomes part of the feminine identity.

In summary, the family is here described as a focus of economic and political relations, as well as of personal ones. But the family does not stand alone. Women have a place in the labour market too, albeit a relatively weak one. And the family is connected to the labour market through the work women do in maintaining labour as well as through the family wage. This chapter therefore describes woman's place through an account of both labour market and family.

The ideal family type of male breadwinner/dependent wife and children is not dead. Women do leave the labour market, especially when they have young children, and a crucial part of women's experience is dependence on a male wage. This dependence is at its most acute when children are small, but is a continuing fact of life for many women, in view of low pay and poor access to jobs. On the other hand, this ideal type blurs some realities. In particular it blurs the importance of women's part in paid work, and the varieties of family patterns that exist. There are many women breadwinners too.

Women's work and women's liberation

The argument of this chapter is that women are subordinate in paid work and in the family, and that subordination in both spheres is connected. This continuity implies that the increase in women's paid employment does not necessarily mean a step on the way to women's liberation. It may be, as Pahl argues, that women can use their position in the paid economy to 'shift the sexual division of labour in the household' (Pahl 1981: 156). As he argues, many women

> 'need their position in the formal economy in order to be in a position to renegotiate their previously subordinate position in the domestic economy. Socializing their husbands into their role as partners in the reproduction of labour power is easier when, at a pinch, they could manage without their husbands altogether.' (Pahl 1981: 159)

The statistical evidence already cited does indeed point to some shift in the domestic division of labour where women have paid jobs.

But the use of the word 'partner' in this analysis is hardly borne out by the evidence. Employment helps women to reduce their dependence on men at home – and this figures strongly in women's accounts of working for pay. But women are not in the same economic league as men and they do not win independence; they do not shift the burden of domestic responsibilities to a major degree; and they do take on responsibilities (such as keeping themselves and their families out of poverty) which may be very unliberating. They certainly work more hours than men and more than women at home, and often face oppressive conditions in the workplace.

The point of this section is to argue against the simplicities of the view that paid work for women is automatically liberating. Women do not, on the whole, step out of oppressive relationships in the family into liberated relationships in paid work: family relationships appear to be only slightly modified by women's greater economic independence, and paid work is especially exploitative for women.

Another difficulty attaches to the view that liberation for women lies in competing with men in paid work; for such a view tends to denigrate women's traditional work, and appears as an attack on those women whose lives revolve around the 'family'. As Flax remarks, in discussing some 'radical feminist' writings:

'None of these writers considers the gratifying and humane elements of women's traditional work and how these could be preserved or even turned into part of the attack on patriarchy, given that the oppressive social relations within which such work occurs must be destroyed. These failures cause feminism to be perceived by some women not as an attack on women's oppression but as an attack on themselves and/or a denial of their own experience.'   (Flax 1983: 232)

Such a view seems itself patriarchal, to grow from a set of values which puts the production of things above the production of people, and prefers to see women make things while babies are left to test-tubes. Feminists have tended to become less concerned about getting women off the reproductive hook and more concerned to challenge the relations within which reproduction takes place, and the way these relate to productive relations. This still means critically analysing the family, but the abolition of private life, and the wholesale mechanization of reproduction, seem unattractive.

One way of understanding the complexities of these issues is to ask women themselves: to look at their attachment to the house-wife role, the family, paid work, their experience and identity. One tendency in women's writing about women has been a concern to reflect women's experiences as well as to describe the material reality of women's lives. The tradition of works such as *Round about a Pound a Week* and *Maternity: Letters from Working Women* is continued in more recent work.

The increase in married women's paid employment has led to a concern with women's identity as housewives and paid employees. Among a number of recent studies examining the experience and consciousness of women in varied situations are Angela Coyle's *Redundant Women* (1984), Pauline Hunt's *Gender and Class Consciousness* (1981/1983), Anna Pollert's *Girls, Wives, Factory Lives* (1981), Marilyn Porter's 'Standing on the Edge: Working Class Housewives and the World of Work' (1982), Sue Sharpe's *Double Identity: The Lives of Working Mothers* (1984), and Sallie Westwood's *All Day, Every Day: Factory and Family in the Making of Women's Lives* (1984). Some of these works compare women in different situations; others are concerned with the way women's lives straddle factory and family, work and home; all examine the way women's identities are constructed in both spheres.

The increase in women's paid employment is not just a matter of women's choice – it also has to do with wider economic movements as well as the economic needs of families. But women are choosing paid work and are valuing it. The lives of women employees may not be exactly liberated, but they are perhaps a little less oppressive than those of most women at home. Two of the few studies which compare women in both situations are very clear about this. The Department of Employment study found that 'non-working women . . . had higher stress scores than working women' (Martin and Roberts 1984: 93). And in the conclusion to her chapter on women at home, Pauline Hunt concludes that they are 'oppressed in their personal relations to a much greater extent than is the case with their economically active counterparts. The houseworker's life is centered round the husband's activity. Her leisure and work are tailored to suit his. She cuts her coat according to the cloth he provides' (Hunt 1980/1983: 99).

It was argued earlier in the chapter that housework and looking after people are work, economic activity; the other side of this coin is that they are also identity. Work is who you are as well as what you do. Sadly, for women who are houseworkers, the housework identity is a demoralizing one. Comments made by Pauline Hunt's interviewees suggest the impact on self-esteem of working 'backstage':

'I think I'm most boring actually, because I don't have an awful lot to say to my husband. I don't go out very much. . . . So I can't talk to him. It's not like going out to work and spending the day out.'

'You don't want to talk to me. My life's not interesting. I've never been able to say I go out and earn a wage.'
                                                    (Hunt 1980/1983: 81)

Low morale and poor mental health among women at home looking after young children are well documented (see Chapter 3). We know rather less about those who care for other dependants, though their morale seems unlikely to be better. The wife/mother identity on its own is socially stigmatized and dependent. Thus, despite its human rewards, it is often demoralizing.

Sue Sharpe summarizes the views of women she interviewed in her recent study:

'The women I talked to described the nature of their lives as mothers and workers. They spoke of the significance of work, not just from the financial point of view, but equally as much in terms of the social and psychological meaning it had for them. Although a few would have preferred not to be working, and some would have liked to improve the nature of their jobs and the conditions under which they worked, the majority would not have considered giving up work altogether. In many cases the experience of full-time mothering had proved less than satisfactory and they had no inclination to return to it, especially if their children were no longer dependent. Through returning to work, these mothers had experienced a number of other benefits apart from a wage, which had often had positive repercussions on the rest of the family. They talked, for instance, of their gains in economic independence and growth in self-confidence; the importance of having a separate identity from the home and family; feelings of being in touch with the outside world; and improvements in their relationships with their husbands and children.'   (Sharpe 1984: 240)

The jobs that most women do are not socially, financially, or intrinsically rewarding. When women are involved in both worlds, as most women are, they may avoid the worst perils of both – the demoralization of dependency in marriage and the bare exploitation of total dependence on wage labour. For more advantaged women the 'double identity' does seem to represent a gain over life backstage. On the other hand, women may find themselves trapped. Pollert describes her tobacco factory women as so hemmed in between various demands that they felt hopeless and helpless to change:

'Their prison was sandwiched between work and home; and the walls seemed high. . . . Packed tightly between their two worlds of home and factory, surviving from day to day, they could conceive of no practical strategy of change.'

(Pollert 1981: 124)

Studies of women's experiences and consciousness reflect the duality of ties to home and labour market. Domestic responsibilities are a powerful shaping factor in women's working lives and married women are not bound to the labour market quite as inexorably as men are. Furthermore, most women's jobs are ill paid and many are boring. It would not be surprising to find women in paid work looking somewhat wistfully to full-time motherhood and life at home. As Sallie Westwood says in her study of factory workers, 'in the home, women felt they organized for real needs and their labour went to support and sustain children and men – real people, not factory owners and profits' (Westwood 1984: 196). Yet, despite all this, women's attachment to paid work is demonstrated in practice and in their own accounts. Angela Coyle found in her study of redundant women what 'extraordinary attachment women have to their paid employment' (Coyle 1984:121), and one of the women she interviewed described her feelings plainly enough:

'The last time I went for a job and she said "We'll let you know", I said, "For God's sake tell people straight. Why don't you tell us we're too old?" You feel as if you're ready for dying. I can't believe it. It's lonely, I even went after the toilet job in town, the public toilets. I've got my name down everywhere. It's depressing. I have many a weep, I can't help it. You just can't believe it's come to this. This has been the hardest time of my life. I mean I've been on strikes in Leeds and that, but I knew we'd get back to work. It's never been like this.'

(Coyle 1984: 119–20)

A recurring theme in several studies is the way in which women bring the family into work:

'Home was something they brought into the factory. It was always with them. After all, it was something more useful to care for people and children than pack tobacco to go up in smoke. But they not only talked about it; they lived out their family lives at work. . . . Men, too, are centred on their families and discuss them at work. But they relate to them differently; their family is part of their concern as father and breadwinner. With women it is the immediate, intimate and daily concern with the actual processes of family care which penetrates and alters their consciousness of work. Work is overshadowed by the family.'

(Pollert 1981: 113)

And Sallie Westwood, in her study of hosiery workers, describes the way women decorated their machines with family photographs, wore slippers, and embroidered aprons for themselves on company machines – all attempts, as she sees it, to 'reinsert their lives, as women and as workers, into the production process' (Westwood 1984: 21).

While the domestication of work seems, to these authors who describe it, to be 'collusive' in its acceptance of women's domestic role, other efforts to humanize work may seem less so. Another recurrent theme is women's concern with working conditions rather than merely with pay. Pauline Hunt argues as follows:

'Women's desire to find satisfaction in the work experience finds expression in their concern with working conditions. . . . As productive workers in the home, women have been less subject to the full force of the calculative relations characteristic of capitalism. In terms of the development of class conscious-ness this is a drawback. It is, however, also in advantage in that it means that to some extent women have been less adequately socialized into seeing themselves as wage earners above all else. Audrey Wise has come near to expressing this distinction by arguing that when women work in industry they put up a struggle to stay human.

'I would say that as a result of their caring for people job in the home women may well return to work with a greater sensitiveness concerning capitalism's capacity to transform workers into the means to profitable ends. . . . Women who are out to find self-satisfaction in their place of work can be more politically assertive than men who see their home as their haven, and who have dismissed industry as a place of self-fulfilment. It is precisely because women are alienated from the home environment that they are more likely to place greater, more positive, demands on the industrial environment.'

(Hunt 1981/1983: 171–73)

Women domesticate the work environment, and demand in it a recognition of themselves as human beings. But their home environment is also a place of work, and women's leisure is less free and less varied than that of men. Women do not therefore experience in the same way as men the fracture between factory and family, work and leisure. Instead, the family permeates work, and domestic life is both love and labour.

Most women employees have a strong commitment to a working identity; but women in employment do not abandon their identities as wives and mothers. In particular, women demonstrate a continuing sense of responsibility for dependants and for the work of maintaining families. This is reflected in the qualified commitment to employment shown in the first of the following quotations, as well as in the more mundane anxiety of the second:

'I see it as if you're going to have a baby you've got to more or less give up sixteen years of your life, they've got to come first, that's how I see it. If it doesn't work, working, then you've got to sacrifice it because you choose to have these children, and I see it that they've got to come first. I mean, if I thought that these kids were in any danger, tomorrow I would pack my job in and go back on social security.'   (Sharpe 1984: 224)

'It's a continuous sort of process of things going on – cycle of clothes and washing and things like this. John will say, "Well you shouldn't be thinking about it", but you've just been trained to do it, you can't switch off, but that's what it is. That's what most women have to contend with all the time . . . they're doing the organizing, that's what they've got to keep in their heads as well as holding down their jobs.'

(Sharpe 1984: 226)

Access to the labour market, then, is not enough. It may improve some women's lives. But liberation for women means changes in reproductive relations as well.

Explaining women's place

Explanations of women's place can centre on the public world, particularly the labour market, or can focus on the private world and the domestic division of labour. They may be based on the material realities of production and reproduction, or on the consciousness of women born into those material realities. This section looks briefly at two of these approaches to explanation: at attempts to explain women's position in the labour market, and at attempts to explain why women do the unpaid work of caring. In general the first type of explanation is materially based and applies to the public world; the second is psychologically based and applies to the private. My own view is that explanation needs to take account of the interactions between public and private work, between production and reproduction, and between material world and private consciousness.

Theories of the labour market

The considerable literature explaining women's position in the labour market is reviewed in Beechey (1978) and Breugel (1983). There are, of course, people who want to put the 'blame' squarely on women themselves, on their qualifications or their aspirations, their productivity, or their preference for low-paid work. One can pick out two conclusions from Breugel's review of these ideas: first, drawing on a study by Greenhalgh that compared the wages of single women and married men,

> 'none of the gap appeared to be explained by differences in personal attributes. Single women had as much experience in the labour-market on average as men (25 years), they had more formal educational qualifications, and had just as often been in their current jobs over a year. They were also more likely to live in Greater London, where wage rates are generally higher, and yet they earned only 73 per cent as much as married men.'

The second conclusion was that, 'Wage and promotion discrimination within firms is only a small proportion of the total discrimination' (Breugel 1983: 148). Put together, these conclusions point to differences between employers, rather than differences between men and women, as the main factor in women's lower pay. Job segregation would seem to bear crucially on the poor status, pay, and conditions of women workers.

Alternatively, then, one can look to the institutional factors that shape the labour market, rather than for some fatal flaw in women. Instead of seeing the labour market as operating neutrally between men and women of different capacities, the market may act with great particularity. Thus some theories have suggested that labour markets impose choices on men and women, and 'confer a biography on individuals' (Barron and Norris 1976: 50). Both 'dual labour market' theories and the Marxist concept of the 'industrial reserve army' point to employers' interests in maintaining a pool of unskilled, low-paid workers to whom they have few commitments and who can easily be sloughed off. So firms may build on divisions of sex and race to create a sector which is insecure and low paid. In Britain, Barron and Norris argue, this secondary labour market 'is pre-eminently a female labour market' (p. 48). The various characteristics of women's work, such as its 'low skill' and its insecurity may be explained in terms of employers' needs rather than in terms of women's abilities and work commitments.

A study of day release, across a variety of settings in business, distribution, chemicals, engineering, and textiles firms gives interesting examples of these sorts of processes operating within firms. Firms in the business sector operated two distinct labour markets:

> 'The two banks we surveyed recruited two broad categories of clerical staff: "non-career" staff, the majority of whom were 16-year-old girls with (normally) four GCE "O" level passes or equivalent, and were seen, as one bank officer put it, as "machine and counter fodder"; and "career" staff, the majority of whom were 18-year-old males with one (or more) GCE "A" level passes. Both these banks deliberately recruited less able and less well qualified girls in order to avoid demands for day release.' (Benett and Carter 1983: 34–5)

Throughout this study are examples of firms not telling girls about training opportunities, using service requirements and age limits to deter the younger female recruits, and using marriage or prospective marriage to throw doubt on girls' commitments to their jobs. By contrast, firms are shown as taking somewhat older male recruits and grooming them for management, explaining training and promotion opportunities.

Such firms are operating a 'dual labour market', and these processes go some way to explaining how some groups of workers come to be disadvantaged. However, there are features which cannot be explained on this basis. For example, sex segregation between firms has already been pointed to as a fundamental feature of the labour market, and is probably more important than segregation within firms; also, some 'women's' careers do, in fact, have career ladders. Most important, this approach lacks an explanation of the specific use of women as the disadvantaged workers.

In a parallel but more radical account Braverman draws directly from Marx in describing capital's need for a pool of cheap labour, which can be drawn into the labour force, or expelled, according to the exigencies of capitalist accumulation. Braverman sees women's labour as one main component of the reserve army which is thus created for capital's use (Braverman 1974). Unlike dual labour market theory, this analysis takes the explanation beyond the firm to major structural upheavals in the labour market and capitalist development.

Feminists have argued that this approach appears to marginalize women's paid labour, and underplays – or confuses – the long-term and permanent shift towards the employment of women's cheap labour. Beechey's conclusion, in her review of Braverman, is that the 'industrial reserve army' concept is useful if restricted to situations in which women are drawn into and expelled from the labour market for specific periods. The two world wars are a clear example of this. The longer term, secular shift towards the use of 'unskilled' female labour, she concludes, can better be understood in terms of 'deskilling', that is, of capital's attempt to control labour power by breaking down traditional skills into simple tasks, carried out by lower paid workers under strictly controlled conditions (Beechey 1982/1983: 69–70).

Such theories, then, go some way towards looking beyond the personal characteristics of men and women, and challenging assumptions about women's lesser productivity. They do begin to take account of the fundamental divisions in the labour market that have been described earlier in this chapter. However, no theory based solely on the labour market is able to explain why it is women who provide such a useful resource of cheap labour and component of the industrial reserve army. The theories lack a component that is specific to gender.

From a feminist point of view, then, such theories are useful but partial. They point to a material context which women play no part in shaping; they connect women's position to the forces of capitalist development in a specific historical manner. But they rest upon presuppositions about the sex/gender system. It is impossible to understand women's position in the labour market without presupposing a domestic division of labour in which women take the major responsibility for reproduction, and a family in which women are dependent on men. It is the designation of young women as future mothers which provides the ideological justification for discriminatory recruitment and training policies. It is the ability of the family to reabsorb women (with little cost to capital) that makes them such an exploitable and large component of the industrial reserve army. And it is economic dependence and domestic/people work that makes them such a useful pool of low-paid, insecure, part-time employees. Labour market theories do presuppose the domestic division of labour and the economic dependence of women – indeed, they largely take it for granted.

Theories of mothering

Instead of beginning in the public world, some feminists begin in the private. Feminist theory here attempts to explain women's responsibility for looking after people. In particular it attempts to explain the difference between mothering and fathering. It attacks assumptions that mothering is simply an inevitable fact of nature or biology. Women's responsibility for nurturing children and caring for adults goes far beyond the biology of reproduction and lactation. The importance of mothers, and the relative absence of fathers in parenting need to be explained.

Dinnerstein's *The Rocking of the Cradle and the Ruling of the World* (1976/1978) and Chodorow's *The Reproduction of Mothering* (1978) are key works. Both draw on psychoanalysis in attempts to explain why women mother. Broadly, the argument is that mothering reproduces itself. Because women – for whatever reason – have cared for children in the past, it is women's presence in the child-rearing process, and men's absence, which reproduce gender differences in children. This will only be changed if men become as much involved in child-care as women.

Chodorow's analysis begins from the social fact that women mother. It also argues in the Freudian tradition for the importance of the psycho-dynamic processes of early childhood in the making of identity. She particularly argues for the importance of relationships in establishing who we are. In western industrial societies, where women have prime responsibility in the private world and men in the public, relationships between mothers and children and fathers and children are asymmetrical.

> 'An account of the early mother–infant relationship in contemporary western society reveals the overwhelming importance of the mother in everyone's psychological development, in their sense of self, and in their basic relational stance. It reveals that becoming a person is the same thing as becoming a person in relationship and in social context.'   (Chodorow 1978: 76)

In addition to gender differences in parenting, there exist gender differences in development. Relationships between mothers and sons and mothers and daughters vary in systematic ways, always conditioned by the asymmetry of parenting. Briefly, girls, in the comparative absence of fathers, have difficulty separating themselves from their mothers and become preoccupied with relational issues. These preoccupations help girls to develop the capacity for mothering, and lead them to seek motherhood. Boys have to identify with fathers for the sake of masculinity. In order to achieve this they become preoccupied with separating themselves from mothers. In doing so they close off their capacities for emotional attachments and become concerned with figuring in the public world.

> 'I argue that the relationship to the mother differs in systematic ways for boys and girls, beginning in the earliest period. The development of mothering in girls – and not in boys – results from differential object-relational experiences, and the ways these are internalized and organized. Development in the infantile period and particularly the emergence and resolution of the oedipus complex entail different psychological reactions, needs and experiences, which cut off or curtail relational possibilities for parenting in boys, and keep them open and extend them in girls.'   (Chodorow 1978: 91)

According to Chodorow, then:

> 'A psychoanalytic investigation shows that women's mother-
> ing capacities and commitments, and the general psychological
> capacities and wants which are the basis of women's emotion
> work, are built developmentally into feminine personality.
> Because women are themselves mothered by women, they
> grow up with the relational capacities and needs, and psycho-
> logical definition of self-in-relationship, which commits them
> to mothering. Men, because they are mothered by women, do
> not.'   (Chodorow 1978: 209)

The merit of this approach is that it points to fundamental issues
of personality in mothering, and to the importance of relationships with children. Women may well find the relationships
within which mothering takes place unsatisfactory, and want to
change them; but they are likely to continue to want to mother.
And women are likely to go on believing that children need
relationships as well as physical care. Change, then, depends not
just on finding women a place in the public world but also on
changing the relationships of reproduction in the family.

The difficulty with the focus on mothering is a tendency to
blame women for their own plight. Little is made of the
advantage to men of shuffling off child-care and domestic
labour, and dominating the public sphere. Furthermore, while
Chodorow recognizes the social context in which women choose
to mother, her analysis is at the level of psycho-dynamics. In
other words, she takes for granted a public world in which
women's opportunities are limited.

Mothers and breadwinners

There is, then, an absence in psycho-dynamic accounts which
parallels the absence in accounts of the labour market. Labour
market theories presuppose a sex/gender system in which
women have major responsibility for children, and a sexual
division of labour built upon that. Psycho-dynamic accounts
presuppose a public world in which men dominate and women
have few opportunities. The prescriptions associated with the
first tend to underestimate the personal investment people have
in existing relations of reproduction. The prescriptions associated
with the second tend to underestimate the importance of the
material context in which people make that investment.

The obvious conclusion is that we need to develop understandings of both public world and private, and of the relations between them. But while we may learn from both the approaches just discussed, there is a danger of circularity. Women do low-paid work because they are responsible for the unpaid work of caring for people; women are dependent in the home because their outside employment is insecure and low paid. This is, indeed, the way the vicious circle is experienced. The condition of women's lives is to be caught between dependency in the family and low wages outside. But as an explanatory account this is inadequate.

One way out of this difficulty is to look for the historical roots of the present configuration of public and private life. The bread-winner/dependent form of family life emerged in response to the physical separation of home and work which went along with industrial processes. The interests of capital ruptured the domestic economy, to produce a separation of production and reproduction, of public and private spheres. Industrial capitalism did not necessarily mean employing only men's labour, but the tendency in the latter part of the nineteenth century was for women to be excluded from paid employment. Trades unions played some part in this. It was certainly in the interests of working men to press for a 'family wage' that would maintain women and children. In so far as women were obliged to be dependent on men's wages, it was in their interests too, however ambivalent that experience was. Historically, then, both capital and trades unions played their part in producing the economic form of the family that we know. State policies, too, have reflected and promoted this economic relationship, through arrangements for social security, child-care, the 'family' care of the elderly and handicapped, and so on.

If it is understood historically, the existence of this kind of family economy does not have to be seen as an immutable, functional necessity of the capitalist mode of production. It is, rather, what emerged from the interaction of the pre-existing family with the processes of industrial capitalism. The fact that the family economy that emerged was strongly favourable to men points to the advantages of men in the pre-capitalist era. It also points to the contemporary interests of men in keeping it so. Men at home and men at work benefit from the division of labour. The structures of labour, of capital, and of the state are male-dominated structures; they tend to reflect men's interests in the labour market and in the family. The breadwinner/dependent model of family life ensures men's dominance at home and at work. It is not likely to crumble in the face of one or two pieces of legislation.

If the particular form of male domination that we have today emerged out of these historical processes, what of the more general existence of male domination in other histories? It also seems necessary to explain men's need to dominate women, a need which transcends the limits of the particular family form of western capitalism. It does seem to make sense to locate this generalized form of male dominance in the reproductive sphere. I am most persuaded by Mary O'Brien's attempt to ground it in the material facts of the reproductive process (O'Brien 1981). The need to dominate women, she argues, arises from the absence of continuity for men in the reproductive process – the potency principle. Control over women is a route to control over reproduction.

These more general reflections, while they show the limits of analysis of our particular family system, do not invalidate it. The particular form in which women experience oppression as women in western capitalism is that of a fracture between public and private life, and the breadwinner/dependant form of family which goes with that.

In practice, these sharp lines are blurred. Women have won for themselves a place in the public world – albeit a disadvantaged one. They have won concessions in the family – though not a transformation. And public and private are reflected in one another in all kinds of ways.

But 'support for the family' in social policy can almost always be interpreted to mean support for the most rigidly demarcated breadwinner/dependent model of the family. And that model, I have argued, is at the heart of the way women experience oppression in western capitalism. That is why state 'support for the family' is seen by feminist as state oppression of women.

Feminist social policy has found more fruitful ways of analysing relations between state and family than the bland assertion of state support. Chapter 1 has already begun to outline some of these approaches.

One approach has been to analyse the kind of family pattern that underlies state policies; and the effects of state support for such families on women inside and outside them.

Another is to analyse the boundary between state and family.

As a corollary of the fact that women and social policy 'share' a concern with reproduction, social policy defines a key boundary between public life and private life. Through social policy are decided such questions as whether – or at what age – the raising of children is 'educational' and part of the public world, or whether it is nurturing and a 'private' responsibility; or at what point the sick and elderly become part of the health industry; or which family relationships entail dependency. Nurturing and caring activities may be part of paid public work or unpaid private. The boundary thus drawn is of the greatest significance in women's lives and measures the real extent of state support for reproductive work.

A third approach is to examine the extent of public control over reproduction and over women's work.

The idea of support for the family, then, has to be replaced with a critical analysis of the nature of relations between the state and the family.

3

Caring and Social Policy

In simple terms, caring is looking after people: people capable of looking after themselves but who choose not to – teenagers, husbands, perhaps – and people who need intimate daily care for health and life – babies, the very old and frail. Such looking after involves work, often hard work, and it involves relationships which are likely to be profoundly important to those involved. It is often assumed that the state has 'taken over' a great deal of such work from the 'family', and that men have taken over much from women. This chapter is about the division of caring work, between state and family, and between men and women. And because caring work is mostly done by women, it is concerned with the meaning of such work in women's lives, the material context in which women accept it, and its material consequences.

Some of the most interesting recent work in feminist social policy has centred on caring, or 'human service' or 'people work'. Two particularly important essays are by Hilary Graham, on 'Caring: A Labour of Love' (1983), and by Margaret Stacey on 'The Division of Labour Revisited or Overcoming the Two Adams' (1981). Both these essays claim a central significance for caring work, in society and social policy. According to Graham, 'caring is not something on the periphery of our social order; it marks the point at which the relations of capital and gender intersect. It should be the place we begin, and not end our analysis of modern society' (Graham 1983: 30). Graham goes on to quote Stacey: 'We shall never be able to understand the social processes going on around us so long as we tacitly or overtly deny the part played by the givers and receivers of "care" and "service", the victims of socialization processes, the unpaid labourers in the processes of production and reproduction' (Stacey 1981: 189).

A second point shared by these authors is a critique of the ways in which existing conceptual categories and disciplines fragment and obscure the meaning and importance of caring. Stacey sees this in terms of reconceptualizing the division of labour. She argues that the way sociology divides work from family, public from private, leaves us with inadequate means of understanding work that straddles the two. Work that takes place in the private domain tends to be uncounted and unanalysed; or if it is analysed, it is described in inappropriate terms borrowed from the world of industry. The whole division of labour is thus understood in terms of work in the public domain. We need, she thinks, to 'rethink what constitutes work' (Stacey 1981).

The point is followed up by Graham in her argument that we need a 'reconception of caring' (Graham 1983: 23). Disciplinary boundaries, she argues, have fragmented our understanding of caring which demands 'both love and labour, both identity and activity' (Graham 1983: 13). Social policy has studied the work aspects of caring, the material constraints within which women make choices about caring, and the material effects on women's lives that flow from these responsibilities. Psychology, on the other hand, has focused on the emotional aspects of caring; it sees the responsibility for others as the key to female identity. Caring is what makes women women. Both approaches are inadequate. The account of caring as work fails to face up to the 'emotional component of human service' (Stacey 1981: 173). It 'tends to underplay the symbolic bonds that hold the caring relationship together. The roots of people's deep resistance to the socialization of care is thus lost' (Graham 1983: 29). But analysis in terms of feminine identity and self-fulfilment neglects the material aspects of caring; it runs the risk of concluding that caring is an essential, natural, part of women's identity and of legitimizing women's place in the material world. Instead of these separate accounts, we need an analysis which can contain both love and labour, which can take seriously both the emotional and material understandings of caring and of why women do it.

Unfortunately, for the present, we have to rely mostly on accounts that are conceived in traditional categories. However, these authors do point in important directions, which can be followed to some degree. First, Stacey points to the need to connect the division of labour at home to the division of labour in the public world; to understand social policy developments in terms which incorporate both, and which analyse the changing boundaries between state and family in caring for people. Such a look at the division of caring labour shows that a large part of state social policy consists in taking a small part of caring work into the public sphere. Health services in particular, but also education and social work, consist in turning some specialized aspects of caring work into 'professional' employment; and in their absorption into a masculine hierarchy, though with a large female labour force. At the same time, large parts of educational, health, and caring work are still undertaken within the family. Here they may not be thought of as 'health work' or 'education work' or even as work. Nevertheless, for children under five, the greater part of health and educational care is given by mothers; schoolchildren may spend 'fifteen thousand hours' at school, but they will spend more waking hours than that at home; and at the other end of life, the most dependent elderly people are more likely to rely on relatives than on social services:

> 'The extensive and intensive care provided by the family forms the basis on which the professional services have evolved. Professional health workers, like doctors and health visitors, do not provide an alternative to the family; rather, they have a range of skills which they employ in order to improve the quality of care that families provide. Doctors diagnose and prescribe treatments for the patients who come to them; they do not nurse the sick. Similarly, health visitors listen and advise: it is left to mothers to put their advice into practice.'
>
> (Graham 1984: 7)

The state has not, therefore, taken away the work of caring from families or from women. Males of all ages, and females young and old are likely to require care and to be looked after at home by women. The small percentage of children and elderly who are cared for out of families – at great expense – are still cared for mainly by women. Caring work cuts across the boundaries of family/employment and family/social policy; understanding its pattern is central to understanding social policy.

The second direction in which this writing points is to putting both love and labour aspects of caring in the balance, even where we lack the material for a more integrated account. The unsharing of caring can be counted and costed; but those who bear that cost are not clamouring to hand their children or their mothers over to the government. To count the very small part that social policy plays in the care of young and old is not to call for comprehensive institutional care for the under fives and over sixties. It should be assumed that caring relationships matter profoundly to those involved in them.

This chapter concentrates on the very young and the very old. These are the groups who are most dependent on others for day-to-day life; they are also the groups whose care government departments are most anxious to shrug off. They are therefore predominantly the province of the domestic world. Their care largely involves relationships including women; and those relationships and the labour involved have profound long-term consequences for women's place in the public world.

The chapter also looks at the ideas of 'maternal deprivation' and 'community care'. To anticipate a little, the most striking features of the division of caring labour are its allocation to women and its location in the home. The idea that care of young and old belongs to women and to the home is widely held and believed in as a 'natural' phenomenon. Such ideas appear as unquestioned assumptions by those who take on care, as well as in scientific and political discourse. In this chapter the section on children is prefaced by a discussion of one formulation of this idea – the maternal deprivation thesis. The section on the elderly is prefaced by a discussion of another – 'community care'. There are, of course, other formulations of motherhood and domesticity which could be considered. But these two are of special import-ance: 'maternal deprivation' because of its widespread dissemi-nation and 'scientific' authority; 'community care' because of its insistent promulgation by government departments.

The connection between the ideas and the politics of caring is not a clear one. 'Maternal deprivation' theory cannot be credited with all responsibility for state policy towards under fives and their mothers and fathers. Neither can ideology be seen as something foisted on a gullible population by a penny-pinching government which wants to keep women at home. (For a critical approach to such ideas see Riley 1983.) But these are key concepts which have helped to keep the bulk of caring work in the domestic arena and in women's hands. They are the background against which government success in keeping out of caring work can be better understood; their critique is also one foundation for a critical analysis of caring policy and, indeed, for any vision of a different future.

This chapter, then, looks at the care of the very young and very old; at some key ideas about caring as women's work and as domestic labour; at the question of who does it, in terms of boundaries between social policy and the family, as well as between men and women; at the material context and impact of caring work in women's lives; and at what caring relationships mean to those involved in them.

Caring for young children

Maternal deprivation

The ideology of domesticity, of woman and home, is at its most intense when it invokes the needs of young children. Here there are droves of 'experts', from 'Locke to Spock' as one recent writer put it (Hardyment 1983) and, indeed, beyond. Child-care writers, Freudian psychologists, and developmental psychologists have all devoted a great deal of ink and opinion to children's needs. Children's needs for mothers are the usual starting point, and often the finishing point. Their needs for fathers are an occasional afterthought; the rest of the world frequently seems immaterial.

A key reference point for this literature, and the undercurrent for more popular journalism on the subject, is John Bowlby's famous work on *Maternal Care and Mental Health* published by the WHO in 1951 (Bowlby 1951/1965). Bowlby's work highlighted the profoundly damaging effect of poor institutional care on young children. Unfortunately, it also pointed to 'maternal deprivation' as the key to ill effects on institutionalized children, at the time and in their later lives.

Briefly, Bowlby's argument, as popularized in the revised version of 1953, was that 'what is believed to be essential for mental health is that an infant and young child should experience a warm, intimate, and continuous relationship with his mother (or permanent mother-substitute – one person who steadily "mothers" him) in which both find satisfaction and enjoyment' (Bowlby 1953/1965: 13). To be without such a relationship was to suffer 'maternal deprivation' (p. 14), which could happen even when the child lived with its parents. The relationship with mother, or mother-substitute, was the relationship that mattered. In the young child's eyes, according to Bowlby, 'father plays second fiddle' (p. 15); the father's part is defined, not as relating to his child, but as providing for 'the economic and emotional support of the mother' (p. 16). Therefore, the book did not 'treat in detail the child's relation to his father' (p. 15). The significance of maternal deprivation was long term; 'what occurs in the earliest months and years of life can have deep and long-lasting effects' (p. 17). Maternally deprived children would be damaged adults who might damage their own children in the same way. 'Deprived children, whether in their own homes or out of them, are the source of social infection as real and serious as are carriers of diphtheria and typhoid' (p. 239).

Bowlby did make distinctions between degrees of deprivation (though not adequate ones). His main evidence concerned children who had wholly lacked loving care from anyone, but he made it clear that his argument concerned less serious deprivations, and uttered rather ominous-sounding warnings:

> 'The absolute need of infants and toddlers for the continuous care of their mothers will be borne in on all who read this book, and some will exclaim "Can I then never leave my child?". Though far more knowledge is required before a proper answer can be given, some advice is perhaps possible. In the first place, we must recognize that leaving any child of under three years of age is a major operation only to be undertaken for good and sufficient reasons, and, when undertaken, to be planned with great care.'   (Bowlby 1953/1965: 18)

Today's child-care books strike a more homely note, but their habitual tone of reassurance is not enough to disguise a persistent anxiety about mothers who do not spend 100 per cent of their time with their small children. And their debt to the thinking of Bowlby is plain enough. Dr Jolly, for example, in one of today's widely recommended manuals, advises: 'Babies and small children need loving individual care from one person who handles them most of the time.' It is immediately clear that the one person is a 'mother, or mother-figure'. Next it seems that going out to work might be all right: 'The baby with a working mother is all right if he has someone else to provide this focus and interest, as long as she is warm, understanding and permanent.' But lest that be seen to be too encouraging, there follows a catalogue of hazards:

> 'But the relationship between the two of you might be less intimate, more of a "special relationship" than the deep friendliness that develops between two people who are constantly together. Mummy is probably a more romantic figure if she is not always available and is not associated with the kitchen sink, but she is also a more remote figure. She may find herself being more indulgent than she knows is good for the child because she is anxious to enjoy him while they are together. However,

the opposite can happen – a mother falls over backwards to avoid "spoiling" her child and ends up by being stricter than comes naturally to her.' (Jolly 1975/1977: 177)

After more pitfalls, the mother is told that 'it is normal to feel intellectually rather lazy and even "cow-like" for a year or so after having a baby. You may not feel like doing anything more demanding than reading magazines.' And in case there should be any doubt: 'Don't force yourself to take on work because you feel it is expected nowadays' (Jolly, 1975/1977: 178). Perhaps it is as well that fathers going out to work do not provoke so much anxiety.

There is another side to this ideology of motherhood. If children need mothers, women also need children. This idea, too, has firm roots in the psychoanalytic tradition, as well as a pervasive hold in popular advice literature and journalism. The Freudian idea is that women reach mature femininity through bearing sons. More popularly, romantic notions of women fulfilled through motherhood lie behind everything from cornflakes advertisements to the British Medical Association's advice on 'You and Your Baby' (see Oakley 1974a: 187–190, for a discussion of these issues).

The maternal deprivation thesis has now been extensively researched; the research is authoritatively reviewed by Rutter (1972/1981). The effects of day care too have been studied, particularly by developmental psychologists. Fortunately, the evidence is altogether more cheerful than the prognostications of Bowlby and those child-care 'experts' who follow in his intellectual tradition. No one argues that children thrive without love and care, without security and stimulation – or that they should be asked to do so. What is argued is that the maternal deprivation thesis is too diffuse in its meaning, attaches too much importance to bonding with a single mother-figure, and is too pessimistic about the long-term irreversibility of damage inflicted on young children at supposedly critical periods. It can also be argued that it is culturally hidebound, operating within the framework of a culture where children's resources are highly limited – where, if they do not have good mothers, they are likely to lack all the essentials for human development.

Rutter's work, however, assesses the meaning and effects of 'maternal deprivation' from within the cultural perspective of child-rearing in twentieth-century Britain and America. In other words, his work is a critique of a body of theory, not a critique of western child-rearing practice. He accepts Bowlby's notion that children need to develop attachments, and that disruption of such attachments is distressing. But children have other needs, and it is not at all clear that the mother must provide everything. In considering the distress which children display in hospitals and nurseries, Rutter remarks:

> 'The evidence that distress is much reduced by the presence of a brother or sister or a friend even when the mother remains absent strongly suggests that there is nothing specific about mother separation. Indeed it is most curious that studies of children in hospital or a residential nursery are nearly always considered as examples of separation from mother when in fact they consist of separation from mother and father and sibs and the home environment.' (Rutter 1972/1981: 50)

Neither does separation in itself necessarily have dire consequences for relationships between parents and children. Briefly, Rutter concludes, in relation to short-term consequences of 'maternal deprivation': 'theories of mothering have frequently been too mechanical in equating separation with bond disruption, too restricted in regarding the mother as the only person important in a child's life, and too narrow in considering love as the only important element in maternal care' (p. 53). In relation to long-term consequences, of supposed defective personality development, Rutter argues: 'Bonding, caretaking and play are three separate functions which may or may not be performed by the same person. It is hypothesized that so long as all three are available, it is of no matter, with regard to the prevention of "affectionless psychopathy", who provides them, and in particular it does not matter if the mother does so' (p. 108). Rutter's conclusion is that:

> 'the evidence strongly suggests that most of the long-term consequences are due to privation or lack of some kind, rather than to any type of loss. Accordingly the "deprivation" half of the concept is somewhat misleading. The "maternal" half of the concept is also inaccurate in that, with but few exceptions, the deleterious influences concern the care of the child or relationships with people rather than any specific defect of the mother.' (Rutter 1972/1981: 121)

The idea of 'maternal deprivation', then, belongs to a society in which children separated from mothers are separated from love, care, and play. When these consequences are disentangled it appears that, given the chance, children can develop attachments widely in the world, that their care can safely be shared, and that it is at least as stimulating for them to share play with other adults and children as to rely wholly on their mothers. Studies of day care tend to suggest that it is often more stimulating. The tendency of Bowlby's writing is to associate mothering with biological processes (for example, by comparison with 'imprinting' in animals). This distances his argument from the ways in which patterns of child-care have to do with culture. This may not make patterns of care much easier to change, but it does suggest that the consequences of different patterns may be less dire than he supposed. Children allowed to form more diverse relationships may even be more protected than others from the hazards of separation and loss.

While the 'maternal deprivation' thesis does not positively propose that children will be unalterably damaged if their mothers spend some hours out of each twenty-four away from them, it has induced wariness. Subsequently, researchers have more carefully differentiated the effects of day care from those of residential nurseries. Rutter has added a chapter to the recent edition of his book; and research has also been reviewed by Hughes (1980) and Clarke-Stewart (1982). Rutter argues that it is incorrect to assume that families who use day care are the same as those who do not; and he points out that day care itself is varied. Most existing work does not, therefore, allow simple conclusions. However:

> 'good quality day care does not disrupt a child's emotional bonds with his parents; moreover, children continue to prefer their parents over alternative caregivers. Furthermore, even day care for very young children does not usually result in serious emotional disturbance. On the other hand, there are indications that to some extent day care influences the form of children's social behaviour (in ways which may be either helpful or deleterious).'   (Rutter 1972/1981: 178)

Hughes and Clarke-Stewart are rather less cautious. Clarke-Stewart's review of a wide range of studies finds very consistent results in the direction of day care children showing greater intellectual and social competence (Clarke-Stewart 1982: 66–75). Hughes concludes that children benefit from nurseries by their wider circle of relationships and play facilities; but they also benefit indirectly because mothers benefit (Hughes 1980: 60).

'Maternal deprivation' is an important part of the background against which policy for young children has developed in Britain. Bowlby's work was not an isolated phenomenon, but it was unusually popular in form and effect. Riley writes that it is:

'popularizing . . . which has an impact in the world, and this which has to be examined if the entanglements of psychology with social policies are to be unravelled. It is not pure psychoanalytic theory which has been most visible; it has been Bowlby's work with its particular characterizing of maternity, the family, emotions, institutions, zoology.'

(Riley 1983: 6–7)

Bowlby's work supported – though it was not wholly responsible for – a belief that a young child must at all times be at home with its mother, a belief which later became 'so dominant that for years it has held sway in debates about nursery provision' (Riley 1983: 110).

The division of caring labour: mothers and the state

Over 99 per cent of children live with one or both parents. Local authority care befalls a small minority; and even among children in care about half will be cared for by parents, guardians, or foster parents (Graham 1984: 24). Some part of older children's care is undertaken by the state education system. But this does not apply to the youngest, most dependent children.

Government documents argue that it is no part of state business to provide care for children under five, unless there is special need, or an educational benefit. The fact that they were saying this in 1945, when hastily closing down wartime nurseries, shows that policy has not owed everything to Bowlby (see Riley 1979: 1983). But the 'evidence' of 'maternal deprivation' has added authority, and sometimes hysteria, to the policy of reserving government funds for better uses. In 1945 the Ministry of Health told local authorities: 'The ministers concerned . . . are of the opinion that, under normal peacetime conditions, the right policy to pursue would be positively to discourage mothers of children under two from going out to work' (Ministry of Health 1945, quoted in Fonda 1980: 110). In 1968, maternal deprivation thesis in pocket, the same Ministry held that nursery provision 'must be looked at in relation to the view of medical and other authority that early and prolonged separation from the mother is detrimental to the child (and) that wherever possible the younger preschool child should be at home with his mother' (Ministry of Health 1968, quoted in Hughes 1980: 46).

The practice of the 1950s and 1960s confirmed the policy rhetoric. In Ministries of Education and Health there evolved policies which left the great majority of care for the great majority of children with mothers. The Ministry of Health developed a set of criteria for day nurseries to include only those children with special needs: children of single parents where the parent had to take paid work, children whose mothers were thought incapable of care, and so on (see Bone 1977: 2). Nurseries were not for children of ordinary mothers, or for women who preferred employment to full-time child-care. Policy in the Ministry of Education had a similar drift, in effectively excluding children of employed mothers. Responsibility for pre-school children not thought to have special needs was transferred to the Ministry of Education after the war; but nursery schools did not operate a full working day, and catered only for children of age three plus; they thus depended on the existence of fairly full-time mothers, and were irrelevant to the needs of most employed mothers and their children (Riley 1979; Tizard, Moss, and Perry 1976: 76–9).

Subsequent policy tended further in this direction. The pattern of nursery school provision shifted from a norm of full-day sessions to one of half-days. 'By the 1970s part-time education for under fives had become not just a regrettable practical necessity, but a policy justified on educational grounds' (Tizard, Moss, and Perry 1976: 76). Notions of cultural deprivation brought nursery education to the fore in the war against poverty; but it was clear that this education was to compensate for inadequate mothers, not to encourage them to become more 'inadequate' by taking employment or spending more than the odd couple of hours away from their children. Thus the one flurry of activity for the under fives promoted very part-time schooling, which could be used only by very full-time mothers.

The state, then, does not provide day care for ordinary children in ordinary families. The few existing facilities go to those in special need (day nurseries) or give mainly part-time 'education' to older under-fives (nursery classes, nursery schools, and reception classes in primary schools). These two forms of public provision come under different administrations and cater for a small proportion of the age-group.

Day nursery places are the main full-time provision, but the few available are generally reserved for children in special need. In 1981 they catered for 1 per cent of the age-group. Nursery schools and nursery classes in primary schools offer many more places, but largely part time, and only for children of two and over (by legal restriction), or four and over (in common practice). These together took 9 per cent of the age-group. A large contribution is made by reception classes of ordinary primary schools, which took 7 per cent. Together the state sector catered for 18 per cent of the age-group (figures recalculated from Central Statistical Office, *Social Trends 1985*: 20, 45). Local authorities also have a role in controlling and servicing the private sector. There is, though, no commitment to a general service for children under five and their mothers. Children living at home, it is assumed, will have a mother constantly available. Of course, children may be removed from home and cared for wholly by local authorities, but between this drastic measure and constant maternal attendance there is – as far as state services go – a chasm.

In part the chasm is filled by private arrangements, by the 'informal networks' currently beloved by writers of government documents. Registered child-minders fill the gap for mothers and children needing substantial periods each day (3 per cent of the age-group). Unregistered ones probably look after half as many again. Playgroups offer many, but very part-time places. The most informal, and very common arrangement for children of employed mothers is care by relatives and friends (Bone 1977: 22; Jackson and Jackson 1979: 87; Martin and Roberts 1984: 156). But while 'informal networks' fill part of the chasm, nothing fills the whole of it. Many mothers accept inadequate and stressful arrangements, and many more would like day care than use it.

'Even when all nurseries, playgroups and other services are taken together, the total number of places available still falls far short of the number desired by parents . . . surveys carried out in London, Rochdale, Oxfordshire and Fife – as well as the nationwide OPCS survey – indicate that places are wanted for about two-thirds of all pre-school children in the country. Yet . . . there are altogether places for only 40 per cent of all children, and over a fifth of these are in reception classes not primarily intended for under-fives. . . . Even those children whose circumstances classify them as "priority" admissions for council day nurseries – for example, children of single parents who have to work, or children who are considered to be severely "socially disadvantaged" – are by no means guaranteed a place. In 1976 there were nearly 12,000 priority children on the *waiting lists* of council day nurseries, almost half the total number of places available.'   (Hughes 1980: 115)

Shortage of resources is a common enough refrain in discussions about social services. But what characterizes these services is more absence than shortage. It clearly reflects the ideology of mothers' responsibility, and fear of undermining this principle. While practice reflects ideology, ideology is reinforced by practice: children should not be separated from their mothers; caring services will therefore be provided on the barest minimum level; in the absence of decent facilities, everyone must concede that children should be with mothers.

Unfortunately, many women are in a double bind. Staying at home to look after children full time may have ill effects on their mental health (see Brown and Harris 1978) and therefore on their children. Paid employment may be the only way to keep them and their children out of poverty. At this point class differences may be crucial. Some women can buy themselves out of the dilemma; others cannot. Women who cannot, and their children, bear a heavy cost in inadequate care arrangements and disrupted family lives.

In 1978, the Central Policy Review Staff admitted that 'there are major problems of child neglect and widespread use of unsatisfactory child-minders' (Central Policy Review Staff 1978: 18). The Jacksons' study of child-care in Huddersfield more graphically describes some of the stresses of working alternating shifts, an arrangement that appeared 'an important feature of family life':

'our impression was that this group of children may be especially disadvantaged. They were more likely than any others to be left alone in the house, either when the parents' shifts overlapped or when both parents were temporarily on nights. Of course very few parents would openly admit to leaving their children alone, but we had plenty of reason to think this happened much more often than we were told. Hardly better off were the children left in the care of very young brothers and sisters; one of these child child-minders was only six years old herself.'   (Jackson and Jackson 1979: 94–5)

The Jacksons attribute these arrangements to lack of alternatives. Nursery classes and playgroups excluded themselves by their short hours, and were anyway few and far between in the working-class district they studied. Child-minders had to be paid, but were the main alternative for those who needed more than the family could provide.

Unfortunately, the drift of many arguments for public sector provision tends towards an attack on child-minders. It is not hard to find inadequate child-care in any setting – child-minding, local authority care, or family – but it is unfortunate to attack child-minders, who may be victims of the same forces as their charges. Some parents are left with little option but to accept inadequate arrangements, or to bear with patterns of work and family life that are extraordinarily stressful. The harshest cost of withholding state support for child-care is borne by such parents and children. But all mothers of young children bear some cost, in terms of very limited alternatives. To stay at home may be to suffer isolation and depression, as well as to jeopardize future employment and pensions; to take full-time employment may be to bear the 'triple-shift' of work, husband-support, and housework/child-care; to work part time is to join the most exploited and low-paid part of the labour-force. Underlying all these choices is the model of a family in which women care for children, without contribution by men or services, and in which men do paid work and 'provide'. Day care for children exists only where there are special 'problems' or where it is thought to be educational, i.e. where mothers may be feared inadequate. The model is clearly an inaccurate one, unattainable where the father cannot support the children, undesirable for women and children alike, undesirable, indeed, even for some men. In so far as the model does not fit the real world, where women with children do go out to work, it imposes heavy costs on those who cannot make decent arrangements for their children.

Embedded in state provision for children, particularly the under fives, is a peculiar contradiction. On the one hand is the ideology of motherhood as an essentially private, domestic affair: children are not for sharing. This ideology is reflected in policy statements and in the nature of nursery provision; its maintenance is cornerstone of defence for a certain kind of family pattern. On the other hand, children are the future, producers and reproducers. They are also, therefore, a very public concern. State interest is shown by massive expenditure on children and adolescents in the educational system; but it is also shown, tentatively, for under fives by the protective element in day nursery provision (for children with 'inadequate' mothers) and by the compensatory element in nursery education (particularly marked in Plowden). One ludicrous outcome of this contradiction is the sudden shift, in both ideology and provision, between the ages of four and five. At four, more or less continuous maternal care is preferred, and a half-day place at a nursery school is good fortune. But woe betide a parent who decides thereafter that she would prefer to keep her children at home.

State policies for young children reflect the idea that successful development depends on continuous care by mothers. The counterpart – usually assumed – is that women's fulfilment lies in devoting themselves wholly to this task. The idealization of this – historically somewhat peculiar – intimate and isolated relationship underpins the place of women in domestic life, and therefore in public life too.

The division of caring labour: men and women

That the under fives belong to mothers rather than to fathers is widely assumed. Indeed, the previous section is about mothers and the state rather than about parents, because government departments share and promote this assumption about the sexual division of labour. There is, however, an alternative version of the family available – a version that has men becoming much more involved, sharing the labour of child-care while women share the labour of breadwinning. Thus, according to some studies, we have 'symmetrical families' and 'highly participant' fathers. There is, no doubt, some basis in reality for this alternative version, for the sense that families have changed. Men do some things with children that they used not to do. There is, as Harris describes, 'a blurring of the division of labour' (Harris 1983: 231), and a greater sense that sharing ought to happen. However, the argument of this section is that child-care still belongs to mothers, in the sense that it is still overwhelmingly their continuing responsibility; and that the material and power relationships built upon this have not substantially changed.

Mary Boulton argues that many studies overestimate the participation of fathers for two main reasons. The first is that, in a culture which sees children as mothers' business, any participation by fathers is thought remarkable. Thus fathers who take any part at all may be rated as very much involved. The second reason is that child-care tends to be described as a series of tasks, rather than as a relationship and a responsibility; and taking a part in some tasks is not the same thing as sharing responsibility (Boulton 1983: 147–48). Boulton concludes from her own study as follows:

> 'The number of men described as giving each pattern of help . . . suggests that children are still almost exclusively the women's domain. In only nine families was there anything approximating to parenthood as a 'joint enterprise', while in almost half of the families the husband left the care of the children to his wife alone and in a third he did no more than support his wife with moderate help. There is little evidence from this study, therefore, to suggest that the sharing of child care between husband and wife is now widespread.'
>
> (Boulton 1983: 145)

If husbands do not, in general, share child-care, neither do others. For all the debate about 'nuclear' and 'extended' families, one thing is clear. The 'reproductive group' as Harris puts it 'has shrunk to its nuclear core'. 'In industrial societies in comparison with other cultures, and epochs, the reproductive group is quite remarkably restricted in form' (Harris 1983: 183).

State services, men, 'extended families', thus play no major part in the care of the under fives. It is not surprising, then, to find that mothers recite a litany about responsibility for their children, a responsibility in which there is no one to share (see, for example, Boulton 1983: 78ff.). Motherhood in industrial societies is characterized by an intense and singular relationship and responsibility.

Caring for the elderly and handicapped

'Community care'

An ideology that romanticizes caring for the elderly and handicapped seems more improbable than one that romanticizes motherhood. However, the idea of 'community care', while less developed than romanticized notions of motherhood, fulfils a very similar function in legitimating minimal state activity in the private sphere of home and family. It also disguises minimal men's activity.

The notion of 'community care' belongs to social policy documents rather than to women. It does not have the widespread allegiance of 'maternal deprivation'; nor is it in any sense 'needed' to persuade women to look after dependent relatives and friends. Its use has been in justifying low government spending on the elderly and handicapped, and in disguising policies whose real effects are to burden and isolate individuals. Irony is plentiful. For community one can read its virtual opposite. The heavier the demands of caring, the less likely the 'community' will care to be involved (Equal Opportunities Commission 1982a: 17–18). An expression which appears warmly to encompass everyone disguises the fact that, whether as paid workers or as relatives, it is generally women who do the 'caring'. And for 'care', when it comes to state activity, one may often read neglect.

'Community care' has been casting its warm glow over government documents for almost as long as we have had a 'Welfare State'. Titmuss found official use of the term in 1950 (Titmuss 1968: 107). He was probably the first to hint that it served an ideological function: 'And what of the everlasting cottage-garden trailer, "Community Care"? Does it not conjure up a sense of warmth and human kindness, essentially personal and comforting, as loving as the wild flowers so enchantingly described by Lawrence in *Lady Chatterley's Lover*?.' The concern of Titmuss's essay 'Community Care: Fact or Fiction?' was to begin to uncover the reality which this 'comforting appellation' (Titmuss 1968: 104) so well disguised. The need for this exercise becomes more urgent as 'community care' is sprinkled ever more liberally through government documents, apparently to deal with an increasing population of dependent people.

The idea of community care would have no power but for its basis in widely shared values. Its use in the 1950s and 1960s in the critique of inhumane institutions was not altogether sham. And the ideal of people in general supporting the elderly and handicapped is hardly contentious. What is contentious is the implication of a state of affairs which has never existed (i.e. a comprehensive network of community services in support of work in the private world of home); and the disguising of a sexual division of labour disadvantageous to women.

The rhetoric of 'community care' has undergone some change. In the 1950s and early 1960s it was part of an assault on large-scale, isolated institutions. 'At that time the emphasis seemed to be mainly upon replacing large and often geographically remote institutional facilities with smaller units of residential provision, located in built-up areas which would, if possible, be familiar to individual residents' (Finch and Groves 1980: 489). By the late 1960s and 1970s the emphasis had shifted towards ideas of community involvement. By the 1980s care by the community was to take the place of state involvement. For example, a recent White Paper, *Growing Older*, takes community resources as its theme, with cuts in public services lurking not far below the surface. Chapter 1 concludes:

'Providing adequate support and care for elderly people in all their varying personal circumstances is a matter which concerns – and should involve – the whole community; not just politicians and officials, or charitable bodies. It is a responsibility which must be shared by everyone. Public authorities simply will not command the resources to deal with it alone; nor, even if they did, would it be right or possible for official help to meet all individual needs.'

(DHSS 1981a: 3, para 1.11)

And the very last remarks of the paper are:

'improving the lives of elderly people must involve the whole of society. The government hopes it will help people every-where to take stock of the implications – for themselves and for others – of the growing numbers of elderly people, and encourage them to consider what they can do to meet the challenge and the opportunity it poses.'   (DHSS 1981a: 64, para 9.23)

When such remarks are taken in conjunction with public spending plans, their implications are quite plain: 'community care' is a substitute for social services.

'Community care', then, has flexible meaning. It may be used to contrast with institutions; to imply publicly provided services in support of caring work; or to imply informal 'networks of provision'. While the rhetoric changes, the underlying meaning is more consistent. As Finch and Groves put it: 'in practice community care equals care by the family, and in practice care by the family equals care by women' (Finch and Groves 1980: 494).

The division of caring labour: the state and the family

The aim of much recent empirical work on caring has been to lift it out of the obscurity of domesticity, and describe it as labour analogous to industrial labour, much as housework and child-care have been described by writers such as Oakley (1974). Researchers have begun to ask who does such labour, how heavy is the burden, what are its relations with paid caring work carried out by central and local authorities, what are its effects on carers' lives, and what are its economic costs? Studies of this kind include several by the Equal Opportunities Commission (1980, 1982a, 1982c, 1984), works by Cartwright and Bowling (1982), Nissel and Bonnerjea (1982), and Glendinning (1983); other work is reported in collections by Walker (ed.) (1982), and by Finch and Groves (1983). Since most empirical work has aimed to discover the work of caring, and to describe it as work, the most general account that can be given of it is this somewhat economistic one. (The problems raised by this frame of reference have already been suggested.)

One way of describing who does caring work is to look at the share borne by state services, relatives, and voluntary/friendly help. This gives some insight into state/family relations as well as into the realities of 'community care'.

Only in institutions does the state bear the full cost of caring for dependent adults. Most institutional care is state organized and state funded. The recent growth of privately organized institutions, funded partly through DHSS payments to residents, is a complicating but so far unmeasurable factor. In most institutions neither residents nor relatives are normally expected to share caring work; in this – as will be shown later – they contrast with 'community care', where the state plays a relatively minor part. The rate of institutionalization is therefore one way of looking at the state's share of caring work. From the public expenditure point of view, it is by far the most expensive form of care, and one which tends to soak up increasing proportions of the budget, irrespective of numerous government documents aimed at giving priority to 'community care' (see, for example, Walker 1983: 158–63). In terms of the cost to government, then, and of the share of care provided by the state, institutions contrast sharply with most 'community' alternatives.

It is not entirely easy to measure rates of institutional care, since old and handicapped people live and stay in a variety of residential settings, under a variety of authorities. These include hospitals, geriatric and general, mental and mental handicap, as well as homes provided by local authorities and a complexity of other private, voluntary arrangements with different degrees and sources of state support. The proportion living in institutions is very low in relation to the numbers of old and handicapped living at home or with other family members – only about 5 per cent of those over pension age. Concentrating on those who are handicapped, Walker concludes that there are 'three times as many bedfast and disabled elderly people living in their own or their relatives' homes as in all institutions put together' (Walker 1983: 165).

Thus a small minority of adult dependants live in state institutions. And the minority seems to be getting smaller. A recent summary of changes in institutionalization by Kathleen Jones and A. J. Fowles (1983) shows a varied pattern for different institutions. It concludes that the number of patients resident in mental hospitals and in mental handicap hospitals has declined considerably over the two decades to 1980; on the other hand, local authority residential provision for this group has increased substantially. The net general effect is, first, a shift from central government funded institutions to local authority ones; second, rather little change in the population of these institutions; but, third, some decrease in institutional places in relation to a population which was growing larger, and growing older. The authors argue that by 1980 the elderly population, in particular, 'had relatively less institutional care available than twenty years earlier' (Jones and Fowles 1983: 97).

The numbers of both handicapped and elderly people are rising dramatically (see, for example, Parker 1981), and the pattern of institutional/domiciliary care cannot be understood without realizing this. More state spending and more institutions can still leave relatives with more of the cost. Growing numbers of elderly, and especially very elderly people, fill government planning documents with an air of anxiety. The DHSS paper *Growing Older* tells us:

'In the last twenty years the number of men and women aged 65 and over has risen by no less than one-third. They now represent about 15 per cent of the population; and their numbers are still growing. Within the total increase another profound change is taking place. Not only are more people living longer, but the average age of the older generation is rising. By the end of the century the number of people aged 75 and over is expected to increase by about one-fifth, and the number aged 85 and over by no less than one-half.' (DHSS 1981a: 1)

Pressures on space in hospitals and homes have led to some dramatic changes, including more rapid turnover in hospitals and a quite different clientele for residential homes. The DHSS explains it in these terms: 'In the past, people entered residential homes while they were still in their sixties. Now, with the expansion of community care and sheltered housing, the age of admission has been rising steadily and the average is approaching 82' (DHSS 1981a: 44–5). The DHSS, then, justify the increasing age of entry to residential establishments by reference to 'community' alternatives, including sheltered housing. The next section looks in more detail at the way dependants and their carers are supported at home. It will just be remarked here that sheltered housing – while it has certainly expanded – has also undergone an ageing process (Finch and Groves 1982: 431). Neither residential care nor sheltered housing are generally available to any but the very old.

Doubtless, more old people are now healthier and more able to care for themselves. But the greatly increased numbers of very elderly and handicapped people, the increasing age of entry to residential care, together with the analysis of numbers in institutions provided by Jones and Fowles, seem to point also to a growing rate of dependency in households. There has been, in this area, a translation from public sphere to private, from state institution to the family. Social policy in relation to care for the elderly and handicapped seems consistent in rhetoric and reality. The state will not adopt the increasing work in the comprehensive form of institutional care.

If, in institutions, care is almost total, with minimal expectations placed on residents or relatives, in the domestic setting, the reverse is the case. State provision in support of caring work at home has always been scanty, and continues so. Health expenditure has been dominated by hospitals and the high technology end of medicine; social service expenditure is dominated by residential care, despite the small proportion in institutions (Walker 1983: 162). Provision is spread thinly, so that those in greatest need do not receive significant support. An official study acknowledges: 'Very few people seem to receive the intensive help that one might expect would need to be given if a real community-based alternative were being offered to long-term hospital or residential care' (DHSS 1981b: 25–6).

The same study drew interesting conclusions about the costs of care at home:

'Our findings suggest that for some people community-based packages of care may not always be a less expensive or more effective alternative to residential or hospital provision, particularly for those living alone. In some cases, the community alternative might only appear cheap because its level of provisions could be considered inadequate. . . . We would stress that the "cost-effectiveness" of a package of community-based services often depends greatly on the presence of informal care.'   (DHSS 1981b: 20, paras 3.27, 3.28)

In other words, the costs of caring adequately for very elderly and handicapped people are very high, wherever they live. Living at home may be better for all kinds of reasons, but does not necessarily reduce the need for care. What it does is to shift the cost of care, from an unambiguous charge on the state to an unrelieved cost to unpaid carers. No longer part of public expenditure, and no longer even part of 'economic activity', it has been translated from the public world of paid work to the private world of unpaid work.

The DHSS research report also admits that state support for carers and dependants has not been keeping up with growing needs. It finds: 'There are . . . significant differences between the increase in the level of provision of domiciliary and day care services (numbers of home helps, district nurses, etc.) and the increase in the numbers of people receiving these services' (DHSS 1981b: 29). Not surprisingly, the 'significant differences' indicate a declining level of service per user.

The DHSS is quite clear that shifting the emphasis from institutional to domiciliary provision implies not merely a change of location, but also putting limits on state responsibility. The idea of 'networks of community provision' is offered by government documents in justification of such a move. The third element in the support system, then, after relatives and the state, is 'the community'. However, the evidence accumulates that it is relatives who provide the bulk of the work and that 'sharing' care is not the common experience. A recent EOC study of people looking after elderly dependants at home found that 11 per cent of its main carers were friends and neighbours (EOC 1984: 10), the rest being spouses or other relatives. And according to an earlier EOC study, those who do caring work find the burden not much relieved by a wider community:

'Only in one case were relatives cited as giving "frequent" help; more commonly it was "hardly ever" or "none at all". Help from voluntary organizations or neighbours was even more rare, and where given, it was on a fairly casual basis. Ironically it appeared that the greater the degree of dependency, the smaller the amount of external help offered.'

(Equal Opportunities Commission 1982a: 17–18)

Parker argues that 'sharing care may be a much more difficult undertaking than is generally believed' (Parker 1981: 24). He cites evidence that elderly people living with relatives are less likely to be visited and helped by others, and more likely to feel lonely than those living alone; that most people who receive help obtain it from only one person; and so on. Very dependent people living at home are much more likely to be very dependent on a single person rather than on any kind of network. The voluntary sector – whatever valuable work it can do – is unlikely to assist the most dependent or to relieve their carers.

It is, then, relatives who do the greater part of caring work, and it is relatives who bear the burden of increasing numbers of elderly and handicapped people:

'The amount of support and care which the female members of families provide for their old and disabled kin is vast, as study after study has shown. Families are reluctant for the old or severely subnormal to enter residential homes or long-stay hospitals; they give dedicated nursing care to the chronically sick and dying and they are ready to offer help which is needed when the time comes for relatives to be discharged from hospitals or convalescent homes. A high proportion of adults who do stay in hospitals or residential homes for unnecessarily prolonged periods have no spouse or close kin.'

(Land and Parker 1978: 355)

This quotation leads to the further point that in practice state institutions support the isolation of relatives caring for dependants. In another article Parker assembles the evidence that fewer services are allocated when dependants live with relatives and that services are withdrawn when dependants move in. He concludes:

'There seems to be a widespread practical presumption that the state steps in to offer care services only when the resources of the family have collapsed or when they have been exhausted.

The converse also seems to apply; namely, that the state withdraws once family resources have been mobilized, or are seen to be on hand.' (Parker 1981: 23)

The state substitutes when no family is at hand but does not support the family's own caring work.

Demographic changes have put pressures on institutions: shorter stays and an older population make the work of hospitals and homes more intensive and more expensive. These pressures have coincided with government pressure over public expenditure. Bloody battles have therefore been waged over resources in institutions. 'Community care' has acted as the safety valve, absorbing the extra work. The slight shift in public resources towards supporting care at home merely touches the surface. The real work is done by relatives alone. It is barely noticed in the official statistics, being outside the 'real' economy, and is supported in the most superficial way by very limited help from state or voluntary domiciliary services.

The division of caring labour: men and women

If one way of looking at caring work is in terms of relations between state and family, another way is by gender. Caring work, paid or unpaid, in institutions or people's own homes, in public sphere or private, is primarily women's work. It is women who are nurses and home helps, run day centres and meals on wheels, clean hospitals and homes, and staff old people's homes.

An Equal Opportunities Commission study in 1980 commented that:

'Perhaps the most notable finding of the survey was that there were three times as many women carers as men. . . . About a fifth of those looking after old people were spouses, and over half were children or children-in-law. It is particularly noteworthy that 27 daughters were responsible for looking after an elderly parent as against only six sons. Similarly five of the carers were daughters-in-law, only two were sons-in-law; four were nieces and only one a nephew, and three were granddaughters while there were no grandsons.'

(Equal Opportunities Commission 1980: 9–10)

Caring for elderly and handicapped people is a relationship that is likely to involve women on both sides: as the main providers of care and as the most cared for. Women live longer than men and predominate heavily among the handicapped and frail. Women who care for dependent adults are quite likely to be elderly themselves.

Caring for adult dependants is a common experience for women. One estimate suggests that 'between the ages of 35 and 64 roughly half the "housewives" can expect at some time or another to give some help to elderly or infirm persons' (Hunt 1970: 424). Another study found that 13 per cent of women of working age had some such responsibility at the time they were interviewed (Martin and Roberts 1984: 112).

An EOC study comparing male and female carers found women carers bearing heavier burdens. They were more likely to be sharing households with dependants and coping with more severe dependency. Women's dependants were more likely to have never done households tasks for themselves, less likely to be fully independent in caring for themselves in personal matters such as washing, dressing, feeding, and toileting, and less likely to be wholly lucid (EOC 1984: 15). Women carers were more likely than men to suffer in terms of paid work, leisure, and health. A study of single carers looking after elderly parents found a similar pattern (Wright 1983). Elderly mothers living with sons struggled longer to do domestic work, in fact to look after the sons. Daughters bore a heavier burden of care, and tended to feel pressure to give up employment.

When women take on these responsibilities, especially when they live with the dependent person, they can expect little help. Nissel's study, quoted by the EOC, found that 'Not one woman said that her husband or children helped in the feeding, washing or washing clothes for the relative, the three activities that took the most time' (Equal Opportunities Commission 1982a: 12). And the 'help' husbands did give – in the more peripheral tasks – averaged thirteen minutes a day. (The women spent over three hours.)

It is not hard to find reasons in the culture and in women's identity which lead them to accept caring work. But the state is involved too. First, state provision for dependants assumes that the greater part will be done unpaid – and married women are the only large group whose labour is no charge to public expenditure. Second, the social security system provides that this is work for women, particularly married women, work that they do as a 'natural' part of their role: thus the Invalid Care Allowance (see

Chapter 7) is denied to married women. Third, the pattern of state support for carers at home confirms the designation, 'women's' work. The existence of a female relative, especially in the same house, lessens the likelihood of social service provision; male carers get more help. The EOC study found that dependants with male carers were more likely to receive domestic help, in the form of meals on wheels, and home helps; and were more likely to be admitted to long-term residential care while still relatively independent. Dependants with female carers were more likely to receive day care and short-stay residential care. As the Commission comments:

> 'In practice, this meant that temporary relief was provided for daughters who were carrying a burden of severe dependency. The services responded by providing day care and periodic relief admissions, in an attempt to ease the burden sufficiently for the carers to be able to continue. In contrast to the provision of home help and meals on wheels, which was provided when the elderly person was still relatively able, day care and short-stay care were provided at a much later stage in the onset of dependency.' (EOC 1984: 30)

In general, 'Male carers tended to receive more support at an earlier stage in the onset of dependency' (EOC 1984: 31). The conclusion in this study lends support to similar evidence collected in earlier EOC work (EOC 1980, 1982a).

Thus, a number of social policies foster women's caring role and its domestic isolation: first, the low and declining rate of institutionalization; second, the low level of domiciliary services and their failure to keep up with increasing levels of dependency; and third, the procedures for allocating those domiciliary services that exist. It seems that only if there is no woman relative available will the full resources of the 'Welfare State' be brought to bear.

It does seem necessary to explain the widespread failure to 'share' care, to support women who do caring work, to fund any real middle way between the total institution and the woman alone. A conspiratorial interpretation would suggest that such policies are 'meant' to keep women in their place. But the idea of the state as a coherent entity with a coherent policy on women's place is not very compelling. I would argue that policies for 'sharing' care involve a threat to traditional notions of the family and woman's 'role', and that the fear of undermining women's commitment to caring work lies near the surface. The quantity and cost of such work, especially in an era of increasing dependency, must reinforce wariness about drawing it into public expenditure. Thus, the interest of government departments in maintaining traditional family patterns is a pervasive underlying element, if it does not amount to a policy for women.

Caring and women's lives

Material matters

The fact that the private world of home, of children, and of the care of people is women's business is crucial to understanding women's place in the public worlds of production and politics. Women who have young children spend a very large number of hours on caring for them. The CPAG recently found that mothers with a child under five spent about fifty hours a week on 'basic life-support tasks' for their children (Piachaud 1984). McIntosh points out that while the period of caring for children under five has diminished with the declining birth-rate, the intensity of children's demands has in some ways increased:

> 'children's dependence on care by their own mothers is far greater and more prolonged than it was in the nineteenth century. Nowadays, children cannot easily be sent to live in another household. They are not company or help to the elderly; they do not care for younger children; they do not work in the home or in anything productive; they cannot be apprenticed or go into service until they are sixteen.'
> (McIntosh 1979: 167–68)

Most women in Britain with children under five do not have paid employment: for them child-care means relinquishing or forgoing access to an independent income and a part in public life. Those who are employed generally work shorter hours than other people, and for lower pay.

While caring for children under five absorbs a rather short period of women's lives, the effects of women's responsibility for children spread very much further. Child-care is at the heart of the sexual division of labour. Responsibility for children keeps women isolated in the home and disadvantages them in the labour market. While raising children must often be more satisfying than the male side of the labour bargain, the ramifications of its social organization spread into every area of women's lives. Anticipating having children may be one factor in girls' aspirations about work and career. Children go on having needs after the age of five, and these too are largely met by women. When women leave the labour market to have children, their return is usually to work with shorter hours, lower status, and lower pay (Daniel 1980: 90–1; Martin and Roberts 1984: 149–52). This results partly from continuing domestic responsibilities, and partly from absence from the labour market during critical years. When, often somewhat later in life, there are elderly or disabled relatives to care for, again the task falls to women. Not only is it in the 'appropriate' sphere, but they are by now even more badly placed in the labour market.

By restricting full participation in the labour market, women's responsibility for children ensures their dependence on men. Women with children, living as single parents, run an exceptionally high risk of poverty (see Chapter 7). Women living with men and caring for children full time lack the resources for change, even if they suffer violence (see Chapter 5).

Thus women's responsibilities in private life, and particularly the care of young children, affect their lives at every point. Motherhood is central, both in the general social concept of woman, and in most women's experience. It casts women into marginal positions in public life. In this it is quite unlike fatherhood.

This chapter therefore began with motherhood and the care of very young children. Most women become mothers, and none can easily escape the effects of the way that motherhood is defined as women's central experience and life's work. The chapter went on to look at the work of caring for the elderly and disabled. This is a necessary counterweight to the emphasis on motherhood. Whatever the long reaches of motherhood in women's lives, the majority of women at any one time are not bringing up small children. Feminist social policy has reflected the personal interests of its writers in motherhood, rather at the expense of older women, and it is important 'to develop feminist analyses of the Welfare State, and of the relationship of the state and the family, which do not leave the elderly invisible' (Finch and Groves 1982: 432). Since both carers and cared for are likely to be women, and quite likely to be elderly, this issue does enable a wider look at women's lives than does motherhood alone.

As with children, the expectation that women will care for

dependants goes beyond the immediate experience in its material impact on women's lives. It seems that when women do caring work it is particularly likely to affect their health and employment as compared with male counterparts (EOC 1984); the age at which women are most likely to have caring responsibilities is also the age at which women counterparts are most likely to be in employment; caring is likely to affect incomes through both employment and pension years.

The task of caring for elderly or handicapped relatives varies greatly in intensity. It is not always a full-time job. But for those caring for the severely dependant it can be quite unremitting work, physically onerous as well as emotionally demanding. The Equal Opportunities Commission remarks: 'These women "come to terms" with problems in ways that would be hardly tolerable to most people, giving up work, forfeiting all social life, never leaving the home for more than an hour at a time, never taking a holiday' (Equal Opportunities Commission 1980: 18). The immediate costs are well described in the Equal Opportunities Commission's various publications (1980; 1982a; 1982c). There are also long-term costs. The commitment is open-ended, its duration uncertain. The results for women's employment, careers, pensions, to name only the most tangible items, must always be significant, often devastating.

Identity matters

Motherhood has been rather more studied than has the experience of caring for adult dependants, and so this section begins with the mental health of mothers of small children, and with their sense of enjoyment and fulfilment in caring for children.

'Maternal deprivation' is not usually taken to refer to mothers. Perhaps it ought to be. Most work on mothering focuses on children. It asks how are children developed or damaged by inadequate mothering and by institutions. It is often assumed that mothers will automatically find their role fulfilling. Feminists have been rather more eloquent about the anguish (as well as about the rapture). But evidence of the anguish of motherhood has now begun to emerge from a number of large-scale surveys. One such is Brown's and Harris's work on *The Social Origins of Depression* (Brown and Harris 1978). This is a community mental health study of women in Camberwell. Its general finding is of very high rates of mental illness among women, many of them unknown to health services. In particular, it finds very high rates among working-class women with young children: 31 per cent of working-class women with a child under six suffered some psychiatric disorder (Brown and Harris 1978: 151–52). This was the highest rate for working-class women and higher than any for middle-class women. Particularly vulnerable were working-class women with a child under six and three or more under fourteen living at home. The authors concluded that 'having three or more children under fourteen at home is directly implicated in increasing risks of depression' (p. 152). The authors identified four 'vulnerability factors' which exposed women to depression. They were a lack of intimate relationships, loss of a mother before eleven, three or more children at home under fourteen, and lack of employment outside the home (pp. 173–81). All these vulnerability factors have to do with the way motherhood is experienced or defined, directly, or – as in the case of work outside the home – indirectly; and it is working-class women who suffer the worst consequences.

Other work confirms this picture. The Department of Employment study on women and employment shows higher levels of 'psychological stress' among women with dependent children, especially single mothers and women in unskilled or semi-skilled work; it also finds higher levels of stress among those women at home than those in employment, this being partly related to the presence of children (Martin and Roberts 1984: 66, 93). The Child Health and Education Study finds that maternal depression is greater among single mothers and those who are 'socially disadvantaged' (Osborn, Butler, and Morris 1984: 73–5). Mary Boulton summarizes other work in this area (Boulton 1983: 1–2), which draws similar conclusions. Motherhood, then, in some conditions and for some women, seems to have damaging effects on mental health.

Such studies are important evidence of the damage done to some women by the motherhood role, as it is constructed in Britain today. The concentration on stress and depression is an important counterweight to the rosy imagery of the more popular media. However, it is not a complete picture. Mary Boulton's own study focuses on women with children under five and gives a complex picture of the mixed experience of motherhood: of frustrations and irritations, of alienation and of fulfilment. She attempts to overcome the division of motherhood into love and labour by reconceptualizing it in terms of:

'Two different modes of experience: the women's immediate response to looking after their children and their sense of meaning and purpose in doing so. The first included pleasure, irritation and frustration in day-to-day lives; the second covered the longer-term sense of meaning, of being needed and wanted.'   (Boulton 1983: 35)

Boulton's main finding about the day-to-day level of experience was that 'more than half the women found looking after children a predominantly irritating experience' (Boulton 1983: 58), compared with just under half who found it enjoyable. At the other level of experience, a sense of 'meaning, value and significance' in looking after children, the conclusions are more positive, though not overwhelmingly so:

'For those who experienced these feelings, motherhood was a unique and rewarding role. This is an important point, for it suggests one reason why women may continue in their role as mothers despite the frustrations and stresses they also experience.
    Not all of the women, however, felt a strong sense of meaning and significance in motherhood: over a third did not and among the working-class women the proportion rose to as high as a half. Children may bring a sense of meaning and purpose but they do not necessarily do so. Though they have the potential to give a sense of meaningfulness and intrinsic worth to a woman's life, children may bring no more than an "appropriate" or socially desirable role. This, too, is an important point, for it belies the expectation and general assumption held about motherhood. A sense of meaning and purpose does not come automatically or inevitably in motherhood. It is not wholly instinctual and there is nothing as straightforward as the automatic fulfilment of a need. Rather, a positive commitment to her children and a sense of meaning and purpose in looking after them must be created and sustained in the values, meanings, and interpretations given to children and child-care by those directly involved in it as well as by the society in which they live.'   (Boulton 1983: 119)

The tendency of western child-care practice is to isolate mothers in their total responsibility for children. For many, there is evidently no one to foster their 'sense of meaning and purpose' in caring for children. Thus, while motherhood is fulfilling and rewarding for the majority, a considerable proportion of mothers are alienated, discontented, or ambiguous about their experience.

We know much less about the experience of caring for elderly dependants. EOC reports suggest that the emotional demands are often heavier than those involved in child-care. There is no parallel to the aspirations for children's development and independence; and there may well be even less involvement by friends and relatives. On the other hand, the EOC report writes of emotional rewards as well as emotional demands (EOC 1982a: 5–7). There is surely a sense in which women choose to care; it is not just a question of 'female self-sacrifice and supreme selflessness' (Graham 1983: 17). The unquestioning way in which women take on this role appears to support the view that women identify with caring:

> 'It is quite apparent that carers rarely ask themselves whether or why they should take on the care of a sick, handicapped or elderly person. Indeed most were surprised and perplexed when the question was put to them at all. One respondent answered "I've always done it. She relies on me having always done it. There is nobody else. I decided to care for her because she's my mother. That's the only reason." '   (EOC 1980: 12)

Social policy provides a material context in which women's practical choice is limited. The lack of acceptable alternative state provision, and the importance of men's wages for women's survival, mean that women's choice is made under stringent conditions. But caring is not just a labour which women are looking for someone else to perform. It involves both a relationship and a dependant whose fates are of the utmost consequence. Any attempt to restructure caring will have to take these issues seriously.

Social policy and caring work

The argument of this chapter has been that caring is central to social policy, to the division of labour and to the construction of gender. The division of labour in the public sector of social policy rests on the broad base of caring by women at home. The care of dependants is a relationship and a labour largely involving women and taking place largely in the domestic sector. Contrasting the private world of home and family with the public world of paid work and 'economic activity' it is possible to show how social policies have manipulated the boundaries between private and public. The fragmentary nature of public provision for the very young, the very old, and the very handicapped may be seen as part of a family policy. However incoherent 'family' policy may seem in certain respects, there is some consistency in social policy's tendency to preserve – at a considerable cost to many of the very old, the very young, and the very handicapped – women's availability and readiness to care for family members within the family, without pay. Such preservation results in keeping women dependent in the family and weak in the public sphere.

4

Education

Education, the family, and employment

Ideas about education

Educational institutions stand at the junction of private and public worlds, mediating between the family and paid employment. Historically it can be argued that 'schooling emerged when the site of production was separated from the major site of reproduction (the family). Schooling provided a link between these two crucial sites – it articulated the family to the now separate sphere of production' (Centre for Contemporary Cultural Studies 1981: 248). Schooling was built as a bridge upon the division between public and private. Today it occupies the same terrain.

This much seems simple in relation to boys. In relation to girls, however, this account of the location of educational institutions serves to reveal ambiguities and to pose questions about the nature and purpose of education. The idea that education can be seen as a bridge between private and public, between family and workplace, can be set against the recurring idea that women belong to the family. The result is to produce two very different models of education for girls. These models coexist, though in a changing way which partly reflects changes in economy and family.

There is thus an ambiguity at the heart of girls' education. This is thoroughly reflected in the literature of educational ideas, some of which is couched in terms of opportunity, even of liberation, while some has to do with girls' future in domestic life. Sometimes these appear as clearly opposite ideals, sometimes in (unholy?) combination. This section explores the contradictions in ideas about education for girls in terms of this polarity. The same contradiction permeates education practice as well as educational thinking. Therefore later sections deal more directly with educational practice within the same broad framework.

One kind of educational ideal for girls is to see educational institutions as a bridge from domestic life, an escape route from oppression, a 'golden pathway to uncountable opportunities' (Oakley 1981b: 134). If schooling provides the route into the public sphere for boys, then it may do so for girls, too, provided that they have enough of it and of the right kind.

Many middle-class eighteenth- and nineteenth-century women – who were excluded from full participation in the universities, who were debarred therefore from the major professions, and whose schooling was mainly concerned with feminine 'accomplishments' – well knew how exclusion from formal education could mean exclusion from public life. Mary Wollstonecraft expressed herself exactly in these terms:

> 'nor will women ever fulfil the peculiar duties of their sex, till they become enlightened citizens, till they become free by being enabled to earn their own subsistence, independent of men; in the same manner, I mean, to prevent misconstruction, as one man is independent of another. Nay, marriage will never be held sacred till women, by being brought up with men, are prepared to be their companions rather than their mistresses.'   (Wollstonecraft 1792/1975: 165)

The part that education played in the feminist politics of the latter half of the nineteenth century is testimony to the strength of this notion of education. The fight for the development of proper schools for girls, the fight for admission to the universities and medical education, the work of building training institutions for women teachers – these were based, at least for some of their protagonists, on the premise that education would give access to the professions and to independence for those women who could not depend upon men or preferred to remain single. It paralleled the other fight for a place in public life, the fight for the franchise.

It was, of course, a movement involving a variety of women with a variety of perspectives on women's education (see Kamm 1958, 1965; Marks 1976; Lavigueur 1980 for a fuller account). Two who stand out as taking a particularly sturdy line on the need for women's education to be equivalent to that of men were Frances Buss, who founded the North London Collegiate School and the Camden School for Girls, and Emily Davies, who was responsible for the schools which are now known as Girls' Public Day School

Trust, and for Girton College, Cambridge. These women fought vigorously against all interpretations of women's education that separated it from men's. Here is Emily Davies's view of a special examination for women established by London University:

'I am afraid that the people who are interested in the education of women are a thankless crew. . . . They do not consider a special examination any boon at all, and will have nothing to do with it. . . . We are really obliged to Convocation for their kind intentions in offering us a serpent when we asked for a fish, though we cannot pretend to believe that serpents are better for us.' (Quoted in Kamm 1958: 88)

Frances Buss, replying to the Taunton Commission's question about whether the education of a girl should 'differ essentially from that of a boy in the same rank of life, with regard to the subjects which are to be taught?' overcame her nervousness enough to make a shrewd reply: 'I think not, but it is rather difficult to ascertain what is the proper education for a boy' (quoted in Ridley 1895: 7). Thus she committed herself to the same education for boys and girls, without accepting boys' classical education as model.

Dorothea Beale, the influential head of Cheltenham Ladies' College, had a different view of women's place in life, and held more flexible views about their education. But her view of the nature and purpose of education was as exalted as that of Davies and Buss:

'The old rubbish about masculine and feminine studies is beginning to be treated as it deserves. It cannot be seriously maintained that these studies which tend to make a man nobler or better, have the opposite effect upon a woman; the "blue-stocking" ghost will I am sure be altogether laid, if brought to the light of day. When a sound system of education has been introduced, people will learn to value rightly ignorant preten-tiousness, and that affectation of contemptuous superiority which is one of the most decisive tests of ignorance.' (Quoted in Kamm 1958: 91)

Of course no sensible woman who was involved with the education of middle-class girls at the end of the nineteenth century could ignore the fact that for most the future lay in marriage rather than a career, and that these would not be combined. Their fight was partly based on the desperate plight of those fairly numerous middle-class women who did not marry, whose main choices were to depend on relatives or to be exploited as governesses. But it is interesting to see how they dealt with the question of the to-be-married majority. Beale, in the passage quote above, made her position quite clear. She went on to argue the merits of her 'sound system of education' for women who would marry as well as for those who would earn their living. Along with other reformers, she believed that this kind of education would elevate marriage, which was seen as a wasteland of small-minded concerns. Education was relevant to marriage and motherhood, then, and that education had nothing to do with 'pudding making and pickling' (Buss, quoted in Kamm 1958: 42). The sort of education which would undermine the privacy and pettiness of domestic life was the same as that relevant to boys and girls who would enter the professions. A proper education for girls was like a proper education for boys. It would fit them for the public world and it would connect domestic life to the public world.

Official support for this view of education for girls came before the century turned. The Schools Inquiry Commission, reporting in 1895, defined secondary education as 'the education of the boy or girl not simply as a human being who needs to be instructed in certain rudiments of knowledge, but (as) a process of intellectual training and personal discipline conducted with special regard to the profession or trade to be followed.' It went on to report that 'the idea that a girl, like a boy, may be fitted by education to earn a livelihood, or, at any rate, to be a more useful member of Society, has become more widely diffused'. In relation to the 'industrial classes' the commissioners accepted that there would be differences in the secondary education required for boys and girls, but argued that it was 'undesirable that this difference should be so emphasized as to obscure the aim common to Secondary Education for boys and girls alike' (quoted in Kamm 1965: 225–26).

Despite such official acknowledgement, the idea that education for girls should fit them for public life was a minority idea, and minority practice. Lavigueur argues that only the Buss tradition carried through idea and practice without concession. Other middle-class girls' schools still owed something to the notion of 'feminine accomplishments'; and schools for working-class girls promulgated a bourgeois notion of the family as a form of social control (see Davin 1979; Lavigueur 1980) which imparted a strongly domestic tone to their ideology and practice.

The idea of educating girls for public life can, though, be traced through most of the official policy documents of this century. An early, and in some ways quite enlightened analysis is provided by the Hadow report (Board of Education 1923), which was explicitly concerned with preparing girls for paid work and for civil life, as well as for domesticity. It recognized the large number of women manual workers who did not always stop paid work as soon as they were married, as well as the numbers of middle-class women following professions. It concluded that the ordinary girl 'should be given an education which prepares her to earn her livelihood' and that specific preparation for domestic life should not 'impede the Secondary School in its task of giving a good general education both to girls and to boys' (Board of Education 1923: 131).

The 1940s – when the idea of domesticity for women was at its strongest – saw an Education Act (1944) which considerably enlarged girls' participation in education. The Norwood report (Secondary Schools Examinations Council 1943), whose three types of children seem all to be boys, and Newsom's book on *The Education of Girls* (1948), had little time for girls' opportunities. But the 1950s began an era in which education and opportunity seemed always to belong in the same breath. It was, then, often applied to girls. This is not to say that the connection – or lack of it – was fully explored, or that it held the centre of the stage, for neither of these is true. It is to make the much more limited point that the expansionist reports of the social democratic era (Crowther (1959), Robbins (1963), Newsom (1963), and Plowden (1967)) naturally included girls along with boys in all their discussions of social deprivations and lost opportunities, and to add that a number of these reports did show a somewhat fleeting concern with the extent to which girls were denied opportunities. Thus the *Early Leaving* report noticed that girls' achievements were less than those of boys (Ministry of Education 1954); the Crowther report was concerned about the lack of day release opportunities for girls (Ministry of Education 1959), and the Robbins report (Ministry of Education 1963b) saw girls as one pool of untapped talent.

The issue of education as opportunity for girls has been raised again in modern feminist politics, asking the obvious question about the relative place of boys and girls in the education system. There has been a concern with girls' relatively poor access to the higher levels of educational institutions, and with their poor representation in high prestige subjects, especially in those high prestige subjects which lead to well-paid jobs (e.g. Kelly 1981). Modern feminist writing has thus complemented the well-established literature on social class differentials in education with similar analyses based on sex. The underlying assumption of this branch of feminist writing is that girls can use education as a bridge to a more secure place in public life, and that the education system can be modified to perform this role more successfully.

This approach has, in a sense, been officially adopted, in that the Sex Discrimination Act requires that coeducational institutions give equal access to any benefits, facilities, or services. 'In most respects, official educational ideology in Britain now supports the axiom of sex equality' (Oakley 1981b: 130).

Thus the idea of education as opportunity, as a bridge from the family to public life, has been applied to girls as well as to boys. It forms a significant theme in nineteenth-century feminist politics as well as in contemporary official ideology. However, it does not hold the stage alone. That schools should prepare women for their place in the real world, and that that place is the home and family, is an ideal for some. For others, who would prefer otherwise, it is a dismal reality, the inevitable consequence of a patriarchal education system in a patriarchal world. These are, of course, very different groups of writers. They share a pre-occupation with girls' domestic destiny and its relation to the education system.

Modern feminists – especially socialist feminists concerned with the reproduction of capitalist and patriarchal relations – tend to argue that the dominant official view (Sex Discrimination Act notwithstanding) has always been the domestic one (see Wolpe 1974; Bland, McCabe, and Mort 1979; Deem, 1981). Frances Buss and Emily Davies may have wanted and provided an education that was similar and equal to that given to boys, but this applied to a privileged minority. The rest were, and have been ever since, in the hands of an education system dominated by men, who were often gripped by fear that education would make women unhappy with their modest married lot.

The idea that education for girls should lead straight back to domestic life can be traced as a leitmotif through official education documents. The idea that education for girls should be for girls' 'real lives' – for marriage, housework, and motherhood – involves emphasis on the different needs of girls and boys, and frequently a denial that education should be a bridge to public life, except for a small minority of abler middle-class girls. Instead there is an elevation of girls' domestic destiny. Housework, as in the Beveridge report, may be elevated into a skilled activity and dedicated calling, a worthy enterprise for young minds – especially young working-class minds.

The expression of this ideal of girls' education recurs, from the nineteenth-century debates about women's access to a kind of education which it was feared would rob them of their health, modesty, and feminine destiny, to more modern concerns about an education suited to girls' interests. This is not to say, however, that advocacy of education for domestic life is always equally intensive.

It is interesting to compare, for example, the Hadow report of 1923 with the literature of the post-war era. Hadow saw education for girls as pointing in three directions, towards paid work, towards domestic life, and towards citizenship. The report argued for a domestic element, but argued that it should take second place:

'We do not think it desirable to attempt to divorce a girl's education from her home duties and her home opportunities. On the other hand, there is a real danger now of her energies being exhausted by home duties, and her interest absorbed by social engagements, to the detriment of her mental development. We do not consider that any distinction can be drawn between the qualities that go to make a good parent and those that go to make a good citizen. No matter what the curriculum may be, the aim must be the fullest and best balanced development of mind, body, and spirit. The training in housewifery and cookery, and even in physiology and hygiene, though it may elicit the qualities of intelligence, skill, thoroughness, unselfishness, and so forth, is not so important as the general training. But there will probably be some gain in efficiency, if the girl associates the arts relating to the care of her home with the thoroughness and intelligence required in other subjects. There is a gain, too, in her feeling that her teachers appreciate the dignity of home duties and have full sympathy with her development in this direction. We must, however, remember that we are only on the threshold of the development of women's work and their opportunities. Experience may even mislead us. We think that in no part of School life is an open .

mind more essential. No preconceived ideas as to the best preparation, even for motherhood, ought to hamper experiment or to dim vision.'   (Board of Education 1923: 125)

Open minds were less in fashion in the 1940s. The Norwood report showed no embarrassment about the 'fundamental importance' of the idea that domestic subjects were a 'necessary equipment for all girls as potential makers of homes'. Referring to evidence received, Norwood argued:

'It is assumed that the majority of girls do not receive at home a training sufficient to turn them into good makers of homes. If this is true – and we cannot disprove it – then the opportunity of some minimum course of training at school is a necessity for all girls as girls and the training at school must necessarily take nothing or little for granted and must start from the beginning. . . . Accordingly we take the view that every girl before she leaves school should have had the opportunity to take a minimum course which would give her the essential elements of Needlework, Cookery and Laundrywork. . . . For many girls much more than the minimum course is clearly desirable'.
(Secondary Schools Examinations Council 1943: 127–28)

More passionately and more eloquently, though also less officially, John Newsom argued the same case in his volume on *The Education of Girls* (Newsom 1948), whose purpose was 'to examine the relationship between the part women play in a civilized community and the education they receive to prepare them for it' (p. 21). He argued that 'The future of women's education lies not in attempting to iron out their differences from men, to reduce them to neuters, but to teach girls how to grow into women and to re-learn the graces which so many have forgotten in the past thirty years' (p. 109).

Newsom (who later chaired the official report, *Half Our Future*) argues that people should be educated with their social function in mind and that the social function of boys and girls is different:

'The fundamental common experience (for women) is the fact that the vast majority of them will become the makers of homes, and that to do this successfully requires the proper development of many talents. This is largely ignored in the education they at present receive.
With notable exceptions, it is true to say that the education of

girls has been modelled on that of their brothers without any
reference to their different function in society. This is a modern
perversion and its corrupting influence dates from the end of
the last century, when the pioneers of a higher education for
women finally secured "equal opportunities" for girls'.

(Newsom 1948: 110)

Thus Newsom neatly exposes the divergent ideals of women's
education. Education as a bridge to public life, education for
equal opportunities, is set plainly against education for women's
domestic function. To be fair to Newsom, the education
he prescribes for wives and mothers is not wholly directed to
alleviating 'the tortures inflicted on husbands and children by
inexpert wives' (Newsom 1948: 127). But the fundamental
assumption is that girls' interest can be captured through
connecting school work to their ultimate, domestic concerns. The
home is a centre of interest

'to whose daily life almost everything we normally call subjects
can be related. Arithmetic concerns household accounts,
cookery, furnishing costs and the garden, all involving the
basic processes in a wide variety of measure, mensuration, the
reading of instruments, percentages and graphs. This is about
all the mathematics most girls will ever need.'

(Newsom 1948: 120)

Subsequent reports have not grasped the nettle so boldly.
Increasing need for women's labour in the 1960s was reflected in
more open-ended views about girls' education (see Deem 1981).
But while the reports of the 1960s wrote of opportunity, they also
continued the domestic theme. They show how divergent
models of education may be meshed, often without acknowledgement. The Crowther and Newsom reports were particularly marked by their emphasis on girls' domestic future as well
as by the language of opportunity.

In general the reports of the 1950s and 1960s failed to place
gender at the heart of their analysis and thus left a space in which
differences could flourish unnoticed. This peculiar void in the
vision of social democracy is well represented by the Newsom
report on *Half Our Future* (Ministry of Education 1963a). This
is a passionate argument about the unjust neglect of socially
deprived children in secondary modern schools. Yet it almost
always treats boys and girls together. It does not investigate the
patterns of differential achievement and provision between the

sexes, or ask whether children may be deprived simply because of their sex. Girls are mentioned separately mainly under 'housecraft and needlework'. Thus, characteristically, the reports of the 1960s were concerned with the opportunities of 'boys and girls', but they were unable to see the extent to which opportunities were in fact different for boys and girls (King 1971). The Centre for Contemporary Cultural Studies note the 'absence of women from the political arithmetic of social democracy' (1981: 249) and remark that 'there was no discomfort at all in the reports about gender' (p. 121). There was no acknowledgement of the tension between education for domestic life, which some of these reports proposed as an ideal for girls, and equality of opportunities, which they all sought for all children.

Thus reports which saw domesticity as no bar to opportunity had in practice little to offer to girls. And the feminist movement was able to find that girls were profoundly disadvantaged by unquestioned assumptions about a domestic future.

Feminism and education

In contrast to the optimism with which early feminists viewed education, the dominant concern of modern feminist theory has been education's part in preparing girls for a subordinate place in public and private life. Their place in public life is to do low-paid, insecure work, and characteristically 'feminine' jobs; their place in private life is to bear the unpaid work of reproduction. As well as specific preparation for both kinds of work, there is preparation for subordination. Most explanatory accounts of girls' education have thus stressed the part that schooling plays in reproducing the relations of production and reproduction. Thus Janet Finch summarizes the argument:

'feminists have been responsible for demonstrating that (the education system) also reproduces the sexual division of labour between men and women. This applies in two senses; education reproduces the conventional division of labour in the family, whereby men are in paid employment and women do unpaid work in the home; and it reproduces sexual divisions within the labour market itself, so that when women do take paid work, they tend to be concentrated in particular types of jobs and at the lower level of organizational hierarchies. The contribution of the educational system to sustaining both of these processes is significant.' (Finch 1984: 152–53)

Whatever part reformers and feminists may want education to play in liberating girls and women, there are powerful constraints. These are strongly felt by girls and are part of the fabric of schools themselves. Schools' location within the structures of capitalism and patriarchy means that, far from achieving 'equality' for girls, schools actually have to produce inequality – they have to produce women who are ready to accept subordinate positions in the family and the labour market. Thus feminist educational theory has highlighted the ideology of domesticity as it runs through official educational documents, and examined those educational practices which prepare girls to be wives and mothers, and to be content with lower paid jobs (see Deem 1978, 1980; Delamont 1980; David, 1980, and for critical reviews of theories of reproduction see Centre for Contemporary Cultural Studies 1981; Willis 1983).

These accounts contribute greatly to our understanding of girls' education. But they are, as the Centre for Contemporary Cultural Studies argues, 'insufficiently alive to the contested nature of such processes and therefore to the centrality of political struggles' (1981: 9). Feminist versions of theories of reproduction sometimes make it appear as if there is no room for anything except the making of wives and mothers. It is less pessimistic – and more accurate – to think of the educational environment as complicated and rich, and of girls and their teachers as more than passive objects of some outside 'structure'. Whatever the constraints of economy and patriarchy, there has been room for enlarging girls' educational experience, preparing some, at least, for a reasonable place in public life, running courses on women's studies, and employing large numbers of women teachers; and there is room for girls to resist the definitions of the future offered to them. These theories rightly break open the liberal conception of schools as simple purveyors of opportunity, but replace it with too crude a version of schools as a device for reproducing girls as wives, mothers, and low-paid workers.

Education in practice – education for public life

Those reformers who saw an education equal with men's as women's route to public life would see many of their aspirations met in modern schooling. (No doubt they would also see a need for new aspirations.) No one now suggests that girls should devote their lives to drawing and needlework, or that they are too frail to take examinations or to attend universities and medical schools. Formal barriers have been assaulted and removed; in their place is legislation which promises equal access not just to educational institutions, but also to the same subjects and materials as boys. So much for an earlier feminist politics whose gains it ill behoves us to despise.

Girls, too, have fulfilled the faith of those women teachers who knew that girls' capacities would not prove inferior. From early high-flyers, such as Philippa Garrett Fawcett, who swept past the male competition in the Cambridge Tripos, long before women were actually allowed to take the Cambridge degrees (Kamm 1958: 96–7) to countless contemporary eleven-year-old girls, whose abilities in basic school tasks average somewhat above those of boys, girls and women have demonstrated the myths of biological inferiority.

This section, then, surveys the contemporary evidence about girls' participation in education and their achievements. Together with the following section it also indicates why we need new aspirations.

In this era of compulsory, and in most cases coeducational schooling, access to educational institutions can be taken for granted up to the age of sixteen. It will be shown that there are very important differences in the 'education' offered. Nevertheless, there is also evidence that girls of compulsory school-age have seized their opportunities at least as successfully as boys. Most of the evidence in the following section is based on reviews by Bone (1980) and Wilkin (1982), and on the official statistics of education. The reader should keep in mind that 'achievement' is only one of the things going on in schools, and that not all children sit examinations.

At primary school girls do as well as, or better than boys on most measures of ability or achievement. The early study by Douglas (1964) showed that girls were more advanced readers, at both eight and eleven years of age. Most subsequent large-scale studies have shown the same result. In mathematics girls and boys seem to have different strengths, but differences are small. Wilkin is able to conclude that, 'By halfway through their schooling . . . there are no outstanding differences between the sexes in overall attainment in these two basic subjects' (Wilkin 1982: 88).

Secondary schooling from eleven to sixteen shows a similar picture, with girls marginally outperforming boys. In 1981–82, 57 per cent of girls leaving school, compared with 51 per cent of boys, had obtained GCE O-level passes (Grades A–C) or CSE grade 1 (DES 1983: Table 12).

Girls' and boys' achievements, then, are quantitively similar during the period of compulsory schooling. There is no evidence here of intellectual inferiority. What does begin to emerge at the GCE/CSE stage is the typification of subjects as male or female. A higher percentage of girls have passes in English, French, the arts, and biology, while more boys are successful in mathematics, physics, and chemistry. The detailed picture can be seen in Figure 1, which is based on O-level entries in London: it shows clearly the relative 'femininity' and 'masculinity' of a range of subjects. This divergence is built upon in later stages of educational life. The period of compulsory schooling, then, is characterized by similarity in the level of achievements, and by divergence in its content.

Divergence comes to be more characteristic as one moves up the educational hierarchy. As Ann Bone remarks:

> 'The end of compulsory-age schooling marks the age at which schoolchildren are most explicitly directed into the channels which will eventually place them in the "economic division of labour" and it is then that girls come up most heavily against the notion that "there is no point in educating girls". From that moment they start to trip over the educational hurdles.'
>
> (Bone 1980: 91).

The higher reaches of the educational world, then, come to be dominated by boys and men. This begins in the sixth form, and becomes more marked at every level up to the university professoriat.

Among school-leavers at A-level, a slightly higher proportion of boys attempt, and a considerably higher proportion of boys gain, three or more passes. Gender patterning of subjects is more marked than at O-level. For example, in 1978 girls won 39.6 per cent of the maths passes at O-level, and only 23.4 per cent of those at A-level (EOC 1981b: 2–3).

Higher levels of education are characterized by much wider institutional diversity than are schools. Colleges of further and higher education, polytechnics and universities offer courses at a variety of levels and with very distinct career implications. Here the issue of access to key resources comes into the open, and here gender becomes overt as an organizing principle.

Formal education after school-leaving may take the form of day

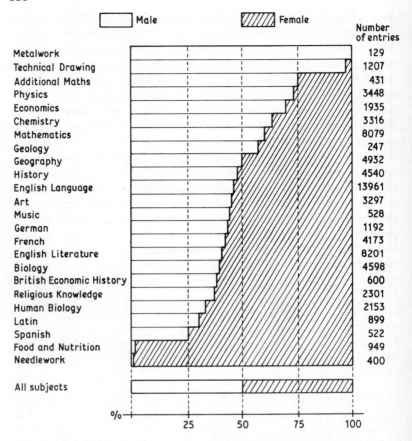

Figure 1 Percentage of entries in O level subjects by sex, inner London, summer 1976

Source: ILEA, *Examination Results in the ILEA, 1976*

release for those in jobs, of Youth Training Schemes for those who are unemployed, or of full-time higher or further education under traditional educational authorities. The first two of these categories explicitly connect education with paid work; they may be decisive and specific in allocating people to destinations in the public world. They reflect the hierarchy and sex segregation of the labour market more directly than other sectors of education.

The number of male workers aged eighteen who are given day release is about four times that of women workers (16 per cent of all 18-year-old boys were working with day study in 1982–83 compared with 4 per cent of all 18-year-old girls: DES 1983: Table 15). A recent study (Benett and Carter 1983) found that young women were excluded from day release partly because they were excluded from occupations where it was available (one example is that few young women are full apprentices), but also that firms operated a number of policies to discourage female employees from taking courses. These included simply not telling young women and discouraging them if they asked (compared with a careful grooming of young men for career posts); deliberately recruiting young women with poor qualifications (compared with slightly older, more qualified young men); demanding geographical mobility (a deterrent to women seeking to make work a career rather than a job); and demanding a period of service before entitlement (more often applicable to younger, predominantly female recruits than to older, mostly male ones). Young women recruits were thus excluded from training and from career opportunities, while young men were recruited for 'career' posts, groomed, and encouraged. The 'dual labour market' is thus carefully constructed along gender lines.

Youth Training Schemes, on the other hand, are available to all unemployed school-leavers. Their predecessor, the Youth Opportunities Programme, is discussed in a review of *The State and Training Programmes for Women* by Ann Wickham (1982). She remarks:

'Within the programmes the same dispiriting pattern of work opportunities for women is to be found. Far more girls, for instance, go into community work experience schemes, a continuation of women's role in "caring" areas, whilst more boys enter the training workshops. Work experience places in employers' premises make up the majority of opportunities in the YOPs programme and here the tendency is for further reinforcement of occupational segregation. To some extent the MSC (Manpower Services Commission) can claim that this is out of their control, for the Commission has to rely on the voluntary cooperation of employers. Employers, particularly in small firms, are notorious for their maintenance of segregated work roles. Sponsors can only be encouraged, not forced, to make provision for women in "non-traditional" areas.' (Wickham 1982)

This small detour out of education authority full-time courses is made for two reasons: to give more prominence to those who play a small part in traditional 'achievement' statistics; and to show how the linkage of these courses with work and opportunities makes explicit the impact of a segregated labour market on the educational route followed by girls. Girls in general seem to be turned away from the highest educational courses and qualifications as the reality of the labour market looms. Working-class girls are likely to find themselves in women's jobs without prospect of further advance or of formal education after the age of sixteen.

In the full-time sector girls' presence is much greater. A higher proportion of girls than boys go on to some form of further or higher education (DES 1983: Table 11), though they tend to take lower status subjects, at lower status institutions, for poorer qualifications, leading to more lowly paid jobs. Thus in 1983–84, 41.6 per cent of university undergraduate students were women (University Grants Commission 1984: 6). On the other hand, teacher training, nursing, and secretarial courses are dominated by girls (DES 1983: Table 11; EOC 1981b: 9). The trend for education and nursing courses to become degree courses has increased the amount of degree-level work done by girls. However, recent cutbacks in training teachers, and in arts and social science degree courses are affecting girls more severely (EOC 1982b); neither of these trends is yet fully reflected in official education statistics.

Schooling for opportunity, achievement, liberation even, from the domestic world, 'works' for some girls. Girls do as well at school as boys up to the age of sixteen; they take the educational route to public life in similar numbers. The route, however, has a different stream for girls, leading away from the higher reaches of public life. Even the highest achievers – those with degrees – have a characteristically female destiny – the education system, whither graduates tend to drift, even those who start elsewhere (Chisholm and Woodward 1980). In so far as education 'works' as a route to public life, too, it does so unequally. Its small relevance to working-class girls is reflected in their tiny representation at universities as well as in the culture of adolescent girls at school (see p. 129). In 1971, King analysed the relationship between sex and social class in access to education. Using official statistics of entry to courses at O-level or above, he concluded:

'At each level of education the sex-gap is bigger for the working class than the middle class, and the class-gap is bigger for girls than for boys. As the level of education rises the sex-gap widens for both classes, but widens more for the working class. The class-gap also widens for both sexes, but more for girls than for boys.' (King 1971: 171)

Two simple facts emerge: to be working class and female is to be particularly disadvantaged, and disadvantage becomes clearer as one mounts the hierarchy. King's evidence is supported by an analysis of the university population where, as the Robbins report noted, working-class girls number very few (Ministry of Education 1963b: 51); even the Open University has been unable to attract women manual workers, who make up only about 2 per cent of its intake (Arnot 1983a: 20). For the great majority of working-class girls education leads to unskilled work and (in the absence of other viable ambitions) dreams of home. One consequence is profoundly to affect women's relationship to men: in Britain only a few women, those few being middle-class, 'acquire the kind of education and jobs which enable them to enjoy economic independence from men' (Deem 1978: 136). The practice quite closely reflects that ideology which distinguishes different routes for the minority of 'able' girls and the majority.

Some key features of girls' achievement and access may be summarized as follows. First, up to sixteen girls 'achieve' as solidly as boys. Second, after sixteen follows a decline in achievement, as measured by A-levels; and a stratification process develops whereby higher status courses and institutions are dominated by men, and working-class girls have especially poor access to such heights. Third, there is a patterning of male and female subjects – increasing with age – which reflects the traditional segregation of the labour market to which pupils look. Despite coeducation and comprehensive schools, the content of girls' and boys' education is highly distinct and matches the segregation of the labour market. The educational bridge, it turns out, has two lanes. Even when girls are being prepared for the public world, it seems they are being prepared for 'women's jobs'.

If low aspirations characterize girls at the sixteen-plus stage, there is another side. Some women do turn to education later. Adult education, the Open University and other courses available to 'mature students' form a significant avenue for a minority. The somewhat shaky (Bone 1980: 97)) statistics of enrolments in adult education shown women as dominant at 68 per cent. And women's educational interests are not limited to the part-time and lower level. Griffiths concludes that 'many women who did not go on to degree-level work on leaving school, or who had not the qualifications to do so, are nevertheless interested in studying for a degree' (Griffiths 1980: 131), and Bone finds that '48 per cent of women students attending major establishments of further and higher education in 1976 were over 24 compared with 29 per cent of men students . . . Within the figures on the age of students at major establishments of further and higher education, there is evidence of two phases in women's education which echoes the phases of women's working life' (Bone 1980: 97). Griffiths found an increased proportion of women applicants for Open University places, to 44 per cent in 1977. A high proportion of those taking OU degrees developed or fulfilled career aspirations, and many spoke in terms of opportunities that had been missing earlier. The respondent in Griffiths' study who wrote 'It has meant that I have started to find myself as a person, and has opened up the world' (Griffiths 1980: 141) clearly saw her experience as one of liberation.

Education for the family

Two crucial features of the preceding account need explaining. First, there is girls' declining success from the age of about sixteen, the apparent turning away from achievement by those who have shown every evidence of their ability. Second, there is the subject stereotyping which makes the content of girls' education and their qualifications very different from those of boys.

Both are critically related to girls' adult lives and are age related. The period of looking forward to adulthood is one of contracting horizons, of negotiating with the realities of a segregated labour market, of intensified 'femininity' and preoccupation with a romantic and domestic future. It is when girls look beyond school that their commitment to academic achievement may decline. This does suggest the need to look outside educational institutions as well as in them, and to exercise caution in assessing the impact of sexed schooling on the identity and aspirations of girls – after all, it is only as they near leaving age that girls' limited aspirations become apparent.

However, schools do offer girls and boys an education in a certain kind of family life, as well as a different educational experience. There are a variety of ways in which schools teach girls to be women: in which they point girls towards a domestic future and away from extended 'careers'; and help girls to develop an identity of inferiority. If Marxist writers have stressed the schools' part in preparing boys for their place in productive relations, feminists have argued that they prepare girls for their place in reproductive relations. There are aspects of the curriculum devoted to family life and so on (David 1983; Finch 1984: 175–77). Less obvious, but more deep-rooted, are the myriad practices and elements of the 'hidden curriculum' which differentiate between girls and boys, and point them to different destinies. This literature is briefly surveyed here, and is treated under four headings: books, curriculum, school structure, and classroom interaction.

Books

Analyses of school textbooks and, in particular, reading books are reviewed in Spender and Sarah (1980) and Lobban (1978). It is impossible to disentangle what children actually absorb from different sources, but school reading books are an interesting example for the essential role they play in the daily lives of the youngest schoolchildren. While the account here is restricted to school reading books, these may be taken to typify the treatment of women in a whole range of school materials, from the treatment of history as the history of wars and male politics, to the choice of English texts at A-level (see Spender and Sarah 1980: 29–31). Analysis of the reading books demonstrates three main features: that the books are mainly populated by male characters; that they offer children a caricature of gender roles in adult life; and that the few female characters are more often denigrated.

Lobban has reviewed analyses made of nine 'widely used' reading schemes and 200 reading books. The ratio of male to female characters varied from 2:1 to 4:1, and male central characters were five times as common as female ones.

'Child and adult sex roles were rigidly and traditionally sex-differentiated. Boys and men were shown as active, aggressive and courageous, while girls and women were shown as nurturant, passive and timid.' Perhaps even more crucial for children's view of their adult selves, girls were offered a highly restricted range of images. In two of the modern reading schemes, 'a total of 33 different occupations were depicted for adult males and these were both varied and realistic ways of earning a living. A grand total of 8 occupations were shown for adult women, and these were mum, granny, princess, queen, witch, handywoman about the house, teacher and shop assistant.' Domestic indoor images of women contrast with adventurous outdoor images of men. Lobban's analysis also showed that 'the male characters in the books were accorded far more prestige than the female characters who were more frequently shown as more uninteresting, stupid and evil' (Lobban 1978: 54–5).

> 'The books and materials used within our schools abound in crude and inaccurate images of women and men . . . the inequality of the sexes is subtly maintained by providing one sex with a few tarnished images with which to make sense of the world and their place within it and by providing the other sex with a range of glorified images. It is not surprising that the two sexes should learn the lesson and develop very different views of the world and very different self concepts.'
>
> (Spender and Sarah 1980: 25–6)

Curriculum

The Sex Discrimination Act entitles girls and boys to equal access to all facilities in mixed schools. In theory, then, the whole range of the curriculum is open to girls and boys on the same basis. In practice, a segregated curriculum is entrenched. Through the schools, as well as through outside pressures, girls are taught what are sex-appropriate subjects and they learn the benefits of conforming. Schools contribute through a number of practices, of which illegal discrimination is only one.

Illegal discrimination seems most likely to appear in the 'craft' subjects. These are the subjects most overtly connected to domestic work and manual labour, as well as to some kinds of 'male' technical jobs. An HMI report, based on survey work from autumn 1975 to 1978 (the Sex Discrimination Act came into force in December 1975), found that differentiation in the curriculum was mainly 'confined to the craft subjects, with woodwork and/or metalwork for boys, and home economics and/or needlework for girls. Some mixed schools made this distinction prescriptive; others provided an organization which would have allowed pupils to cross the traditional boundaries had they chosen to do so.' Prescriptive (and thus illegal) segregation occurred in 19 per cent of the schools studied, and 'differentiation by sex in the craft subjects occurred in practice if not by design in something ove 65 per cent of the 365 schools'. (The 365 schools included a considerable number of single-sex ones where the question does not apply in the same way, so the real percentages in mixed schools were higher (Department of Education and Science 1979: 14–15).)

Schools have several ways of indicating to pupils which are the most 'appropriate' subjects. Relatively few of the schools in the above study ensured that all pupils tried all crafts. The number that imposed sex discrimination by fiat was more or less matched by the number that effectively imposed it by timetable. Blocking 'male' subjects against 'female' ones makes the 'wrong' choice uncomfortable. While overt discrimination may be more or less confined to craft subjects (the above report did find 'only three' schools where girls were 'obliged to take biology and boys physics' (DES 1979: 14)), the more or less subtle encouragement to fit in is more pervasive. And while illegal discrimination may well be on the decline, there is every evidence that a sex-segregated curriculum (arrived at by other means) is becoming more entrenched. Physics and chemistry are very much a male domain, even by the fourth and fifth years of secondary school. The same study found that 48 per cent of fifth-year boys were studying physics compared with 10 per cent of fifth-year girls. The evidence was of subtle pressures rather than deliberate exclusion. Some science teachers thought boys should do physics and girls biology, or that physics was too difficult for girls; girls were not encouraged or advised of the career implications; and sometimes physics was set against typing or home economics, with a clear understanding by staff and pupils that girls were meant to do the latter (DES 1979: 167–69).

The move to comprehensive schools has gone along with two other developments that are relevant here. First, comprehensive schooling has justified itself in part by the choice of subjects available to pupils; second, coeducation has often happened along with comprehensive development. All this has been part of an apparently liberal creed, but the effects on girls' education appear ambiguous at best.

To take the first issue, the 'freedom' to choose typing may bring less freedom in later life than the 'freedom' to choose mathematics and physics. The HMI report quoted above described the following situations as not untypical of a 'considerable number of schools':

'in one full range comprehensive school nearly 20 able girls had been allowed to choose courses which consisted of 15 periods a week of commercial subjects to the exclusion of physical education, religious education or physical science and only optional mathematics. In another full range comprehensive school 20 per cent of the fourth year pupils did not take a subject in the humanities while 50 per cent of the girls undertook no science.'

(DES 1979: 210)

In such circumstances, 'freedom of choice' becomes a mechanism by which power relations are perpetuated.

Furthermore, it has been argued by a number of feminists that the trend to coeducation has intensified and pressures on girls to do 'feminine' subjects (Shaw 1980; Spender 1982). There is a little evidence to suggest that girls in single-sex grammar schools are more likely to take physics than girls in mixed grammar schools (DES 1979: 168). And there is further evidence that 'girls from girls' schools are more successful in science than those from mixed schools' when measured by examination success. Girls from direct grant and independent schools were 'outstandingly successful' according to one study (Harding 1980: 93). It appears that girls may retreat from male subjects in mixed classrooms, as well as retreating from success when in competition with boys.

School structure

A fundamental feature of educational institutions is that (girls' schools apart) they are patriarchal structures. Men command the heights, particularly at the university apex, but also in the 'women's world' of primary education. This has profound implications for the nature of educational institutions and of girls' experience in them. One is the lesson rammed home to every child every day that it is men who have authority and prestige, and women who are helpmeets.

An allied feature of school structure is its analogy with the patriarchal family, and its 'familial ambiance' (Miriam David 1980). The male headmaster is balanced by the female deputy, mother and father to a somewhat extended brood. Here is an education in a certain kind of family life. Sex differences are 'taught as much through the hierarchical and patriarchal relations within school and by the expectations made of girls' and boys' progress through schooling as through specific issues' (David

1980: 245). The involvement of women as teachers is itself a lesson in motherhood. It is 'based on the assumption that caring for children, especially young ones, is a feminine attribute; more-over, women teachers, especially those who have married, are best equipped to impart knowledge about wifehood, mother-hood and domesticity' (David 1980: 240).

This account is too universal. School structure and ideology are changing phenomena, and they relate to aspects of economy as well as family. The picture is therefore complex. But their relationship to norms of family life can be analysed both as features of contemporary schooling and historically as in Miriam David's account.

Classroom interaction

The lessons about gender that children are offered in books, in a sex-divided curriculum, and in aspects of school structure are complemented by those of teachers. Whatever else we teach, we also offer lessons in girls' inferiority. In ordinary classroom interaction boys take the lion's share of attention and esteem. Girls learn to devalue themselves and to keep quiet.

Michelle Stanworth's *Gender and Schooling: A Study of Sexual Divisions in the Classroom* (1981/1983) involved interviews with teachers and pupils in seven A-level courses at a college of further education. The questions related to individual pupils and teachers rather than to gender. Teachers and pupils were asked for impressions of each other; pupils were asked about classroom experience, and for assessments of themselves and each other.

Two outstanding features of teachers' accounts were, first, that teachers, and especially male teachers, more often expressed concern for and attachment to boys, and were more distanced from girls; second, that teachers had difficulty imagining any future but a domestic one for girls.

The greater distance from girl pupils emerged in direct ques-tioning about preferred pupils, but also emerged in accounts of classroom interaction. For example, teachers asked about first impressions of students had always found some hard to place, and these had always been girls. One teacher remarked:

'In fact, it was quite a time before I could tell some of the girls apart . . . they were friends, I think, and there was no way – that's how it seemed at the time – of telling one from the other.

In fact, they are very different in appearance, I can see that now. One's fair and one's dark, for a start. But at the beginning they were just three quiet girls.' (Stanworth, 1981/1983: 27)

Teachers' visions of girls' futures were dominated by marriage rather than by careers. Male teachers, in particular, found it hard to visualize girls in employment (two-thirds could not) and when they did, their imaginings were somewhat traditional:

'One girl who is ranked as the top performer in both her main subjects, and who wants a career in the diplomatic service, is envisaged by her teacher as the "personal assistant to somebody rather important". . . . No matter how conscientious and capable female pupils are, they are perceived by their teachers to lack the authoritative requisites of "masculine" occupations.' (Stanworth 1981/1983:32)

Pupils' interviews demonstrated that 'both male and female pupils experience the classroom as a place where boys are the focus of activity and attention – particularly in the forms of interaction which are initiated by the teacher – while girls are placed on the margins of classroom life'. When asked to name pupils who were treated positively by teachers in a variety of ways, all pupils tended to name boys. On these pupils' accounts, boys were more likely to be asked questions, more likely to be regarded as highly conscientious, more likely to be the objects of concern and praise, and more likely to be the ones with whom the teachers got on best (Stanworth, 1981/1983: 37–8).

Of course, connections between teachers attitudes, their interactions with pupils, and pupils feelings about themselves cannot be traced straightforwardly. However, it is hard to resist the conclusion that the classroom can be a crushing place for girls. Pupils of both sexes in Stanworth's study did underestimate the abilities of girls. While girls and boys were judged equally capable by teachers, 'all pupils have a clear idea of the rank order of their own sex in academic performance, but in the vast majority of cases, girls downgrade themselves relative to boys, and boys upgrade themselves in comparison to girls' (Stanworth, 1981/1983: 51). One girl expressed the way she saw the connections: 'I think he thinks I'm pretty mediocre. I think I'm pretty mediocre. He never points me out of the group, or talks to me, or looks at me in particular when he's talking about things. I'm just a sort of wallpaper person' (p. 37). The author concludes that: 'whether women succeed at any academic task or whether they fail, neither they nor others who appraise them are left with confidence in their ability, with faith in their capacity to sustain a good performance or to change a poor one' (pp. 51–2).

Education for the family – the girls' view

Girls' experience of education has been less studied than that of boys. Furthermore, as Fuller (1983) has pointed out, it is particularly difficult to understand the ways in which girls resist schools' definitions of them, since the noisier kinds of resistance are a feature of boys' behaviour rather than of girls'. But a look at education through the eyes of girls and women may counter any tendency to see girls as passive objects of indoctrination.

Several accounts stress the way romance, and anticipation of marriage and motherhood appeared to limit the need for achievement, and in some cases to make achievement actually undesirable.

Spender and Sarah, describing the educational autobiographies of contributors to their volume, *Learning to Lose*, report:

'Without exception our autobiographies reveal an absence of aspiration in terms of work. It seems that none of us took it seriously. We found ourselves at work in our twenties but we were surprised by what we found ourselves doing. No one mentions making a choice about work. . . . Underlying all our educational accounts was the understanding that there was another job, besides paid work, for a woman. This is never lost sight of and it stands in sharp contrast to career considerations. Wherever there was conflict it seems that "future security" demanded that it be resolved in favour of the feminine role.'
(Spender and Sarah 1980: 7–8)

Another retrospective view, this time from young working-class mothers (mainly aged nineteen to twenty-one) is given in this account by Dorothy Hobson:

'The other women in the study had all been to secondary modern or comprehensive schools. In some cases they had had ambitions to try to get more interesting jobs when they left school, but they had eventually abandoned those ambitions and taken the conventional jobs for working-class girls: in offices, shops or factories. Their experience of comprehensive education had not made them have ambitions for jobs which could be termed as middle class. Some of them had wanted to become hairdressers or nurses, but even these ambitions had been lost and they had in their own words "ended up in an office" or as Anne says "I always knew I'd end up in a factory". . . . A . . . common reason why the women I had talked to had changed their mind about any ambitions which they had for jobs after they had left school had been the crucial factor of meeting a boy, who in some cases they had later married. The moment they started "going steady" or "court-ing" was the time when they changed their ambitions, or perhaps realized their real ambition, which was to get married. When she was at school, Pat had ambitions to join the Air Force, but these were abandoned when she met her future husband just before she left school.

D: Did you work when you left school?
P: Yes, I worked in, I was going to join, I had me heart set on joining the Air Force but, er (laughs), I met me hubby and things went from there.

It was as if her real "career" was "marriage and motherhood" and once she met the man she later married, there was no need to continue with her ambitions for an alternative "career". Pat had "accepted" her future seemingly even before she left school.'   (Hobson 1981: 105–06)

Sue Sharpe's study of girls in four Ealing schools concludes that these attitudes are shared by girls and schools alike:

'Whatever level of job (boys) are steered towards, they look unambivalently towards a working future. Girls, however, are still schooled with the marriage market in mind, although this may not be acknowledged consciously. This inevitability in their lives provides as much excuse within the school, as for girls themselves, for their ultimate under-achievement.'
(Sharpe 1976: 130)

At a later stage, as young factory workers, women in Anna Pollert's study show strikingly similar attitudes; this is despite the fact of working alongside older women for whom romance, marriage, and motherhood have not proved escape routes from crushing manual jobs.

'None of the girls went so far as to conceive of themselves as full-time, long-term wage-earners. They had little thought of their lives as middle-aged women, or that they would want to, or have to, work. . . . The tragic irony was that the older women, who had shared exactly the same illusions when they were young, had not entirely lost them. Instead of warning the girls that work might not be temporary, they sympathized with their focus on marriage as life's "solution", and if anything reinforced their identification with the roles of housewife and mother. . . . So if the girls failed to see that in the long run they could spend most of their lives as unskilled wage workers, the older women, who knew better, carried on the illusion of "not working for ever" – until it was too late.'

(Pollert 1981: 104–06)

Girls at school who see their world in terms of romance, marriage, and motherhood are not perverse – although they may be limiting their own futures. Their attitudes are – in some respects – widely shared. From educational policy documents, such as Crowther and Newsom, to the older women factory workers in the Pollert study, the idea is reflected that girls' real place in the world will be in marriage and motherhood. If the harsher realities of continuing manual labour and isolated domesticity are too hard for older women to acknowledge, it is not surprising that girls seize the romantic version of their futures offered by a willing media (see McRobbie 1978a, 1978b, 1980, 1981). McRobbie found that youth club girls she studied gave 'an ultimate if not wholesale endorsement of the traditional female role and of femininity' (1978b: 97). Their endorsement of romance, as purveyed in such magazines as *Jackie*, was one of the ways in which girls saved themselves from an unexciting vision of the future; though they knew that marriage 'did not measure up to its claims', they could not see a future without it. Their assessment was based on the economic and sexual realities of life for working-class girls: since women's low-paid work does not give them the possibility of independence, marriage is (almost) the only way of moving from the parental home (McRobbie, 1978b: 105–07).

White girls seem to share an underlying assumption that the future will be domestic; and to share a tendency to limit career horizons accordingly. This appears to cut across class differences, though the evidence about middle-class girls is slight. Studies of black girls, on the other hand, suggest a rather different set of assumptions about the future, and a rather different response to school. Both Fuller (1980, 1983) and Sharpe (1976) describe the black girls they interviewed as having a clear commitment to paid work and to aspects of schooling which would help their job prospects.

> 'The girls were all strongly committed to achievement through the job market, being marked out from the other girls not so much by the type of jobs to which they were aspiring as by the firmness with which they held their future job ambitions, and by their certainty that they would want to be employed whatever their future domestic circumstances might be.'
>
> (Fuller 1980: 57)

Sharpe found that both West Indian and Asian girls wanted to stay at school longer than the white girls she interviewed, and she, too, found definite career ambitions. Of Asian girls she writes: 'most girls also expressed the wish actually to use their future qualifications to make something of their own lives. . . . Almost all had some idea of the job they might take up' (Sharpe 1976: 287). The girls, according to Fuller, used educational qualifications as a means of gaining control over their future, while resisting other aspects of school life.

These studies of black schoolgirls raise all kinds of issues about the interactions of race, class, and gender in schools, as well as making clear the ethnocentric assumptions of much of the literature. They also offer a useful antidote to over-deterministic theories of schooling which leave no room for girls to negotiate the structures of patriarchy and capital within which they find themselves. Black girls, who appear to be doubly oppressed, appear also to negotiate their position in a different way from their white counterparts, and in a way that does appear to give some effective independence.

Education as a male world

Educational institutions have frequently been analysed as middle-class institutions bearing middle-class culture. Less often is it noticed that they are male institutions bearing male culture. Male dominance of the institutions and of the learning that they purvey deserves a little more attention. For it is this which gives rise to a rather different idea of education for girls than has been discussed so far: an idea of an education that is separate, different, and equal.

Male dominance of the institutions is easy to see and not too hard to document. Universities are not merely the apex of the hierarchy; they are also important for their gatekeeping role, their influence on what happens in schools, and their part in defining what constitutes 'knowledge'. They are a more obviously male world than the schools. Only 16 per cent of lecturers and assistant lecturers are women; 7 per cent of readers and senior lecturers and 2 per cent of professors (University Grants Commission 1984: Table 22). Rendel concludes that the feminist 'sees no improvement during more than half a century' (Rendel 1980: 143).

Education's political authorities, as well as its academic and professional government, are in male hands. Eileen Byrne has pointed out the extent to which both local education committees and central government advisory and policy committees have been male dominated (Byrne 1978: 171–72).

From the most overt political mechanisms – the democratically elected authorities – to the most covert – the assumptions written in to the 'knowledge' which is taught – the same analysis can be made. From a history that is a history of men's wars, to a literature that is dominated by men's books, to a social science that is constructed around men's position in the division of labour, the 'knowledge' purveyed is that women have no place in the world.

The same education as men, then, may be damaging; it will be an education in inferiority. Girls are disadvantaged in institutions dominated by men, in classrooms dominated by boys, and in knowledge built on male experience. Separate education for girls could not unpick this in an instant. But it may be that educational institutions for girls and women would give girls more space and women more power. These arguments are more fully debated by Sarah, Scott, and Spender (1980) and Arnot (1983b).

5

Housing

Housing the family

Housing policy

'The concept of the home is another aspect of the concept of the family' (Aries 1960/1973: 390). Houses reflect ideas about families and affect the ways people can live in and out of families. One powerful set of ideas which links house, home, and family is the ideology of domesticity and of woman's place. 'In literature, from highbrow to popular, the wife–mother–house–mistress image often merged with the physical symbol of the house so that it became difficult to visualize the woman as having a separate identity from the house; in a sense she became the house' (Davidoff, L'Esperance, and Newby 1976: 155). The ideology of domesticity connects people's needs for housing with their membership of particular kinds of families. It permeates the policy documents, house construction, and housing policy in practice. Housing policy, then, is family policy.

This chapter will argue that housing policy is predicated on families with male 'breadwinners', and identifies others as special problems; this puts particular pressure on women to become and remain attached to male breadwinners. Women's housing prospects are tied closely to their family status.

But housing policy is not one-dimensional. First, administration is fragmented. The public sector has about one-third of dwellings in Britain, and governments exert only indirect control over the rest; even in the public sector, many decisions are decentralized to local authorities and their housing managers. The variety of agencies makes it hard to identify a single housing policy; so women seeking housing apart from men, for example, may receive very different treatment in different areas.

There is a second source of ambiguity. Housing policy in general may favour male-breadwinner families. But the government's own public sector housing is the chief resource of women without male breadwinners. Women as mothers – though not women alone – are seen as having a special claim on local authority housing; here, ideas of maternal deprivation work to women's advantage. And punitive treatment of single, separated, and divorced mothers has probably decreased. One index of this is that young women having babies outside marriage now less frequently 'choose' adoption; the possibility of independent housing may be one reason. So public housing authorities offer some support to women's reproductive work, even where women do not conform to the ideal type of family life. But conformity is still privileged: 'British housing policies . . . can be seen to be shaped by a pervasive conviction that certain kinds of family should be accorded priority' (Land and Parker 1978: 349).

The preference given to two-parent families with children can be studied as an ideology underlying planning documents, as well as in detailed practice. Thus, the Ministry of Reconstruction in 1945 said that 'the Government's first objective is to afford a separate dwelling for every family which desires to have one' (quoted in Land and Parker 1978: 349–50). The 1977 Housing Green Paper opens with the same theme: 'The Government believe that all families should be able to obtain a decent home at a price within their means' (HMSO 1977: 1). The same document goes on to discuss the needs of some groups outside the implied norm (including single people and couples without children) and suggests that, 'The needs of some, though not all, of these people can often be met by using property which is difficult to let to families' (HMSO, 1977: 79). Clearly, 'families' come first. A management textbook is explicit about the family patterns and personal qualities of successful applicants for housing: 'It will be appreciated that the personal suitability of the applicant and his wife are a guide to the type of dwelling to be offered' (Macey and Baker, quoted in Merrett 1979: 224–25). As Land and Parker remark: 'Family priority in the allocation of public housing is so familiar and unexceptionable that its size and importance as a policy are liable to be overlooked' (1978: 350).

Owner-occupation has dominated housing policy in the post-war period. Privately rented accommodation has declined severely. Waves of public sector building have produced a significant public stock; but council house sales, demolition of structurally deficient developments, and recent public expenditure policy have drastically restricted access here for new tenants. Thus owner-occupation has grown to nearly two-thirds of the total housing stock.

Access to owner-occupation depends, of course, upon income. It is available, therefore, to better-off men and to women largely through men. Women without men are much less likely to be able to buy houses. Although the number of successful women mortgage applicants has gone up, in 1981 the proportion of females to males was still only 1:10 in the UK (according to the sex of the first-named applicant) (Austerberry and Watson 1983: 63).

If low income is the most obvious and important barrier, the management practices of building societies may also be added. Building society preferences are not quite identical to those of local authorities (they probably prefer couples without children), but they too have ideas about 'families' and favour families who fit their stereotype. One example is the practice of calculating a loan offer according to a multiple of the income of the higher earner in a couple plus a multiple of the lower earner's income. Often the multiple for the higher earner is much greater than that for the lower. In practice, this keeps within the Sex Discrimination Act while taking minimal account of a wife's earnings. But an EOC consumer study suggested that building societies practise more overt discrimination: '36 per cent of all Building Society branches discriminated in some way against a couple with a higher-earning wife' (EOC 1978: 6); only 8 per cent applied a single multiple to the couple's joint salary (p. 9). And the officials compounded discriminatory practice by their explanatory remarks: 'We believe, and I think you'll find most Building Societies do too, that women's income cannot be relied upon to be permanent because of babies' (pp. 23–4). Austerberry and Watson quote further evidence that building societies discriminate against career-oriented women and those who have suffered marital breakdown (1983: 63).

Thus women without men have limited access to owner-occupation. Access is largely through men and preferably through being part of a 'building-society-preferred' couple. Limited access matters to women whose marriages break down, as well as to those choosing to live outside marriage. A policy relying on owner-occupation thus has particular significance for women. The decline of the privately rented sector – once the resort of those outside 'standard families' – has severely cut back housing access for women alone and women with children. Local authority policies are now crucial for women without men. Alternative options have withered away.

Housing policy within the public sector, therefore, needs examination. Detailed practice is decentralized and hard to document. However, there are two main stages at which local authority preferences for 'standard families' may be felt. The first is selection of households for council housing; the second is allocation to particular properties. On the first point, waiting lists which stress length of residence and allocate points according to family size tend to tell against women alone with children (because they tend to move often and lack one adult member compared with other families), and virtually to exclude women alone (unless they are elderly). On the second, Merrett concludes:

> 'Rather than being homogeneous in its social geography, the council sector reveals a clear internal spatial patterning of people. The most noted aspect of this tendency is for various minority groups, such as "unsatisfactory tenants", "problem families", black people, single-parent families, the low status, and so on, to inhabit the poorest and lowest status areas and dwellings.'   (Merrett 1979: 225)

The author stresses that 'applicants have different degrees of power or ability to control the dwellings they are allocated' (Merrett 1979: 224). Those in desperate need accept places that would be turned down by those under less pressure. In the absence of alternatives to council housing, women without men may be under special pressure to accept inferior housing. So it is officially admitted that 'all fatherless families tend to be to some extent stigmatized and hence given the most stigmatized lettings' (Housing Services Advisory Group 1978: 8). Such housing disadvantage is the counterpart of the preference for 'standard families'.

Both allocation and building policies in the public sector have favoured two-parent families with children (with special housing for the elderly a rather recent exception). Thus they have largely excluded single people and have disadvantaged one-parent families. Since poorer people – including most women without men – depend very largely on the public sector, and since housing is one of the fundamentals for any kind of living, public sector housing policies are a powerful conditioning factor in women's lives.

Design for domesticity

The shape of the 'standard family' is suggested by the shape of the 'standard dwelling'. The overwhelming preponderance is of two- or three-bedroom units in both public (80 per cent) and owner-occupied (86 per cent) sectors (McDowell 1983: 154, quoting technical housing volumes 1977). The dwelling is likely to be a house, semi-detached, terraced, or detached (in that order). A higher proportion of local authority units are one-bedroom (reflecting the priority given to elderly people) and flats (30 per cent), reflecting high-rise policies in the 1960s. Apart from a small minority of 'special needs' housing, such as warden-assisted flats, the emphasis is on self-containment, rather than on shared or communal facilities.

Two themes run through feminist commentary on this topic. One is a critique of male-dominated design for female living. The other is its connection to ideals of domesticity and family life.

Women's reproductive work makes the home women's place more than it is men's. Yet the planning and design of homes is almost entirely a male preserve. This has led to very practical criticisms about safety, lack of space for children to play, and isolation in high-rise flats. It has also led to criticisms of the lifestyle on which house design is predicated, and which it partly shapes:

> 'Women are isolated probably more effectively than ever before in any civilization in history. We are boxed up with our children in high-rise flats, surrounded by empty corridors and wastelands of empty space, imprisoned in tenement blocks or marooned in suburban semi-detached homes, surrounded by other people's hedges and gardens where neighbours hardly know each other.'
> (Feminist Group of the New Architecture Movement, quoted in Brion and Tinker 1980: 9)

Davidoff and colleagues (Davidoff, L'Esperance, and Newby 1976), and McDowell (1983) push this discussion out to connect housing design and policy with ideals of family and domestic life. Davidoff, in an historical account of the ideals of domesticity and community, argues that these ideals 'laid the groundplan of retreat from the unwanted and threatening by-products of capitalism (and progress) – destitution, urban squalor, materialism, prostitution, crime and class conflict' (Davidoff, L'Esperance, and Newby 1976: 145). Ideals that became powerful in the period of capitalist expansion – as home and work were wrenched apart – live on in the twentieth century. 'The more that the wider society grows in centralized corporate and state power, in size of institutions and in alienating work environment, the more that the home becomes fantasized as a countering haven' (pp. 172–73). The 'Beau Ideal', as the authors call the combination of domestic and community ideals:

'was a model, a way of composing reality that helped to create that reality in a very concrete way, often embalmed in the bricks and mortar of houses, the lay-out of roads and services with which we are still living. Both the village and home sectors of this ideal represented a defence against various attacks on the social structure which made, particularly members of the middle class, fearful of disorder in every sphere of social life. The model was seen to stress consensus and affective ties. It thus shifted attention away from exploitation of groups and emphasized individual relationships. It denied the reality of, and thus made less viable, the existence of households with other structures namely without male heads, with working wives and mothers.'

(Davidoff, L'Esperance, and Newby 1976: 173)

The authors trace the exploitative underside of the 'Beau Ideal' and the consequences for women's ability to maintain themselves outside the domestic haven, and for their isolated lives within it. They also stress its physical effects, in the design of homes, suburbs, and garden cities.

Urban space and domestic life

If housing design reflects an ideology of female domesticity, the shape of cities puts domesticity in its place. Its place is to be separate from public life. Increasingly, the structure and organization of cities reflect the sexual division of labour in concrete form. Housing estates, garden cities, and suburbs segregate domestic life; they ensure its privacy, its disconnection from the public world of work and politics. Linda McDowell argues that, 'Probably the most important feature of this division of cities has been the growing separation of home and work' (McDowell 1983: 143). The period after the Second World War, in particular, saw a 'vast programme of peripherally-located single family state housing (which was surely) related to women's post-war withdrawal from the labour market' (McDowell 1983: 156).

In segregating domestic from public life, the shape of cities also helps to segregate women from public life. Men may bridge the gap between the two worlds, daily travelling to work, retreating to a haven of rest. But for women home is work as well as (sometimes) haven. Women who must be at the school gate, or keep an eye on elderly relatives, women who have work to do in the haven, cannot so easily divide their lives.

Marriage and marriage breakdown

Women in marriage

In marriage women share with men accommodation, privilege or disadvantage, detached owner-occupied house or council flat in vandalized block. Husband's occupation is a key variable in determining access and tenure; differences between women are more striking than similarities.

Thinking of women outside marriage – or wishing to be outside marriage – changes the perception. Most women outside marriage share disadvantage. Their situation illuminates women's housing position in marriage: it shows how much housing security depends on accepting and staying in marriage. But there is a further twist for married women: the effect of their unpaid work may be to reduce or eliminate paid work, independent income, and thus access to alternative housing.

Women's dependence on men for housing therefore affects women in or out of marriage. Those out of it share disadvantage in access, quality, security. Those in marriage share the lack of anywhere else to go.

Formally, there has been a tendency – ever since the Married Woman's Property Act in 1882 – to increasing women's title to property within marriage and to a share in the matrimonial home. An increasing proportion of homes, both rented and owner-occupied, are in joint names. Where they are not, a married woman's contribution to marriage, and need for housing, is now recognized as giving some rights. Such changes make women more than chattels. They do not, however, change the fundamental economics of women's relationship to men and to housing. And they do not provide security of housing for women on marriage breakdown.

Joint ownership is still not general, despite recommendations from the Law Commission that it should be. A survey of married owner-occupiers in 1972 found just over half in joint names; 42 per cent were in the husband's name, and 5 per cent in the wife's (quoted in Austerberry and Watson 1981: 53). There remain here practical implications for women on marriage breakdown: a joint owner has a right to half the value of the house, whereas a woman without a title in the deeds may receive only a third.

A married woman in a local authority property is also more likely than in the past to have joint tenure. And the tenure may well revert to her on marriage breakdown, especially if she has children. But the position of local authority tenants whose marriages break down is complex; and joint tenure does not guarantee housing security.

Although women have considerably increased rights to property and tenure in marriage, their fundamental economic position is unchanged. Women's reproductive tasks combine with labour market disadvantage and with state policies to make marriage their main housing option. And once that option is taken, they make it difficult to change to another.

On the other hand, such changes are happening all the time, whether women choose it or not. The frequency of marriage breakdown means that many women are faced with the issue of independent access to housing. The outcome of marriage breakdown, and the housing position of women without men are therefore of considerable significance to large numbers of women, who will at some time in their lives test their independent access to housing. They are also the most salient evidence about women's relationship to their housing in marriage; for they show the extent to which women's housing depends on the marriage relationship. The rest of this chapter, then, is devoted to marriage breakdown, and to the housing circumstances of women alone with dependent children and without. There is a final section about women's housing dependence at its most critical – when there is violence in marriage.

One reservation should be noted at this stage. What is said here about marriages also applies, in general, to cohabiting relationships. But there are ways in which the position of cohabiting women is different, often worse. And there is no space to deal with the legal complexities. The chapter therefore concerns marriage rather than cohabitation.

Marriage breakdown

The clear dividing lines of the advertiser's marriage – woman at home with sink and children, man at work, earning money – are blurred in the real world. Men may be unemployed, women may have jobs as well as children, many people live alone or in couples, pre- or post-children, or without children. Nevertheless, men's privileged access to employment remains, as does women's privileged access to children. (Surely both have their pains.) Marriage breakdown thus tends to break men's relationship with children, and women's relationship with incomes. In addition, there is often the need for two homes instead of one. Without income, women may lose access to housing and the ability to care for their children. Marriage breakdown has very different effects for women and men, in economic terms, in family terms, and in housing terms.

Women's responsibility for children – usually leading to custody – is seen as making need for special protection. Thus divorce proceedings often result in women retaining the family home, at least until the children grow up. These practices which protect homes for children are often seen as giving women special advantages. There are, however, many situations where this does not happen, particularly – since the special protection is directed at children rather than women – when there are no children. Even where it does happen, the security may be temporary: the arrangement may come to an end when the children grow up, or the lack of an adequate income – another frequent result of divorce – may mean that the home cannot be kept. Some of these situations are discussed below. They illustrate the difficulties women have establishing a right to housing that is independent of their relationship to men.

Before divorce

Women and men have an equal right to live in a matrimonial home (unless there is an exclusion injunction as a result of domestic violence) until there are legal separation or divorce proceedings. This applies regardless of tenancy or title, whether these are in joint names or sole. Thus both sides have the security, until court decisions, of the right to stay. On the other hand, men are more likely to have the economic power to leave without risking destitution.

Women, by contrast, may be trapped in marriages which they

regard as over. Women's Aid has shown that women will stay in violent relationships and even return to them, because of material obstacles to their escape. What has been less advertised is the way these constraints may apply to women whose marriages are merely miserable. Men may choose to go; if they do not, women may have little choice but to stay in the relationship. As Barbara Rogers remarks: 'If your home goes with your marriage or even your husband's job, as so many do, then the pressures to stay become overwhelming even in situations of violence or extreme unhappiness' (Rogers 1983: 97).

It is possible to take out divorce or separation proceedings while remaining together in the home – in the hope that the divorce proceedings will ultimately bring sole tenure; in practice, this option may seem intolerable. The Catholic Housing Aid Society study remarked that 'few that came to CHAS saw it as a realistic option and in only one instance was a solicitor known to advise it' (CHAS 1974: 22–3). Likewise the Housing Services Advisory Group conclude that the right to stay

'has not proved effective in cases where the husband has refused to leave. Usually the woman ultimately leaves with the children . . . . In many cases the situation has become violent and she is actually afraid to stay . . . As a result, it is very common for marital break-up to be accompanied by the homelessness of the wife and children while the man remains in the house.'   (HSAG 1978: 11)

Finding independent accommodation pending divorce proceedings may prove as difficult as staying together in the home. Economic constraints will generally rule out the owner-occupied sector; availability may rule out the privately rented sector. Hence local authority policies will be crucial. Local authorities have control over most temporary accommodation (except Women's Aid refuges), as well as over permanent rehousing. They will have to make decisions about women who already have tenancies as well as women approaching from other sectors. Their decisions will affect how long people wait in temporary accommodation, as well as the kind of housing they are offered. All these, however, are local matters. The Department of the Environment may draw up guidelines, but what happens in practice is a matter of local control and, consequently, variation. Neither is it very easy to find out what does happen.

Local authorities have many pressures on their housing stock;

they may well be seen as managing crises rather than carrying through any grand design. But the DOE's own Housing Services Advisory Group suspects that authorities feel responsibility for the future of marriage:

> 'In cases of marital disputes local authorities are very anxious to avoid the charges that:
>
> (a) they have encouraged the break-up of a marriage by allocating a separate tenancy to the wife prematurely and
>
> (b) that they influenced the judge's decision on custody of the children by allocating a tenancy to the wife.
>
> In their anxiety to avoid these charges, local authorities have sometimes swung too far the other way, so that a wife and children have remained homeless for a long period of time.'
>
> (HSAG 1978)

Of course, the preservation of marriage, in this case, is a one-sided affair. Men's greater economic power makes them less subject to such practices. These are policies which keep women in marriages at men's behest.

Temporary accommodation is a key local authority responsibility. Here, by providing refuges, Women's Aid have demonstrated the lack of an acceptable place for women to go when they suffer domestic violence. But without violence, even temporary accommodation may be hard to come by. The CHAS report remarked that:

> 'many of the women without a separation or divorce came to CHAS because they found themselves hopelessly trapped when their marriage broke down. The right to remain in the matrimonial home until a marriage is dissolved is often interpreted by the local authorities as meaning that, while the home and the marriage exists, a woman cannot technically be considered as homeless. Sometimes local authorities are also worried about the possible accusations that they have pre-empted a court decision by prematurely siding with one party in a dispute. The result is that in these circumstances they seldom offer temporary accommodation.'   (CHAS 1974: 23)

Where temporary accommodation is provided, it is likely to fill the 'less eligibility' criterion. Hostels and bed and breakfast accommodation may be seen as crisis solutions; but they may also be seen as deterrents to homelessness. Relatively long periods in such temporary accommodation may be a way of stemming the flow of 'marriage breakdowns' and of testing women's need and determination to end a marriage.

Local authority policy towards existing tenants whose marriages falter is also important. Authorities may offer separate tenancies to each partner, but this is a matter for local decision. A study of homeless women found some who had had joint local authority tenancies, but they:

> 'had been driven to leave their homes through domestic circumstances becoming intolerable. Their ex-partners, and co-tenants, had forced them out through violence or through moving another woman into their home. Because they had no dependent children, councils had given them no assistance in transferring their existing tenancy or rehousing them to somewhere where it was feasible for them to reside. They had merely been told that as they had a tenancy they should return there.'   (Austerberry and Watson 1983: 42)

The security of tenure belonging to council tenants under the 1980 Housing Act means that marriage breakdown is not grounds for authorities to evict either partner in a joint tenancy. A decision about tenure may have to await divorce proceedings. Local authorities are not enthusiastic about making two tenancies where one existed before. One result is that women in intolerable marriages, with or without children, may leave their joint tenancy, and then be refused another one. Even if the tenancy reverts to them on divorce, this may be too late to prevent homelessness.

Women leaving men often have little choice but to turn to the local authority for housing: but there is too little information to draw a general picture of the response they meet. No doubt many women are rehoused humanely. There are, however, a series of practices that reluctant authorities can use to persuade women to go back 'home'. There may be refusal to allocate a sole tenancy where there is already a married couple tenancy; refusal of temporary accommodation; long waits in temporary accommodation, such as bed and breakfast arrangements; demands for the repayment of rent arrears; discriminatory allocation policies. The impact of such measures on women is altogether different from their impact on men.

Many relationships end by mutual consent; many are ended by mens' initiatives; women who want to end relationships need their men's consent. In any of these situations women may well achieve adequate housing and financial arrangements. But where men do not consent, no doubt, many decide that the risks are too great to take. The risks – of homelessness, and of declining housing standards – are demonstrated by those who try, especially by those who are forced out by violence. Women's ability to bring relationships to an end is curtailed in a way that men's is not.

Divorce and owner-occupation

The ability to retain owner-occupied homes on divorce is a major element in women's housing independence. The fundamental problem is one of income. Without a man's income, women risk losing their homes. According to Jo Tunnard: 'The experience of the Citizens' Rights Office and other agencies which work with one-parent families suggests that . . . divorce and separation carry a relatively high risk that the mother and children will lose an owner-occupied home' (Tunnard 1976a: 40).

All forms of property settlement leave some women exposed to this risk. One way is to sell the home and share the proceeds. This may well leave the woman without enough to buy again. A second is to have the home transferred into her name, in return for reduced maintenance or none at all. Tunnard argues that this is usually the best arrangement, but it can leave women with high mortgage payments, and possibly arrears to settle. Third, she may pay her husband for his share – clearly a financial mountain. Last, she may occupy the house until the youngest child leaves school, with the property to be sold and settled at this stage. This postpones her housing difficulties until she is older, even less likely to be able to find an adequate income, and not likely to be accepted by local authorities as in priority need (being now without children) (see Leevers and Thynne 1979; Austerberry and Watson 1983, for a fuller discussion of these issues).

Jo Tunnard argues that it should be possible for women to stay in owner-occupied homes, with reasonable property settlements and with the policies that exist on paper in building societies and local authorities. Building societies can accept interest-only payments indefinitely, the interest can be paid through benefits, and local authorities have wide powers to buy houses, or to guarantee mortgages. In practice, arrears may mount without women even being informed (where the mortgage is in the man's name), building societies may repossess, women do not always receive their full benefit entitlement, and local authorities are reluctant to use their powers. Solicitors often advise women to sell, rather than helping them to hold on to their homes (Tunnard 1976a, 1976b).

There is not enough information to draw a general picture of the results of divorce for women's housing. It is clearly possible for women to emerge with adequate housing and the ability to finance it. On the other hand, divorce can lead to loss of the owner-occupied home and severe housing stress.

Tied to the job

Numbers of women live in accommodation that is tied to their husband's job. Tied accommodation for men and women means that house security is tied to job security. However, it has an extra twist for the woman. House security is also tied to marriage. This must act as a disincentive to women to leave marriages; it also leaves them vulnerable when men desert or die. The largest of these categories are in agriculture, the police, the armed forces, the church, the prison department, the National Coal Board, British Rail, and the fire service. 'Service regulations allow husbands unilaterally to declare themselves estranged from their wives. The wives thus become illegal occupants of the married quarters' (Brion and Tinker 1980: 12–13). If men's work takes them abroad, women may be yet more vulnerable. One homeless woman who had lived in Kenya for twenty-three years in service accommodation described her fate when the marriage broke down: 'I got the boot. I was packed on the aeroplane like a brown paper parcel and sent home' (Austerberry and Watson 1983: 9). In these situations women have no entitlement to tenure or alternative accommodation; they have no stake in housing property; and unless they have children living with them, they may not be accepted as in priority need by the local authority.

Divorce and separation tend to lead women towards the local authority sector (Brion and Tinker 1980: 15). Despite the barriers that local authorities put in the way, and despite their tendency to offer inferior accommodation in these circumstances, this is women's main resort – often because it is their only resort. Some of the most detailed evidence about women approaching local authorities is published in accounts of victims of violence in marriage, and it will be discussed under that heading at the end of the chapter.

The housing conditions of women whose marriages have broken down are part of the next two sections on women without men. Women with dependent children are the subject of much government-sponsored and highly empirical literature on 'one-parent families'. Women without dependent children are much less studied. What is known is discussed separately.

The housing conditions of women without men

Women with dependent children

One-parent families flout the family ideal, that children belong to couples. They flout another norm, which says that families are headed by men, for most one-parent families are headed by women. If, as this chapter argues, housing policy gives preference to families of the traditional kind, then 'one-parent families' may well expect to be disadvantaged.

One-parent families share a dissonance with family norms, and all varieties stand in some sense outside the economic and family relationships on which housing finance and allocation are predicated. However, the differences between one-parent family types are marked as well. After all, those families formed without marriage, those formed from the breakdown of marriage, and those formed by a parent's death all stand in a different relationship to marriage itself. Not surprisingly some are more stigmatized than others, and some are more able to hold on to the privileges accorded to married couples. Single mothers are least likely to be able to find independent accommodation at all; and widows, although they may suffer severe financial deprivations, are rather more likely than others to have, and be able to maintain, independent accommodation.

While the fundamental difficulty for one-parent families is lack of income, housing problems are consequent and severe. They are stressed by all reports on one-parent families. Thus the Finer committee devoted a substantial chapter to housing and commented that 'housing problems closely rival money problems as a cause of hardship and stress to one-parent families' (DHSS 1974: 357). Subsequently, the Housing Services Advisory Committee remarked: 'for many single parents, particularly women, housing remains their major problem, after finance' (HSAG 1978: 5).

The tenure pattern of single parents is a clear indication of their disadvantage and difference from other families. A much smaller proportion are owner-occupiers than is the case for people in general, though there are widows, and separated and divorced women who have managed to keep the matrimonial home. Providing figures is not in fact straightforward, since many one-parent families are disguised in sharing arrangements. However, one study of fatherless families on Family Income Supplement found that 14 per cent of the householders in the sample were owner-occupiers; nearly 60 per cent were local authority tenants (Nixon 1979: 149). This compares with over 50 per cent owner-occupiers among householders in general. The families in this study were on FIS and thus include only those with employed parents; they exclude the most disadvantaged economically (those whose parent stays at home to care for children) as well as the more advantaged ones, with incomes above the FIS limit.

Both the Finer committee and the Housing Services Advisory Group of the DOE were concerned about the concentration of one-parent families in the privately rented sector. Discussing the 'shrinking pool of privately rented housing', the Finer committee remarked that, 'A particularly disturbing feature of this situation is the concentration of one-parent families in furnished accommodation in the conurbations in England and Wales' (DHSS 1974: 363). And the Housing Services Advisory Group report remarks: 'The pattern of housing tenure for one-parent families runs completely counter to this general trend. They are far less likely to be owner-occupiers, are more dependent on local authority housing, and are particularly concentrated in private furnished accommodation' (HSAG 1978: 4). As both Finer and the Housing Services Advisory Group conclude, this makes one-parent families very vulnerable, both to decreasing availability, high rents and poor conditions in the private sector, and to local authority policies. 'If they are rejected by the public sector, there is nowhere else for them to find adequate accommodation for a family' (HSAG 1978: 4).

But official reports acknowledge that one-parent families face discrimination in the public sector. Finer noted: 'Our evidence suggested that unmarried mothers suffer particular discrimination from local authorities in some areas' (DHSS 1974: 382). More generally, the Housing Services Advisory Group reported that, 'There is a tendency for one-parent families not to be regarded as "real" families and for local authorities to allocate housing to them on a different basis than that which would apply to a two-parent family'. This includes, for example, allocating flats instead of houses, and worse accommodation in worse areas: 'there is ample evidence that discrimination against lone parents in the quality of house and area they receive is the rule rather than the exception' (HSAG 1978: 7–8).

Thus few one-parent families have access to the most advantaged sector, owner-occupation; the declining privately rented sector is difficult to obtain, and often provides poor accommodation for high rents; and the public sector tends to offer its worst lettings in the worst areas. The various studies show one-parent families sharing with friends and relatives; living insecure lives involving frequent moves and being at high risk of homelessness; living in poor conditions; and spending a high proportion of their income on housing.

In several studies (DHSS 1974: 358; Nixon 1979: 48) the proportion who share with other households is calculated to be nearly one-third. This compares with almost no two-parent families who share in this way. Sharing is most likely among single mothers and least likely among widows. It is most likely to be with near-relatives (parents, most often). While sharing is less isolated, and usually gives access to better amenities (Nixon 1979: 48–62), it is unrealistic to see it as chosen in most cases and more realistic to see it as homelessness. Girls who have babies out of marriage may lack the resources to leave home or obtain access to a tenancy of their own; women who want to escape from unhappy or violent marriages may find that staying with friends is the only obvious route. It is a route fraught with difficulties, and in most cases can be regarded as a temporary measure only. The Catholic Housing Aid Society reports that 'staying with friends or relatives is a housing trap for one-parent families'. Tensions arise from overcrowding and lack of privacy; there may be an incentive to keeping the arrangements secret from local authorities; and the housing departments may refuse to regard families in this situation as homeless (CHAS 1974: 21). But it is widely reported that women who want to leave unhappy marriages use this route first; they thus become part of the concealed homeless rather than the counted homeless (Austerberry and Watson 1983: 2).

Frequent moves and ultimately homelessness are greater risks for one-parent families than for others. Frequent moves were reported by Finer (DHSS 1974: 364) and in an official study of fatherless families on FIS (Nixon 1979: 134). The latter study found 14 per cent of its sample had moved three or more times in the last five years, nearly three times the percentage found in families in general. This brings obvious problems of insecurity and of childrens' schooling, as well as making it harder to reach the top of local authority housing lists. It also indicates that these families' tenure of their accommodation was insecure. The evidence on those accepted as homeless by local authorities reinforces this conclusion: one-parent families number disproportionately, forming about a third of the total.

Studies agree again about the tendency for one-parent families to live in poor accommodation at high cost. 'All the information we have leads to the conclusion that the conditions and amenities in the homes of one-parent families are less adequate than in those of two-parent families, more especially in the privately rented sector' (DHSS 1974: 364). More recently, the study of *Fatherless Families on FIS* found that far more of their sample were in overcrowded accommodation than was the case for families in the *General Household Survey* (6 per cent at 1.5 people per room or more, compared with 0.6 per cent in the *GHS*; 35 per cent at 1–1.5 people per room, compared with 12.2 per cent in the *GHS*) (Nixon 1979: 56). Finally, a study of low-income families, commissioned by the DHSS, found that 'relatively higher housing and fuel expenditure distinguishes the one-parent families' (Knight 1981: 54). Whereas two-parent families in the study spent 19 per cent of their incomes on housing (already a high figure), one-parent families spent 22 per cent; lone parents at home caring for children spent 24 per cent. The study remarks that one-parent families whose head was out of the labour market 'emerge . . . clearly as a special group' (Knight 1981: 54).

The one-parent family literature, then, much of it government inspired, documents housing disadvantage. One-parent families are less likely than others to find independent accommodation; less likely to be owner-occupiers; and therefore subject to poor conditions and high rents in the privately rented sector; they are subject to discrimination in the public sector, although it is inevitably their main recourse; they risk frequent moves, and – more than others – they risk homelessness (even as defined by local authorities). What shines less clearly through this literature is the way deprivation relates to women, to women's position in public and private life, and to the state's defence of a certain kind of family structure. To some extent the issues are clouded by the

label 'one-parent families' (no mention of women); from this may
follow the lumping together of male-headed and female-headed
families. Male-headed families suffer from some of the same
disadvantages as female-headed ones, because fathers are playing female parts as well – but even those men who care for
children do not suffer quite the same disadvantage in public
economic life as women do, and the position of motherless
families is therefore somewhat different. However, these are
essentially studies about women and their families; they show
that women's access to housing depends crucially on the men
they live with. Without those men, whether by choice or accident, women – even with children – are critically disadvantaged.

Housing policy and housing finance are predicated on fathers
and mothers, and on men's economic advantage in the labour
market. The disadvantage of women without men follows directly from this. But the existence of discrimination in the public
sector should not obscure the importance of local authority
housing to women with children; or the fact that it does go some
way to meet their needs; or the fact that ideals of motherhood can
sometimes be turned to women's advantage. A revived supply of
public sector (and housing association) houses for rent is the best
hope for mothers who live, or may wish to live without men.

Women alone

This section concerns women without men and without dependent children: those who have never married, as well as those
whose marriages have come to an end through separation,
divorce, or death; those who have never had children as well as
those whose children have grown up; and those who are staying with parents, husbands, cohabitees, or friends for lack of
separate accommodation.

Most women need men's incomes if they are to find housing
within the private sector. If they have children, or if they are old,
the state may fill the gap. If they have no man and no children and
they are of working age there may be nowhere to go. Here is a
set of powerful constraints to encourage women to be part of
families: to stay with parents, to marry, to stay maried. In this
way, surely, much potential homelessness is kept out of public
eye and mind.

More women leave family homes of various kinds and stay
with friends. Here are the 'concealed homeless'. Officially, homeless single women are an almost negligible group. There are few

hostel places for women, and so few are to be found in research studies: where should one look for homeless people if not in hostels? Single women are not defined as in 'priority need' according to the Housing (Homeless Persons) Act 1980, unless they qualify according to some other criterion; they are therefore unlikely to appear in local authority homelessness statistics. Thus there is no obvious place where the homelessness of single women is recorded. And as Austerberry and Watson remark:

'The traditional image of homeless single people tends to be associated with men – the most extreme version being that of the male tramp under the arches. . . . Because fewer women are to be seen sleeping rough, there is an assumption that fewer women than men become homeless. Rarely do we stop to question what this means. Are there really fewer homeless women around, do women adopt different solutions to their housing problems or homelessness, or are homeless women simply forgotten or ignored?'

(Austerberry and Watson 1983:1)

The authors argue that women do adopt different solutions and that their homelessness is more concealed than that of men; that single women are nearly as likely as single men to contact London's Housing Advice Switchboard, in need of help; and that there are large numbers of single adults who are obliged to share, being unable to form independent households (Austerberry and Watson 1983: 2–3).

In many ways the situation of women alone is similar to that of women with children, with the added twist that they are unlikely to be accorded any priority by local authorities. One study of homeless women found:

'Only one definite offer of a standard self-contained local authority flat had actually been made to any of the (102) women interviewed, and this an unsuitable "one offer only" made to a seventy-five year old woman who had been on the housing waiting list for four and a half years. She had been in the same emergency hostel for the past six years, since being made homeless from tied service work at the age of sixty-nine.'

(Austerberry and Watson 1983: 45)

Some of these women were offered hard-to-let tenancies, but they were unlikely to be offered ordinary council lets unless they were defined as 'vulnerable'. Ironically, those who were 'vulnerable' were least likely to be able to manage alone (Austerberry and Watson 1983: 51). Thus women without dependent children were much worse off in relation to the local authority sector than women with such children.

There are some strategies which are more likely to be adopted by women without children. One group are those who never leave their parents' homes; this group partly overlaps with women who are 'carers' of elderly relatives. Some of these women face acute difficulties when the relative dies, especially if the home is to be sold for sharing among other kin (Brion and Tinker 1980: 10–11). Another group are those who live in tied accommodation, tied in this case to their own jobs rather than to a husband's occupation. Thirty-three per cent of women in the hostel study had lived in tied accommodation at some point in their lives. For 10 per cent it was their last secure accommodation. 'Frequently women have no choice but to take on tied employment as the only possible option for employment and housing. When the women have to leave the job hostels may often be the only feasible housing option, since their former employment (for example nursing, catering, caretaking) is generally too low paid to enable them to save' (Austerberry and Watson 1983: 13).

Women alone face the same problems as single men in the lack of non-family accommodation and the lack of local authority priority. They are more likely to face low income, too. Women alone face the full brunt of social definitions of women as reproducers. Their unimportance is measured in lack of earnings and lack of children; and it is rewarded with a virtual absence of housing policy. Many women must be deterred from the effort to form an independent household; and many are forced into unstable, inadequate, and unwanted sharing arrangements.

One group of women alone with rather different housing problems are the elderly. Elderly people are officially recognized as being disadvantaged in relation to housing; and it is women who predominate, especially in the older age-groups. More than other women alone, elderly women are likely to have independent accommodation, acquired during a marriage; though there is evidence that old people's homes accommodate some whose main lack is alternative accommodation. More general problems, however, are the relatively low standards of accommodation among elderly people, and that maintenance and access may become increasingly difficult with age and disability (Brion and Tinker 1980: 21–2).

Domestic violence and homelessness

Violence, Women's Aid, and women's refuges

Women's Aid has been the most successful movement of women's practical politics in Britain in recent times. It is most obviously a movement about violence, and the way it is used by men to control women; but it is equally a movement about housing. The widespread development of refuges demonstrated that women were often victims of domestic cruelty. It also demonstrated the difficulty of escape, and the great part control of housing played in keeping women within violent relationships. As Hilary Rose remarks: 'If we examine the history of the development of Women's Aid from its pioneering house at Chiswick to its network of refuges up and down the country, the significance of the economic independence of women and their independent access to housing becomes an important policy issue' (Rose 1978: 527).

The startling success of Women's Aid as a movement was built on its identification of a practical need, as well as on an ideological commitment. Support groups, planning or actually running refuges, spread quickly. It began at Chiswick in 1972, and there was a national meeting of 25 groups by 1974. By 1975 there were 82 support groups planning or running refuges (see Rose 1978: 582–89; Binney 1981). Women's Aid's own national survey in 1978 was able to trace 150 groups running refuges (Binney, Harkell, and Nixon 1981). Women who needed refuge responded quickly too. Protection and shelter (however physically inadequate) drew women in large numbers. Binney calculated that: 'The 150 refuges traced in England and Wales had accommodated an estimated 11,400 women and 20,850 children between September 1977 and September 1978, and had turned away many more' (Binney, Harkell, and Nixon 1981: viii). The result is both a triumph and a problem. Refuges everywhere are overcrowded and uncomfortable. Yet still the women come. Thus has Women's Aid demonstrated how women may need a place to go.

Out of this need has grown a social movement. Women's Aid's ideals have been about mutual support rather than charity, self-determination rather than hierarchy, and open access rather than bureaucratic gate-keeping. The connection with the women's liberation movement is explicit, though its expression may be tempered by the need for support from authority (Rose 1978: 530–31). One basis for the political success of Women's Aid is its identification of a housing/family nexus as well as a family/ violence nexus. If women's access to housing is directly dependent on their position in families, family violence exposes the lack of another place to go.

Refuges, then, provide accommodation, albeit temporary, protection from violence, mutual support and advice. Studies made of the refuges and the women who use them (Pahl 1978; Binney, Harkell, and Nixon 1981) highlight the degree of violence women have suffered, often over long periods, and the practical problems of becoming re-established in secure accommodation.

While this chapter is not primarily about violence, it is difficult to understand the depth of women's need for a safe place without some grasp of its seriousness. In a DHSS-sponsored study of the Canterbury refuge, Jan Pahl writes:

> 'Some women are appallingly injured; they suffer broken bones, knife wounds, and severe bruising; some are hit over the head with furniture, some are thrown downstairs, and one had a nail hammered into her foot. But some women suffer in other ways and may have no bruises to show for it. One of the women who has stayed longest at the refuge, putting up with what are clearly for her extremely difficult circumstances, has never said what it was that drove her from her home; all she has said is that she has not been physically battered; but her need of the refuge is clearly great.' (Pahl 1978: 8)

Binney's study of 150 refuges and of the 656 women living in them at the time found that, on average, violence had endured for seven years. Most women had wanted to leave before, generally within the first year, but despite attempts, had not succeeded in establishing themselves (Binney, Harkell, and Nixon 1981: 5–6).

The evidence of sustained and serious abuse; of women staying long after they feel the need to leave; of repeated attempts to leave violent homes – these prompt the question of what keeps women at home. Clearly there are personal constraints, considerations of children, of hope for change, of pressure from the men themselves. But also there are material constraints, of income and of accommodation.

Asked about the reasons for returning home in the past, 59 per cent of Binney's respondents mentioned accommodation problems. She concludes that: 'The most powerful constraint against leaving had been the lack of somewhere to go, either immediately or in the long term' (Binney, Harkell, and Nixon 1981: 6). A high proportion had no independent earnings: 'Only a third of the women had had any sort of job before leaving home, often part-time. So most women were either wholly or partly dependent on their husband or boyfriend for material resources. Those at home with very young children were particularly vulnerable' (p. 5). Women kept without enough money to feed the family, as some of these were, would find it particularly difficult to find and furnish alternative accommodation. Even if the escaping woman finds a roof, the evidence about the housing and furnishing conditions of one-parent families will give cold comfort.

A prime concern of refuge workers is to negotiate secure permanent accommodation. There are, very broadly, two routes open. One, generally the least satisfactory, is to try to secure tenure and safety in the previous home. The other is to find new accommodation, either through the local authority as a homeless person, or through a housing association. In practice, 8 per cent of Binney's sample achieved the first route when they left the refuge, 44 per cent were rehoused by the local authority, and 11 per cent by housing associations or in the private rented sector. The rest were either still in temporary accommodation or had returned to their violent partner (Binney, Harkell, and Nixon 1981: 78).

The Domestic Violence Act (1976) includes provisions to protect women in their homes. It uses the civil law (the police being reluctant to deal with domestic violence under the criminal law). The procedure is for a woman to seek an injunction: this is an order from the court to the man to refrain from violence, give her access to the home, and possibly leave the home himself (an 'ouster' injunction). The injunction may be backed by powers of arrest, but is often not. If the man breaks an injunction not backed by powers of arrest, the woman will have to return to court to seek his imprisonment. Breaking the injunction may lead to a fine or imprisonment for contempt of court, for an indefinite (but always short) period.

The Domestic Violence Act is about protection more than accommodation. It is more difficult to obtain an ouster injunction than one which merely orders protection from assault. Coote and Gill conclude: 'If you are married and not yet divorced, it is not easy to obtain an order for your husband to leave, unless the home is in your name alone. Judges are very reluctant to evict any husband from a home which is owned or rented in his name or jointly with his wife' (Coote and Gill 1977/1979: 18). Solicitors in another study (Borkowski, Murch, and Walker 1983: 92) remarked on the difficulty of getting an ouster injunction when the man did not attend court. The fact that only 8 per cent of Binney's sample managed to return home with the man excluded is some indication of the difficulties.

Even success in obtaining an ouster injunction does not bring a permanent solution. Just how unstable it is is indicated rather alarmingly by Binney's sample. While 8 per cent were able to go alone to their homes on leaving the refuge, the follow-up a year later showed only 4 per cent still there. First, the man may break the injunction, and the most severe punishment, a short period of imprisonment, provides scant protection. Second, this procedure does not bring a long-term resolution of property or tenure issues. Such resolution will normally await divorce proceedings.

Women themselves are highly sceptical about the Domestic Violence Act. Binney reports:

> 'Many women and Women's Aid groups felt that without police powers of arrest, injunctions were worthless, since there was little to deter a man from breaking one. Women reported that the police had been reluctant to answer calls for help in the event of a broken injunction, and even more reluctant to press charges. The sentences men received when charged, were felt to be so trivial that women had not bothered to use an injunction again. In September 1978, 32 women who had obtained exclusion orders were still living in refuges, either because they were too afraid to move back home or because the men refused to move out:
>
> "I got the injunction. My husband says he'll be back after a few days, so I'm scared to go back."
>
> "I have an injunction with powers of arrest but I can't get him out."
>
> "They won't attach powers of arrest until I'm living there permanently and he tries to get in. I've been back twice and he's broken in both times."'
>
> (Binney, Harkell, and Nixon 1981: 85–6)

Unsurprisingly, most women feel that moving back to the site of violence is not their best solution.

In seeking alternative accommodation, the main alternatives will be the privately rented sector, housing association lets, or

local authority housing. While single parents use privately rented
housing more than other groups, it forms an ever smaller proportion of the housing market and is especially difficult to find for
women with children. Housing associations, with their ability to
serve the needs of people in special categories, are a real alternative; their disadvantages are that they still form a relatively small
part of the general housing market, that their building programmes are subject to public expenditure restrictions, and
that they cannot therefore provide instant solutions. By far the
largest resource of women in these situations must be the local
authority.

The Housing (Homeless Persons) Act 1977

The law appears to provide a definitive solution for women
whose housing problems are caused by violence. The Housing
(Homeless Persons) Act 1977, 'a major landmark in social legislation' (Robson and Watchman 1981), puts a duty on local authorities to 'provide, secure or help to secure accommodation for
homeless persons and those threatened with homelessness'
(Robson and Watchman 1981: 2). The act was born in a climate
much changed by the Women's Aid movement. Included in its
definition of homeless are those who have accommodation, but
are likely to suffer violence or threats of violence from another
occupant if they try to live there. The Housing (Homeless
Persons) Act, then, appears particularly relevant to women who
suffer domestic violence.

Unfortunately, the act is less comprehensive than originally
intended. Local authorities, faced with duties to rehouse the
homeless but no additional resources, were hostile. They argued,
in effect, their need of a gate-keeping role, and they were
appeased by some serious changes in the bill:

> 'These were effectively to transform the bill from a measure
> which provided homeless persons with a right to accommo-
> dation into a measure which presents them with a series of
> obstacles which have to be successfully negotiated before that
> right can be claimed.'   (Robson and Watchman 1981: 2)

All accounts of battered women seeking accommodation from
local authorities show that they are not absolved from the obstacle race (see also Webb 1983), or from delays and difficulties. A
proportion are rehoused by local authorities; 44 per cent of the

women in Women's Aid's follow-up study had been rehoused in this way (one year after the first interview in the refuge).

The problems women face in being rehoused under this act are here considered under three heads. First, there are obstacles to being accepted for rehousing even when local authorities carry out their statutory duties. Second, there is the meaning of statutory duties and the failure to carry them out. Third, the nature of the accommodation offered to those accepted for rehousing and the arrangements for equipping it. These subjects are covered in more detail in several publications (Robson and Watchman 1981; Binney, Harkell, and Nixon 1981; Hazelgrove 1979).

Obstacles presented within the act

Homelessness as defined in the act covers those who share accommodation with someone who is a danger to them. However, the refusal to regard women as homeless was the most common reason given by women in refuges for their rejection by local authorities (Binney, Harkell, and Nixon 1981: 80). First, a woman is covered by this clause of the act only if the threat comes from someone living in the same house. Thus women attacked by ex-family members who have now moved out may be rejected. Second, a housing department may take issue with, or may refuse to take seriously, a woman's claim that she has suffered violence or is threatened. Reports from women suggest that they have great difficulty persuading housing officials to accept their word.

The next hurdle to be jumped is the category 'priority need'. Only those fitting this category can expect the local authority to secure them accommodation. (Duties to those not in priority need are much more limited.) In the act, women are not defined as in priority need simply on account of being battered. They are included, as are other people, if they have children, if they are pregnant, or if they are defined as 'vulnerable'. Women without children may be defined as 'vulnerable', and the Code of Guidance accompanying the act suggests that this may include women escaping violence. In practice, local authorities are very reluctant to accept women without children as in priority need. Very few such women in the Women's Aid study were rehoused (Binney, Harkell, and Nixon 1981: 81).

'Intentional homelessness' is the third hurdle that may trip applicants for rehousing under this legislation. This was a concession to local authorities made during the passage of the bill; it extricates them from rehousing people thought to have pre-cipitated their own homelessness. The rationale is to prevent queue-jumping, but it is also a gate which local authorities can interpose between the reluctant rate-payer and applicants for rehousing. There is little case in the legislation for regarding any battered woman as intentionally homeless, but 8 per cent of the rejections in the Women's Aid sample were made on these grounds (Binney, Harkell, and Nixon 1981: 80). Rent arrears are one excuse for pinning this particular label.

The fourth tripwire is the 'local connection' clause. Local authorities may refuse to rehouse an applicant who has no local connection, instead notifying a more appropriate area. The act protects battered women against being returned to an area where they risk violence. But the wording of the act is material for another gate-building exercise by local authorities wishing to minimize their responsibilities. The act refers to threats of violence which are likely to be carried out:

> 'The imposition of a likelihood of violence test was roundly criticized by Lord Gifford as extraordinary, unworkable, likely to lead to the interrogation of distressed women and allow-ing housing officials the opportunity to analyse this problem according to their own prejudices and subjective views on matrimonial or domestic life.'
>
> (Robson and Watchman 1981: 13fn, quoting House of Lords debates)

The remarks were prescient. A high proportion of the Women's Aid sample had been told that they were the responsibility of another area – 24 per cent of those rejected, second only to the proportion defined as not homeless.

To be rehoused under this act, a woman must cross each of these hurdles. While each appears to have a bypass route for battered women, each may still be put in the way.

Legal and illegal practices

Many of the decisions of local authorities are taken within a grey area whose legality is being tested by the courts. One significant point of uncertainty has been the status of the Code of Guidance which accompanies the act. This describes very good practice which would offer humane treatment to victims of domestic violence; but while authorities are legally bound to have regard to it, the Court of Appeal has decided that it is not mandatory (Robson and Watchman 1981: 70–2). Hence authorities do not need to define single battered women as 'vulnerable', to take one important example.

Among practices of very dubious legality are excluding women whose pregnancy is of less than a certain length, or defining a refuge as accommodation and its occupants as therefore not homeless, or treating all cases of eviction for rent arrears as 'intentional homelessness'. These latter practices have been tried in the courts and found illegal. Authorities may also try to avoid their rehousing responsibilities by instructing women to return to their former home under the protection of the Domestic Violence Act. This is a particularly unfortunate practice, given the in-security of such arrangements.

Finally, authorities may flout the act without risk of serious redress. Their decisions may be challenged, but 'without a genuine deterrent in the form of damages, we suspect some housing authorities may make a cynical calculation of the cost of providing accommodation for the homeless and the damages the court will award against them if they ignore this duty' (Robson and Watchman 1981: 79). In other words, flouting the act is cheaper than fulfilling its requirements.

The accommodation offered

Women who overcome these obstacles are not yet rehoused. They may still be kept waiting in temporary accommodation; held responsible for rent arrears incurred on their previous home, or asked to wait until they have secured legal custody of the chil-dren; and the permanent accommodation offered at the end may still be inadequate or in unsafe or unsuitable surroundings. Finally, the accommodation will need furnishing and equipping, as many women will have left everything in their previous home.

In his discussion of the first of these issues, Robson concludes as follows:

'The Codes of Guidance may urge housing authorities not to force homeless persons to spend a certain amount of time in interim accommodation as a matter of policy. However, this practice and that of housing homeless persons in unsatisfac-tory accommodation continues unabated by the Act. Research by Shelter into how housing authorities have fulfilled their

housing obligations also indicates the persistence of the practice of "dumping" homeless persons in hostels, hotels, guest
houses, mobile homes, short-term accommodation, pre-
fabricated buildings and disused army camps.'

(Robson and Watchman 1981: 82)

Rent arrears pose a particularly severe problem, and one which
is often out of women's control. Local authorities may describe
people with rent arrears as 'intentionally homeless' and therefore
not eligible for rehousing; or rent arrears can delay the rehousing
of those accepted. One problem is that women in deteriorating
relationships may never see the money for the rent. The Finer
Committee commented that rent arrears were almost an index
of marital discord (DHSS 1974: 389). Another difficulty is that
women in refuges may be incurring two rents at the same time,
and most will have barely enough resources to meet one. Authorities may then defer rehousing until the woman has paid the
arrears; 14 per cent of the applications in the Women's Aid study
were treated thus.

An even higher percentage (20 per cent) were asked to wait
until the end of divorce and custody proceedings. All this can
mean long delays.

It is widely reported that the quality of housing offered to
homeless people is inferior to that offered to people on the
ordinary waiting list. Women's Aid believe that battered women
are treated rather worse than others in this respect (Binney,
Harkell, and Nixon 1981: 84). A high proportion of those who had
been rehoused thought the standard of accommodation was
poor, but many had felt constrained to accept their first offer, for
fear of being classed as intentionally homeless if they refused.
Some of the properties were derelict or vandalized (Binney,
Harkell, and Nixon 1981: 89). While this evidence is somewhat
impressionistic, it has some corroboration from studies of housing standards of one-parent families in general.

Finally, there are problems of making the house habitable, of
repairs and equipment. As Hazelgrove notes: 'There is no obligation to arrange for the accommodation to be equipped in any
way, and so the authority is perfectly justified in assuming . . .
that its duty is discharged by arranging for a homeless family to
collect the key to an empty house' (Hazelgrove, 1979: 47).
Although many of the women in the Women's Aid study had
obtained social security grants, especially for furniture, such

payments are notoriously variable. The report remarks: 'Furnishings were often minimal – interviewers often used words such as "sparse", "spartan", or "bare", to describe the homes they visited. Long after moving in, many women could still not afford floor coverings, cupboards or chests of drawers' (Binney, Harkell, and Nixon 1981: 91). Leaving a violent home was expensive.

Several key themes emerge from this discussion of women leaving violent homes. The first is that Women's Aid has made a political success of women's access to housing. A national network of refuges has been established by women themselves. Some support has come from central government and local authorities. The refuges are used to the point of overcrowding; and the need for more of them has been recognized in the main official study of violence in the family (HMSO 1974–75). Furthermore, the refuges are something new. They offer essential accommodation. But they also offer help without condition or bureaucratic barrier; acceptance of women's own assessment of their need for refuge; mutual aid and community. These stand in place of bureaucratic and professional gatekeepers, hierarchy and authority – more typical characteristics of 'social services'. The Domestic Violence Act and the Housing (Homeless Persons) Act have both been passed in the wake of Women's Aid's success. They both acknowledge and make provision for the accommodation problems of women escaping domestic violence.

There are limitations to Women's Aid's political achievements. The refuges have provided an escape route into temporary accommodation. The route to permanent accommodation is still difficult. It often lies through humiliating and protracted dealings with local authorities; through uncertainty; through penal temporary accommodation in bed and breakfast premises; through poverty. It often leads to accommodation which is worse than that from which women have started, and often the poorest that the local authority has to offer.

It has not proved easy to disconnect women's access to housing from women's position in the family, even when violence is involved. However enlightened the legislation may sound, it remains difficult for women to leave. Nothing has been done to alter the financial facts of women's dependence on men for housing, nor the discriminatory practices of local authorities to whom they must turn when men beat rather than support. The barriers erected around women in their marital homes may be seen in one light as economy measures, having to do with the state's reluctance to support women alone. However, it is difficult not to see them also as family measures, having to do with the preservation of the dependence of women in families and the discouragement of their independence from men. There is no intention here of describing a monolithic, patriarchal 'state' developing consistent policies to keep women in their place. There is after all some support for Women's Aid and some provision for women to escape from violent men. And there are social policies which break up families, as well as housing policies which make it difficult for them to break up. But the drift of policies in practice, as distinct from in appearance, is to support traditional family norms, even in the face of considerable public and political concern about the abuse of women. The intention to protect women, written clearly into the legislation, is sacrificed in the small print and detailed practice to protecting 'the family'.

It is worth comparing the position of women who live in violent relationships with the position of women in general. Other women who want to end a marriage relationship may be more successful in persuading their men to leave; they may also find it more possible to share the matrimonial home while awaiting divorce proceedings. On the other hand, women who suffer violence in marriage do have some recourses which are not open to others. They have, most obviously, refuges; and they have the protection of the legislation already described, inadequate though it is. On balance, the housing position of women who suffer domestic violence is not very different from that of other women. In the one case Women's Aid has succeeded in making an issue; the other case is unsung. The housing position of women who suffer violence is not that of a 'problem' group; it is that of women in general.

6

Health

Reproduction, health care, and disability

Reproduction is central to women's social experience. The way women experience both public and private worlds depends upon the social construction of reproductive biology. Upon the biological fact that women give birth is built women's responsibility for nurturing and their weak place in the public world. Reproduction thus forms a central theme of women's health writing and political action. Male control of women's reproductive lives is the focus of this chapter: in contraception and abortion, women are subject to a male-controlled medical and research establishment; childbirth has been taken out of the hands of midwives and mothers, and is now in the control of male obstetricians; and unsatisfactory treatment of aspects of women's reproductive biology – breast and womb surgery, pre-menstrual tension and menopausal distress – flow from the male domination of medicine. Reproduction and its control by men have formed the basis for a considerable literature, as well as a successful politics of women's health.

 but

In some ways, these are hazardous remarks. There are real dangers in an analysis which reduces women's lives to their biology. The relationship between the biological facts of reproduction and the social construction of women as primarily reproducers is a key area for feminist analysis. However, to argue that biological reproduction at present underpins a considerable edifice of gender differentiation is not to argue that these relationships are constant or independent of other such basic social relations as those of capitalism. Reproduction, then, is central to women's lives as they are lived here and now, and its alienation provides the basis for a feminist critique of health care and its domination by medicine.

But the focus on women as reproducers is a limiting and potentially damaging one. Women are not only 'consumers' of medicine's miracles. They are also major providers in health labour, both unpaid and paid, private and public. This case has been cogently argued in relation to Third World women, whose health role in the production and processing of food is absolutely fundamental, but who are treated by western health services as passive recipients of 'family planning' and maternal and child health services (Eide 1979). In the West, too, women are key health makers (Graham 1984, 1985). Health making belongs to the home more than it does to the hospital. From a health perspective rather than a medical one it is health institutions which are peripheral, and women, as mothers, carers, providers of food, organizers of safety, and negotiators are the ones who play the most central role. Women have extensive health roles in unpaid labour.

In paid labour, too, women occupy the majority of jobs in health care. Despite the hierarchy of male medicine, women health workers outnumber men. They also do most of the caring which, I shall argue, is the main real outcome of health institutions. 'Women are the major producers of health care' (Doyal and Pennell 1979: 237). An analysis of these roles, then, is one way of extending the analysis of women and health beyond reproduction.

A second point is that only a minority of women – at any one time – are of reproductive age. The attention lavished on women as child-bearers by medicine and health institutions has a counterpart in the neglect, and sometimes ill-treatment of women past or passing their reproductive years (Evers 1985; Pocock 1983). Unfortunately both sides of this coin are also mirrored in a women's health literature which has not looked far beyond reproduction (for a recent exception see Lewin and Olesen 1985). Women figure largely among the elderly and those with chronic illness. They are a majority among the physically handicapped and those treated for mental illness. Issues of care and cure, of the relative neglect of people with long-term ailments and disability, are an established part of the NHS literature. They may be particularly illuminated by a feminist approach.

Finally, women of all ages have lives which extend beyond reproduction. In particular, they are extensively involved in production, and their largely segregated work experience must bring with it a characteristic pattern of occupational health and disease. This point is not pursued here, mainly for lack of evidence. Undoubtedly this lack follows from the more obvious dangers of men's jobs, and women's exclusion from some of the more hazardous occupations. Two points may be noted briefly. First, the occupational health of women should be considered in relation to all the work they do. For example, interaction between paid and unpaid labour may cause stress, and domestic accidents are especially important for women. Second, there are specific hazards associated with women's jobs: clerical work, hotel and catering, hairdressing and health work. And routine jobs may be especially stressful (these issues are discussed in Doyal 1983; EOC 1979; Lewin and Olesen 1985; Oakley 1983).

Thus this chapter starts with reproduction, but does not end there. It also looks at health and health policy more broadly, to suggest how these may be enlightened by a feminist interpretation.

Reproduction

Women do the work of reproduction; men control it. This is so, at least under western capitalism. The evidence of history and of anthropology is that this is a peculiar state of affairs. Jordan, in her cross-cultural study, remarks that 'giving birth in most societies is women's business' (Jordan 1980: 3). Oakley argues:

'Childbirth, contraception and abortion are aspects of women's reproductive life. In most cultures of the world and throughout most of history it is women who have controlled their own reproductive function. That is, the management of reproduction has been restricted to women, and regarded as part of the feminine role. Such knowledge of anatomy, physiology, pharmacology and delivery techniques as exists is vested in women as a group. This control is usually informal, often invisible and concealed. It operates through a system of cooperative mutual aid, and with a body of practical knowledge and beliefs which is transmitted from one generation of women to another. There are methods of preventing conception, and ways of ensuring abortion if unwanted conception has occurred. When a child is ready to be born it is a woman or group of women who deliver it, and who care for both mother and child in the postnatal period. Women are the experts. Men are not involved, or are only marginally involved.' (Oakley 1976: 19)

The historical and cultural peculiarity of male control over women's reproductive lives is obscured by medicine, the medium through which this control is mainly expressed. Perhaps medicine's greatest success is as ideology: it has overcome tradition and taboo to the point where male control of childbirth and related matters seems (almost) completely natural.

The area of women's most characteristic competence has not been surrendered without a whimper. The battle between mid-wives and male midwives is entertainingly – and one-sidedly – described by Aveling (1872/1967), and seems to have been par-ticularly virulent in the eighteenth century. Recent times have produced radical movements within midwifery (Spinks 1982) and a Women's Health Movement, grounded in reproductive issues, which has had practical and political impact (Doyal 1983; Wilkins 1983).

The Women's Health Movement is a varied and changing constellation of groups. The common purpose has been to chal-lenge medicine's control of reproduction, and to assert the claims of women to knowledge and power over their own bodies. The point is not to go 'back to nature'. It is rather to argue that medicine has usurped knowledge that is particularly useful to women (who are the main users of health services); has made it less available; and has reduced women's power over their own lives. It is also claimed that medicine's narrow approach to women's health problems contradicts women's experiences, with the result that it is often unhelpful or even damaging. One strategy of women's health groups and women's health literature has been self-help: to give women information about their bodies and offer mutual aid (see, for example, Boston Women's Health Collective 1971/1978). Another strategy has been to attempt to modify the way health institutions treat women. Another has been to fight for women's 'right to choose', especially in abortion.

If women's writing and politics have been consistent in their analysis of male control of reproduction, they have been a good deal more uncertain about an ethic of reproduction to take its place. This partly reflects differences between women. Repro-ductive control, particularly abortion, has formed one of the most public issues of women's health politics. And reproductive con-trol may be used to decide for as well as against motherhood. This issue, then, may give rise to very different responses in women very differently placed (Oakley 1981b: 207; Coote and Campbell 1982). However, there is reason for mothers and non-mothers to share an interest in safe and effective reproductive control. First, it is fundamental to health and life, as a reading of women's lives in earlier decades of this century will show. The following is just one account from many published by Margaret Llewelyn Davies

(1915/1978, 1931/1977) and Margery Spring Rice (1939/1981) and recently reissued:

> 'For fifteen years I was in a very poor state of health owing to continual pregnancy. As soon as I was over one trouble, it was all started over again. In one instance, I was unable to go further than the top of the street the whole time owing to bladder trouble, constant flow of water. With one, my leg was so terribly bad I had constantly to sit down in the road when out, and stand with my leg on a chair to do my washing. I have had four children and *ten* miscarriages, three before the first child, each of them between three and four months. No cause but weakness, and, I'm afraid, ignorance and neglect. I was in a very critical state for years; my sufferings were very great from acute weakness. I now see a great deal of this agony ought never to have been, with proper attention.'
>
> (Llewelyn Davies 1915/1978: 61–2)

Literary impressions are borne out by statistical analysis. Better control over reproduction has played a large part in improving women's health and reproductive experience. Women have used it to have fewer pregnancies, better spaced and at safer ages (Elbourne 1981: 25; Huntingford 1978: 244). This has contributed largely to lower infant and perinatal mortality, and to improved child health.

Safe and effective reproductive control is fundamental to liberation as well as to health and survival. This is so whether it is used to decide against motherhood, or by mothers attempting to assert some control over their lives. O'Brien argues that changes in reproductive technology have changed the material basis of women's oppression, and have thus opened the way to revolutionary change. 'The consolidation of rational control over reproductive process is the precondition of liberation, and it is urgent' (O'Brien 1981: 206). It is quite consistent to assert the part played by reproductive control in women's health and freedom, while affirming reproduction as a central part of most women's lives.

If one leitmotif of the literature on reproduction is its control by men, another is its variation by class. Ethnic variations are probably equally important, though less well documented. While feminists have stressed what is common in the experience of women, epidemiologists have described their differences. Women's experience of reproduction is profoundly unequal. Women in social class V (rated according to their husbands' occupations), suffer a stillbirth rate twice that of women in social class I. Their chance of losing a child within the first year of life is very nearly twice as great, too (Elbourne 1981: 97). These figures are for 'legitimate' births. The experience of women outside families may be even worse. One study concludes that babies of mothers who 'were single, separated or divorced or widowed in 1970 . . . had a higher risk of dying than even babies of Social Class V' (Wynn and Wynn 1979: 46). 'Illegitimate' births 'include children born into many diverse situations', but taking separately those who are registered by one parent only shows that these have very high rates of stillbirth (Macfarlane 1979: 340).

It may seem that there is more to divide women than to unite them, that class has a more profound impact on women's lives than being female. There is certainly cause for feminists to confront the differences in women's health and lives which give rise to such very different reproductive experiences. However, there is no need to oppose class and gender as determining factors. It is rather more productive to study their inter-relationships. The very poor experience of those women who are outside families indicates that both family status and class are key factors in reproductive experience. Relationship to men – and particularly relationship to male incomes – provides the connection. Those women whose marriage relationship is to men with high incomes have the best outcomes. Those whose relationship is to men at the bottom of the occupational and income hierarchy share their poor experiences with those without any relationship. Nowhere is the dependence of women upon male incomes so clearly demonstrated.

Another challenge to meet is the trivialization of a feminist preoccupation with the control of reproduction in favour of an apparent alternative – averting tragedy. Preventing the un-necessary loss of life and handicap among the infants of poorer women may seem the only possible priority. Fortunately, again, there is no need for an either/or decision. Medicine has not, in fact, narrowed the mortality gap. There is a good case in epidemiology, in sociology, and in feminism, for looking beyond obstetrics to understand the sad reproductive experience of poorer women.

One recent review argues: 'The most powerful "determinants" of poor outcome of pregnancy seem to lie outside the traditional scope of the health services. They are related to mothers' socioeconomic circumstances, and probably include such factors as diet, vulnerability to infections, and stress' (Chalmers, Oakley, and Macfarlane 1980: 843). Even within the perinatal health services, the authors argue that the stress on obstetric technology is excessive:

> 'Rarely has it been emphasized that technological aspects of care are probably of minor importance when compared with the clinical skills of the individual midwives, doctor, and nurses responsible for providing care to mothers and babies. Clinical experience in identifying true pathology in a predominantly healthy population; clinical judgment concerning the most appropriate course of action for each case identified; clinical skill in implementing the management selected: these aspects of clinical expertise seem to have attracted little explicit attention in the debate about the quality of perinatal care.'
> (Chalmers, Oakley, and Macfarlane 1980: 843)

The relationship of women's health to their reproductive experience – and particularly the impact of nutritional status – is taken up in *Prevention of Handicap and the Health of Women* (Wynn and Wynn 1979). The authors argue that 'the health of women and their children is indivisible' (Wynn and Wynn 1979: 81). They point to correlations between international rankings of diseases in women (such as multiple sclerosis and cancer) and congenital malformations in children (p. 119). Further correlations appear to link mortality with variations in diet – especially consumption of fresh fruit and vegetables – and space heating (p. 112). The importance of low quality white bread in the fall-back diet of poor women in Britain is especially implicated in their bad reproductive experience (p. 38). Furthermore, 'the nutritional state of the mother at the time of conception and during organogenesis is probably far more important to the fetus than the remainder of pregnancy' (p. 37). There is 'a contributory factor of prenatal origin, such as low birthweight, in the great majority of infant deaths' (p. 119). These authors favour a high level of technological facilities at birth as one way of saving life and preventing handicap among those babies born too small. But conclusions intrinsic to their analysis are that women's health – and particularly nutritional status – is a key factor in reproductive experience; and that the pattern of pregnancy and infant health is often set long before traditional health services come into play.

A concern with foetal and infant loss, and the inequality of reproductive experience, then, does not lead necessarily straight to dependence on obstetric technology. It may well lead instead to a much more broadly based concern with women's health.

Childbirth

'Any questions I've asked him is about the size of the baby, and this doctor, he kept asking how tall I was. I said why? He said; just answer that, you answer me. I said no: you answer *me*. So he said, well he said, all we want to know is how tall you are. So I said if I tell you how tall I am will you tell me why you want to know? And he said yes. And I said I'm five foot one. And he hummed and harred and hummed and harred and I said right; you tell me now why you want to know. And he said well we won't be able to tell you till your next visit, he said, we'll give you an internal examination. You won't be able to tell me what?'

('Sharon Warrington' describing an ante-natal exchange in
Oakley 1979: 282)

Reproduction is women's business in a rather special sense. When men conceive and grow a foetus (*in vitro* fertilization) it is still a matter for headlines. Women's bodies are still a necessary part of the process. But women may be deemed to have little else to do with it.

Modern childbirth is managed childbirth, managed by obstetricians who are, of course, mostly male (though in Britain, midwives still play a significant part). A crucial feature is medicalization, for it is the 'need' for technical control, intervention, hospitalization, which takes childbirth out of the hands of women as mothers and as midwives. At the extreme is active management involving a sequence of technical procedures which tend to be connected. For nearly all pregnant women there is regular monitoring throughout pregnancy and a hospital delivery. In a proportion, there may follow chemical or surgical induction of labour, speeding of labour through drugs, and electronic foetal monitoring during labour. Characteristically, the woman lies on her back, often with her feet in stirrups (the lithotomy position). Anaesthetic drugs, especially epidurals which can remove sensation from the lower part of the body, are frequent and especially likely to be necessary if the labour is induced and the woman lying down. Episiotomy (cutting the perineum) may follow. Anaesthetics mean that the attendant will deliver the baby rather than the woman, possibly with forceps (in the latter case the attendant must be a doctor). Caesarean delivery is another possibility, its incidence greatly increased where foetal monitoring has been used (Banta 1980: 189).

Such, then, is 'active management' of childbirth. Dunn reported in 1976, more or less at the height of the fashion for these procedures: 'So frequent are some of these interventions that they have almost become part of the ritual of modern delivery.' For an alternative model Dunn looked to anthropology. He learnt that:

'The recumbent position is rarely assumed among those people who live naturally . . . and have escaped the influence of civilization and modern obstetrics. . . . According to their build, to the shape of their pelvis, they stand, squat, kneel, or lie on their belly; so also they vary their position in various stages of labor according to the position of the child's head in the pelvis.'   (Engelmann 1882, quoted in Dunn 1976: 792)

Dunn reported a clinical trial of ideas triggered by such comparisons:

'They found that the effectiveness of contractions in dilating the cervix was doubled in the standing position, and at the same time the mothers found this position much less uncomfortable and painful. In fact they often had the greatest difficulty in getting their mothers to lie down again. The mean length of labour in their study group of primigravidas was less than four hours and none required analgesia; in other words, rapid, relatively pain-free labours.'   (Dunn 1976: 793)

Of course, mothers who 'stand, squat, kneel, or lie on their belly' have more or less to deliver their own babies. The 'people who live naturally', as Engelmann rather quaintly put it, were not being 'actively managed' by obstetricians.

Dunn wondered, 'have some obstetricians become intoxicated by their new technology, or have they lost faith in the normal physiology of parturition?' (Dunn 1976: 790). Dr Dunn was not the only one to wonder. His particular perspective was that of the paediatrician, concerned about the effects of these procedures upon the health and survival of babies. But other professional groups have also found cause to question. Epidemiologists, too, have asked about *The Benefits and Hazards of the New Obstetrics* (Chard and Richards 1977), arguing that procedures are insufficiently tested, and that interventions beneficial for a minority may be damaging if used in the majority of normal births. And psychologists have asked whether managed childbirth 'may sometimes affect adversely the development of confidence and the emotional bonding of the parents with their children' (Macfarlane 1977: 31). These are questions from within maledominated disciplines, and their concern is with babies' health and development rather than with handing childbirth back to women. However, epidemiological evidence in particular is useful to feminists. Widespread conclusions are scepticism about obstetric management universally applied – as distinct from its use in selected cases; and that improvements in health and survival have more to do with social and economic change than with the application of medical knowledge.

Feminist writing has focused on the meaning of childbirth to women. Life and physical health are a first concern of women in childbirth as well as of obstetricians. But, argue Graham and Oakley, mothers and doctors have contrasting frames of reference for the experience of childbirth. For obstetricians, childbirth is a medical process, with woman as patient and obstetrician as expert; the episode is transitory, ending with delivery. For women, on the other hand, childbirth is a natural event, in which the patient status is problematic; women may feel that they are the experts in childbirth; they will certainly find that childbirth is a major life-event whose repercussions spread far beyond the 'episode' of delivery (Graham and Oakley 1981).

Obstetricians control both the institutions where most births take place, and the course of pregnancy and childbirth for individual women. 'The women interviewed both in York and London reported very few areas in which they were able to exercise choice about the kind of maternity care they had. From the moment they first saw a doctor about the pregnancy, decisions were made for them' (Graham and Oakley 1981: 61). Control by others belongs particularly to modern managed childbirth, where decisions are made within a technical frame of reference available only to the doctor, and where birth takes place within the terrain of the 'expert' rather than the terrain of the woman giving birth (for a contrast, see Jordan 1980: 62).

Women's experiences of the decisions taken for them are not always happy ones (nor, for that matter always unhappy). Oakley's study found relationships between high and medium technology births and depression. She also found that 'not enjoying and not experiencing achievement in labour constitute a further deprivation that, cumulatively with high technology and social vulnerability, provides a hazardous start to motherhood' (Oakley 1980: 279).

Looking at women's experiences of childbirth more broadly, as women themselves did, the same study found them characterized by difficulties (the study is of first births):

> 'It is clear that it is normal to experience difficulties. A quarter of the women in the Transition to Motherhood sample had depression, four out of five reported the "blues", three-quarters anxiety and a third depressed mood. A third had less than "high" satisfaction with the social role of mother, and two-thirds less than "good" feelings for the baby five months after the birth. Only two of the fifty-five women experienced no negative mental health outcome, had "good" feelings for their babies and "high" satisfaction with motherhood.'
>
> (Oakley 1980: 278)

These conclusions say as much about the social construction of motherhood as about its medical management. But they illustrate graphically the narrowness of the vision in which birth is the end-product, and the uncertain longer term effects of medical management on women and babies.

The extremes of medical management have abated (though the picture is not entirely consistent – see Savage 1983–84). Women's political action has almost certainly played a part in this. The National Childbirth Trust has a network of groups which prepare women to take a greater part in their own childbirth. And more politically oriented groups have campaigned for choice, reduced routine 'management', home births. The style of many hospital obstetrics departments has altered and some procedures are less used. It should not, however, be supposed that medical control and ideas have been much undermined. The government's latest enquiry, the 'Short Report', followed long-established custom in listening mainly to obstetricians.

Abortion

'I made a promise I'd never go through that again, but I lost count of the number of people that stopped me to see if I would help them . . . they were working-class people struggling to get on and how can you get on if you have a large family . . . but I got asked by a close friend to help a friend of hers out . . . I

said alright, just this once . . . I know I've made lots of friends, and all I've ever got out of this is the joy of seeing people happy and free from worry.'
(An abortionist, describing imprisonment and after, in Simms 1981: 180)

'Except in a few cases, financial gain was not the main motive in these women's activities. Had large fees been the rule, it was unlikely that so many would have been living in the poor circumstances described in police reports. . . . There is no doubt that compassion and feminine solidarity were strongly motivating factors among women who had acquired this skill.'
(Woodside 1963, on women abortionists imprisoned in Holloway, quoted in Simms 1981: 179)

The above quotations from before 1967 suggest that abortion as well as childbirth has passed from female hands to male control. Given the legal restraints under which abortion was practised, though, this transition has had rather different implications. Neither church nor law have held a consistent position on abortion (see Greenwood and King 1981: 176–78). Legal control began in the nineteenth century and resulted by 1861 in total criminalization. The relaxation of the law in 1967 has therefore increased women's control over fertility and over their lives. This control, however, is conditional. The act which legalized also medicalized. Legal abortions depend on medical approval and are carried out under medical supervision. In general, women have welcomed medicalization, for its increased safety (compared with abortions which took place in secret), and for its legality (though abortion self-help groups are not unknown: see Bart 1981). The women's liberation movement has fought to defend the abortion law to meet a challenge from groups wishing to restrict or end legal abortion altogether. The demand for the right to choose has been central for the women's liberation movement, because of the part that reproduction and its control play in women's lives, and the part that male medicine plays in the social control of abortion.

Abortion, whether legal or illegal, has always played a part in women's attempts to control their reproductive lives. According to Simms:

'The evidence of the widespread practice of abortion was all around. To ignore it meant deliberately averting one's eyes from reality. In whose interest was it to pretend that abortion was not taking place when it obviously was? It is a curious fact that, even now, many MPs, priests, leader writers, doctors and others who might be supposed to know better talk as if abortion only came into existence on any scale with the passing of the Abortion Act in 1967. Before that, in that hazy golden age that prevailed before our present irreligious era of permissiveness and licentiousness, women cheerfully had all the babies God sent them, and did not complain.'   (Simms 1981: 168)

Simms argues that this picture is a fantasy. Apart from the 'back-street abortionists' there were drugs widely advertised in the popular press, with the flimsiest disguises; medical evidence of death and chronic invalidity on a substantial scale as a result of abortion attempts; and Harley Street practitioners to meet the needs of those with resources. There were large class differences in access and available facilities, with middle-class women being least likely to accept all the babies God sent (Simms 1981: 181–82).

Contraceptive technology is inadequate to prevent all unwanted births. Nor does it reach all those in greatest need. Abortion is likely to play a part in fertility control, even in circumstances widely different from those described above. The rest of this section concerns the ways in which access to abortion is currently controlled.

Under the 1967 Abortion Act two medical practitioners must certify that pregnancy is dangerous to a woman's physical health or mental well-being, or that an abnormal child is expected. Since an early abortion is statistically safer than a full-term pregnancy, there is always medical justification to certify if pregnancy is not far advanced. Medical certification, then, at least at an early stage, has more to do with social control than with technical evaluation. The exercise of control has probably become more relaxed over the years since the act (Aitken-Swan 1977: 79–80). But there is evidence of wide geographical variations; punitive use toward some groups of women; delays, whether deliberate delays to 'give the woman time to think' or the delays of bureaucratic inertia; paternalistic counselling, and even of concurrent sterilization (Savage 1981).

While the law decrees that abortion is a medical matter, this does not make it available within the NHS. In 1983 rather fewer than half of the abortions for residents of England and Wales were done in NHS hospitals. In proportional terms this represents a considerable decline since the first full year of the act's working (1969: 67 per cent) (Office of Population Censuses and Surveys (1985) *Abortion Statistics 1983*: 1, Table 2). This represents a view of abortion as inessential within the NHS. It also enables patients to be referred to private facilities for punitive reasons, or to accommodate the moral judgements of practitioners. The regional variation in the proportion of abortions which take place under the NHS is enormous, from 99 per cent in the Northern region to 13 per cent in the West Midlands (residents only) (*Abortion Statistics 1983*: 32–3, Table 20). But there are other interesting variations. Thus the very young, as well as older women, are more likely to have NHS abortions; women of normal child-bearing years are more likely to have to pay. Single women, too, are more likely to go to private facilities (*Abortion Statistics 1983*: 2, Table 3). While women's own decisions may play some part in producing these variations, they are also the product of medical judgements. A recent study reports:

> 'These doctors were usually filtering their patients before refer-
> ral, some because they thought that certain women would be
> refused an NHS abortion, and others because there was a
> strong feeling in the northern AHA (Area Health Authority),
> found rarely in the southern AHA, that if a girl was young and
> fit and could afford it, she ought to pay rather than take up a
> hospital bed.'   (Allen 1981: 70)

Limiting NHS facilities, then, is one way in which the legitimacy of abortion may be kept in question and the 'deserving' may be distinguished from the 'undeserving'.

Another issue is delay. From the woman's point of view an early abortion is nearly always preferable, even an abortion that takes place before she is sure she is pregnant (Oakley 1983: 109–10). Legal abortions, in fact, take place considerably later, a majority at between nine and twelve weeks' gestation. NHS ones are considerably slower than private; the private sector managed to carry out 43 per cent of its abortions on residents at earlier than nine weeks gestation; in the NHS the comparable figure was 23 per cent (the base of these percentages excludes those where gestation was unknown) (*Abortion Statistics 1983*: 6, Table 8). Delay is not only in women's hands. Allen's study questioned both professionals and patients, and concluded: 'There was also no doubt in some respondents' minds that some GPs were using pregnancy testing as a delaying tactic, and this reinforced the impression received by some women. Delay in general was attributed to professionals rather than patients, which again confirmed what the women suspected' (Allen 1981: 73). 'Delaying tactics' may prevent the abortion. More usually, delay may result in using an inferior method, and distress. It may be a form of control, as well as a consequence of control being out the hands of the person to whom it most matters.

Third, negotiations for abortion may be accompanied by unwanted counselling:

> 'Women who had what could be called "negative counselling", in which doctors tried to dissuade them or made them feel ill-at-ease or guilty, remembered these conversations with graphic clarity, and usually with resentment, although some expected it as part of the process of getting an abortion. Some of the counselling described by the women could only be interpreted as punitive . . . some of the greatest praise came for the nurses, the family planning sisters and the medical social workers. Perhaps the warmest comments on counselling were made about the BPAS counsellors. . . . This ability to communicate was not always found among doctors, some of whom made it very clear that they could not imagine how anyone could find themselves in this situation.'   (Allen 1981: 98)

Finally, there is room for suspicion that women may be persuaded into concurrent sterilization. The dual procedure has been declining. The Allen study found no evidence of pressure being applied in the two areas investigated (Allen 1981: 65). However, rates of concurrent sterilization in the NHS are still high, compared with the private sector and internationally. Economic pressures within the NHS and moral pressures on women may both be suspected; 7,351 such operations were carried out in NHS hospitals in 1981. Among resident women with two previous children the rate in NHS hospitals was 22 per cent, compared with 6 per cent in non-NHS facilities. A statistical review of the first ten years of the abortion services concludes: 'By international standards the concurrent sterilization rate was high. Abortion was rarely combined with sterilization in Eastern Europe and Japan. In the USA, where the distribution of women having abortions was similar by age, parity and marital state to that in the UK, the rate was much lower than the NHS' (Fowkes, Catford, and Logan 1979: 218). There must remain a suspicion that women do not always feel free to choose.

It is not intended to suggest that women always meet obstruction, paternalism, or unpleasantness when they seek abortions, or that doctors relish their powers. The intention is to show some of the ways in which medicine can be used to control women's reproductive lives. The legitimacy of such control is the subject of fierce political dispute, with the forces of 'moral re-armament' ready to challenge an apparent liberalizing of doctors' attitudes. One result is that access to abortion has increased, but to a considerable extent outside the health service.

In some ways it is ironic that women should have to fight for abortion. Abortion is, after all, likely to cause distress and, in a small minority, physical damage. Men reproduce, too, and do not have to choose. But while the work of child-rearing is put so firmly in the hands of women, reproductive control is crucial to women's lives. The Abortion Act and its working present two faces of the Welfare State: liberalization has been a real gain, but it has been partial, and accompanied by an increase in medical control of women's lives.

Contraception and infertility

Problems of fertility and infertility also illustrate the theme of reproduction as women's work, medically directed. Male contraception and sterilization do, of course, exist. But the efforts of the dominant structures – drug companies, research establishments, even the NHS, have gone into female contraception. No drug or internal device has yet been thought safe enough to give to men. Nor is there much knowledge or therapy for male infertility; female infertility, on the other hand, may be the subject of extensive investigation and treatment.

On an international scale, 'population control' demonstrates rather starkly how women, and their reproductive systems, can become the objects of policy rather than its subjects. The control of reproduction is fundamental for women as well as for international agencies and governments concerned with expanding populations. Too many births, and too close together, are a serious threat to women's health; too many children may – depending on economic conditions – be a serious threat to precarious living standards.

But there are other women's health issues in developing countries, infertility, for example, safe childbirth and, in some countries, sexual mutilation. The attention of international agencies, and of the academic researchers whom they support, is focused almost entirely on 'family planning'. Programmes which appear to be about women's health and their access to health services are likely to stem from, and to centre in population policies. Even then, it is rare for women to be asked their views.

That women are degraded by this narrow concern with their fertility, and that their health interests are not best served by it, is indicated by the depo-provera affair. Injectable contraceptives are very convenient for population controllers; this particular one lasts a long time (several months) and can be administered quickly and cheaply. The developed world restricts its use (albeit inadequately) because of side-effects. Yet in the underdeveloped world it is one of the most commonly used contraceptives. It seems unlikely that women are always given the relevant information, or the proper follow-up:

'Reports indicate that nearly half the mothers in Africa who are using birth control currently use DP. Thousands more use it in Asia and Latin America. Aggressive policies of distributors like the International Planned Parenthood Federation (IPPF) and of Upjohn, the manufacturers, contribute to wide "acceptance" of the drug. . . . It is undoubtedly the case that contraceptives are big business with an enormous potential market, and there is particular potential for aggressive marketing techniques in the Third World.'   (Rakusen 1981: 78)

Women in Britain have more protection than this. But the equation between women and reproduction has its consequences here too. Vasectomy and female sterilization are both available within the NHS; but female sterilization is more often free. Some professionals were 'very concerned that some women are being sterilized because they could get it on the NHS, when it would have been better for their husbands to have had a vasectomy' (Allen 1981: 91). The male operation is simpler and safer. But, concludes another study, 'The medical profession is not entirely convinced . . . that the male should be sterilized at all' (Aitken-Swan 1977: 198).

Both men and women suffer the anguish of infertility; and the reproductive systems of both may fail (in roughly equal proportions). But again it is seen as a female problem:

'We have little information about how or why a man has a poor sperm count. Indeed, we have far less information about men than we have about women and their problems. There have been very few attempts to interfere with male fertility. Consequently we remain very ignorant about how the male reproductive system works and what can go wrong, and so little is available in the way of tests or treatment.'

(Pfeffer and Woollett 1983: 65)

Both men and women may well feel ambivalent about this state of affairs. Women may want control over contraception, since it is they who bear most of the costs of reproduction. And infertility investigations and treatments involve hope as well as distress. However, the point, for the moment, is that development has been very one-sided; reproduction and its control have been deemed women's business; the sensibilities, and indeed the physical health, of men have been protected more than those of women; reproduction has been made men's business only in so far as they are the professionals in charge of facilities and research.

The effects of reproductive technology on women's health are contradictory. Reproductive control is the most important basis for improved health; yet the means to it involves risks. The contraceptive pill has profound effects on the way a woman's body works; we hardly yet know of the long-term risks of extended use, though studies are beginning to sound ominous. The intra-uterine contraceptive device (IUCD), too, has known complications, including an increased risk of serious infection. Only barrier methods (the sheath and the cap) are without risk to health. Reproductive technology, then, leaves a lot to be desired. There are, as Oakley argues, 'important questions' to be asked about 'who controls contraceptive technology and which developments are likely to be in women's best interests'; the last few decades may even have seen a decline in women's reproductive health. The evidence for this comes from calculating reproductive mortality. Though maternal mortality has declined, reproductive mortality (including maternal deaths, deaths associated with spontaneous or induced abortion, contraception, or sterilization) for women aged 35–44 has gone up (Oakley 1983: 114, quoting Beral 1979).

Providing health care

'Emerging in the late nineteenth and early twentieth centuries and taking on greater force since the Second World War with the establishment of the "welfare state", some of the human services which were formerly provided in the private domain have been translated into the public domain and therefore into the waged sector. . . . This translation has also involved the transformation of the services into skilled activities for which extensive training is required.'   (Stacey 1981: 174)

Margaret Stacey is surely right to connect the 'Welfare State' with an accelerated 'professionalization' of health and education, with an increasing emphasis on a technology which has to be learnt systematically, and with a shift to the 'public domain'. But this translation has roots deeper than the end of the nineteenth century. An exclusively male medical profession had long since gained privileges and ascendancy over female healers; even 'male midwifery', or what we would now call obstetrics, was poised to dominate the female kind (Donnison 1977; Leeson and Gray 1978: 19–32; Oakley 1976; Versluysen 1980). The Welfare State gave these established tendencies further impetus; it consists largely in activities which have also been designated 'women's work', and have had more immediately to do with reproduction than with production.

Professionalization, exclusive rights, and technical expertise have gone along with male authority. But the process has not been simple; it is not just a matter of private – public, natural – technological, female – male. In practice women are in the public sphere, too, and they are particularly involved in the 'caring' jobs. Neither has there been a continuous, one-way shift of responsibility. For, particularly in times of recession, combined with a growing 'dependent' population, there have been pressures pushing responsibility back the other way, towards 'community care' or, more briefly and accurately, towards women. The way women have reacted to these latter pressures should be enough to keep us from an over-pessimistic view of the Welfare State stripping women of their functions.

A third reservation is expressed by Graham. The domestic sector has always provided the material basis for health; this is not just a feature of 'the cuts'. An emphasis on the male super-structure in the professions may obscure the continuing import-ance of unpaid care and of women's work at home (Graham 1984, 1985). The effects of the developments described in this section, then, are complex.

Medicine

When 'caring' takes place outside the domestic sphere it comes under the ultimate control of men. Medicine, devised as a male profession, now dominates the NHS. The 1858 Medical Registration Act regulated entry to the profession – indeed, established the profession; it admitted very varied groups of men, with diverse skills, class, and educational backgrounds. Few had university degrees, except the physicians; some were quite uneducated. On the other hand, it excluded all women, although there were women who had seven-year apprenticeships or formal training in midwifery at a continental school such as the Hotel Dieu (Versluysen 1980: 186–87). Thus legal and administrative apparatus gave men exclusive rights to controlling positions. More lately, women's legal right to practise medicine has only modified their subordination. And the state has further endorsed medical domination over other health professions and over state health services.

While men control the heights, women have extensive roles throughout health care. The pattern of women's paid work is a kind of caricature of domestic labour. Women clean and tend, nurse, and teach young children. Only, whereas in the home there is mental as well as manual work, love as well as labour, in the public world the higher faculties are peeled away. Doctors are paid to think and to organize. Nurses and cleaners have only to do, at someone else's behest. The status of love, in the world of paid work, is more ambiguous.

'The exclusion of women from health care was an integral part of the process of medical professionalization; thus, they have had to fight to be allowed back in' (Oakley 1983: 120). The fight has resulted in increasing numbers of women doctors. They now make up about a quarter of the number practising medicine (Elston and Doyal 1983), and 43 per cent of medical school undergraduates (University Grants Commission 1983–84: 18). But medicine is still dominated by men (in the West, at least; Leeson and Gray remark that medicine becomes more female as you go east (1978: 43)). Until the Sex Discrimination Act, overt discrimination at first excluded and then limited women's entry. The consequent structuring of medical careers around male lives, and the control of the hierarchy by men, have posed considerable barriers to women doctors (Leeson and Gray 1978: 33–48).

Women have found it especially difficult to climb the hospital hierarchy. Only about 11 per cent of hospital consultant and senior staff are female, compared with about 25 per cent in the lower ranks. If routes to the top are blocked in hospitals, there are, it may be thought, more women in other branches of practice: 18 per cent of general practitioners are women; more are to be found in community medicine (in child health, family planning, school health, and administration) (DHSS, *Health and Personal Social Service Statistics 1982*). Within hospital medicine, higher proportions of women consultants work in specialities relating to children and mental disorder; men fill the senior posts in surgery and general medicine (see Table 2). Not only are these high status branches of medicine, they are also expensive; here NHS priorities are decided in practice (rather than in theory). The distinction between 'male' specialities and 'female' ones is of sex roles as well as of status and power. Thus women have gained entry to medicine, without access to power; and thus have their positions in medicine been restricted to lower status jobs and certain 'feminine' roles.

One of the ironies of 'medical manpower', as it is called, is the way that arguments about efficiency have been used to justify excluding women and neglecting changes in the career structure, needed by men and women, but particularly by women. Thus, as Oakley points out:

> 'to see the problem of women doctors as women's problem is to ignore several other salient facts aside from the domestic inequality of medical women. Among these is the insignificant attrition of medical womanpower due to reproduction compared with the loss of medical manpower consequent on emigration, death, alcoholism, suicide and removal from the Medical Register, and the exploitation in the NHS (and other health-care systems) of women doctors to solve the persistently recurring problems of structural imbalance between the supply of, and demand for medical staff in different specialities and at different status-levels.' (Oakley 1983: 123)

Part-time work has been readily accepted as normal for consultants – in order to accommodate private practice or work in several hospitals – but not for those still on the career ladder (Leeson and Gray 1978: 38). Thus women are hampered in their climb to those jobs which might fit better with some women's lives.

Table 2 *NHS hospital consultants, England and Wales, 1980: most 'feminine' and most 'masculine' specialities* (Source: Medical Staffing Statistics 1981; this is an amended and updated version of a table that first appeared in Oakley 1981b)*

speciality	% women consultants	total no. consultants (men and women)
most 'feminine'		
child and adolescent psychiatry	37.2	296
mental handicap	24.3	152
anaesthetics	19.5	1,625
radiotherapy	19.1	188
medical microbiology	17.4	293
paediatrics	16.4	519
radiology	13.7	825
haematology	13.7	335
dermatology	13.5	207
mental illness	13.3	1,083
most 'masculine'		
traumatic and orthopaedic surgery	0.5	648
general surgery	0.7	954
urology	0.7	146
plastic surgery	1.2	82
neurosurgery	2.3	88
cardio-thoracic surgery	2.7	112
neurology	3.2	157
nephrology	3.2	63
ear, nose and throat surgery	3.5	372
general medicine	3.7	1,045

*Specialities with fewer than fifty consultants have been excluded.
Source: Elston and Doyal 1983: 42.

Perhaps a greater irony lies at a deeper structural level. Medicine's claim to efficiency depends partly on neglecting questions about what exactly it is efficient at and who benefits from its products. Those who have questioned medicine's achievements (Cochrane 1972; McKeown 1976/1979; Dubos 1968/1970) have tended to conclude that claims to give health and prolong life are often insufficiently tested, and often, though not always, unjustified. Care and repair are more likely products than cure and immortality. On the other hand, care and repair are not high medical priorities. Medicine is, after all, predicated on cure; the nineteenth-century division of labour gave cure to male doctors and care to female nurses, but it put doctors in charge. Medicine's control over those areas of 'health care' which have more to do with care than with high technology (particularly mental handicap, but also large stretches of the 'chronic sector') has had some baleful consequences. Likewise, those who have asked about who has access to medical treatment have invariably concluded that hierarchy, professionalization, and technology go with an unequal system of delivery. The effects of this are most tragically apparent in the Third World, where a health system based on western precedents draws resources away from the majority, who are rural and poor. But it is true on a less grotesque scale in Britain, as described, for example, in the *Black Report* on *Inequalities in Health* (Townsend and Davidson 1982). Thus can one criticize rather profoundly the 'efficiency' of the medical supremacy over health care. (Go uk)

The other side of professionalized medicine is the growth of huge groups of mainly female workers, doing work that is thought 'less skilled' and is certainly less rewarded. It is also work that is closer to patients, and has analogies to women's domestic work of caring, cleaning, and household management, as well as to women's traditional 'healing' tasks.

Midwifery

Some instances can be thought of as deskilling women's health work. The clearest case of this is the near destruction of midwifery as an autonomous activity, and its reconstruction as a handmaiden of obstetrics. Looked at in terms of history and anthropology, the western designation of childbirth as men's business seems one of the odder quirks of the industrialized world (though, of course, it does have a logic of its own). 'Traditionally all midwives were women . . . the men-midwives, as their name implies, were intruders into a women's world' (Leeson and Gray 1978: 52). Men had to fight tradition, taboo, and even disdain in the medical hierarchy for this form of practice (Versluysen 1981).

However, they had all the advantages of patriarchy. First, they had access to the resources necessary to establish lying-in hospitals. In the eighteenth century the case for hospitalized childbirth had little to do with increased safety and more to do with men's bid for control (the argument is alive in relation to the present day, for that matter, and is debated in Kitzinger and Davis 1978). As Versluysen argues:

'The type of institution most suited to the medical midwife's various professionalizing requirements, namely the restriction of competition from female practitioners, the establishment of doctor-control over client preferences, the acquisition of clinical experience, and the depiction of childbirth as potentially hazardous, was some sort of hospital provision for maternity patients.'   (Versluysen 1981: 32)

Thus hospitals were gained on men's behalf, and they entrenched the model of female midwife as subordinate to male doctor. The process took a long time to complete. In 1950, 38 per cent of births still took place at home (Central Statistical Office, *Social Trends 1 1970*). Now 99 per cent take place in hospital (*Social Trends 15 1985*). In the 1980s home confinements have become a minority privilege.

A second advantage used by men was their monopoly of instruments. Instrumental delivery is necessary to life in a minority of cases. From eighteenth-century forceps to the modern labour ward, the control of instruments has been in male hands. From the eighteenth century, too, dates the hot dispute about how often instruments are really necessary; and the results of unnecessary use. Technological advance which substantially increased safety came long after the eighteenth century, and long after men were well in control; but male midwifery and obstetrics have always based their claims, especially over complicated childbirth, on the merits of their technology.

A third advantage to men was access to universities. As with instruments, this was probably of political use in excluding opposition before it was of practical value as medical training. By the end of the nineteenth century, university training had become the passport to medical practice, and women's exclusion a subject of famous struggles. At the same time medicine took obstetrics under its wing.

Finally, men have had state sanction. Medicine had, by the Medical Act of 1858, an autonomous, professional establishment. Its pre-eminence over other health practitioners, including, eventually, midwifery, was enforced by statute. The first stage was the incorporation of midwifery into basic medical training,

188 · Social Policy

under the Medical Registration Act of 1886. In contrast, 'female midwives found their subordinate status confirmed by the 1902 Midwife Act which put a majority of medical men on the council responsible for the training and education of midwives, thereby making clear that neither skilled women nor mothers could regard birth as their own concern any more' (Versluysen 1981: 43). Then the 1918 Act insisted that it was a midwife's duty to fetch medical help in case of difficulty. Her business was with 'normal' deliveries, not with complications. The subsequent narrowing of the definition of 'normality', until it is no longer applicable until after the birth, has further weakened the midwife's position. In particular it has justified the shift to hospital childbirth, which has put her more closely under medicine's wing and fragmented her job.

Thus men had the advantages of access to resources for hospitals; of monopoly control over instruments and later more sophisticated technology; of absorption by the medical establishment; and of state protection for medicine's authority over female midwifery. These advantages – some of which were of dubious advantage to the women delivering babies – have subordinated female midwifery.

But they have not, in Britain, led to midwifery's destruction. Midwives still deliver the great majority of babies (about 80 per cent) in Britain. But – being absorbed into a hospital regime organized around obstetrics – they have lost autonomy and suffered fragmentation. The breakdown of the midwives' job into antenatal clinic, labour ward, post-natal ward, and community midwife neatly illustrates the focus on obstetric risk rather than on continuous care. It also damages the job: many midwives do not deliver babies in the normal course of their work (Savage 1985). However, midwives retain a place from which to fight back (Spinks 1982; Holland and McKenna 1984). And schemes such as the 'domino' arrangement (where community midwives take their own patients into hospital and deliver them) show that it is not impossible to reinstate a more autonomous and complete midwifery.

Nursing

The most obvious gender division in the health labour force is between male doctor and female nurse. The sex-role stereotyping is plain: father/mother, decision-maker/assistant, earner/houseworker, with 'pin-money' wages, intellect/emotion, cure/care.

The specialization and elite status of medical men required the development of more humble occupations. 'It was in the nineteenth century that rigid distinctions were finally enforced between "curing" and "caring" functions, which were allocated to male doctors and female nurses respectively' (Versluysen 1980: 188).

As Carpenter argues:

'At this time doctors were becoming increasingly interested in the diagnostic aspects of illness rather than treatment, and were thus prepared to allow some functions to be delegated under their control. They were little interested in and ill-equipped by their training to deal with matters of ward and hospital administration. Then, as now, their focus was largely upon symptoms. The emergence of a new occupation which was prepared humbly to carry out clinical and administrative tasks offered great advantages for doctors.'

(Carpenter 1977: 167–68)

Nursing's handmaiden status is more or less written into its constitution.

'Nursing is a unique non-industrial female occupation. It was established and designed for women, and located within a labour process – health care – already dominated by doctors, all of whom were men. Success depended on both creating paid jobs for women who needed them and situating and defining those jobs in a way which would pose no threat to medical authority.' (Gamarnikow 1978: 121)

The emergence of professional nursing had something to do with the aspirations of women trapped in the bourgeois family ideal, though without a place in it. But it also involved the acceptance of specifically female roles: 'nursing emerged as a compromise. Although some leading individuals were involved in the feminist movement, the main thrust of nursing reform was largely congruent with the prevailing male definitions of woman-hood' (Carpenter 1977: 165–66). Prevailing definitions of woman-hood, however, involved the possibility of a certain domestic autonomy, even authority. 'The family analogy became a major leitmotif in nursing literature' (Gamarnikow 1978: 110), and there was precedent in the bourgeois family for a female authority figure 'whose supervision of servants complemented but did not subvert the authority of her husband' (Carpenter 1977: 168). Thus

Florence Nightingale saw the reform of nursing in gender terms: 'The whole reform in nursing both at home and abroad has consisted in this; to take all power over the nursing out of the hands of the men, and put it into the hands of *one female* trained head and make her responsible for everything' (Nightingale 1867, letter quoted in Abel-Smith 1960: 25).

Subsequent developments in nursing have tended to strip female authority. The so-called 'Salmon' reforms have replaced matrons with a hierarchical structure in which 'management skills' replace nursing skills as criteria for promotion. NHS reform has further elongated the hierarchy, and entrenched the managerial ethos. These developments have favoured male nurses, whose position was previously peripheral. Men have not yet taken over the top places in the hierarchy, but they are working their way up. Thus, while 10 per cent of all nurses are men, the percentage of male registered nurses is 16 per cent. The highest percentage of men is to be found at district nursing officer level, where 36 per cent are male. At the regional level the percentage of male administrative nursing staff is 27 per cent (Elston and Doyal 1983:41).

Parallel developments are the increasing technical requirements of some nursing work, concurrently with an increased load of basic nursing for the chronic sick. Growing differentiation within nursing has resulted, with a proliferation of untrained nurses, now nearly as numerous as SRNs, and predominantly female. While some nurses have shared to a degree in the technology and status of medicine, others (the SENs and auxiliary nurses) have 'practical' work and low status. Doyal argues that the new division of labour in nursing has dimensions of class and race as well as of gender:

> 'The nursing workforce itself has become highly stratified and differentiated. . . . Overseas nurses have played an important part of this rationalization, facilitating the creation of a labour force divided between career nurses on the one hand and deskilled "practical" nurses on the other – a division which frequently occurs along both class and race lines.'
>
> (Doyal, Hunt, and Mellor 1981: 64)

The new division of caring gives cause for concern:

> 'One does not have to be an admirer of traditional nursing to recognize that the stratification of nursing work and its frag-

mentation into basic nursing, clinical nursing and managerial-ism is against both the interests of the majority of nurses and their need for creative work, and ultimately of a caring service for patients; "job satisfaction" is being appropriated by a minority of clinicians and managers.'   (Carpenter 1977: 189)

'Supplementary' professions and 'ancillary' workers

Divisions of health labour do not end with doctors, nurses, and midwives. The professions 'supplementary to medicine' – radiography, physiotherapy, dietetics, orthoptics, occupational therapy – are also predominantly female. 'The pay is poor and the career structure limited. In short like nursing in the past, the professions seem structured to have a constant turnover of young women, ever replaceable by the next generation' (Leeson and Gray 1978: 52). The designation 'supplementary' indicates unambiguously their position in the hierarchy; though the intellectual justification for making dietetics, for example, 'supplementary to medicine' may well be obscure.

Numerous, too, are the 'ancillary workers' – caterers, cleaners, and porters. These form about 30 per cent of the hospital labour force. High proportions of these workers were born overseas, and high proportions are women (Doyal, Hunt, and Mellor 1981: 58–9).

Thus women do most of the caring work, even within the paid sector. But in the paid sector they do it directly under male control. The medical hierarchy has always been male-dominated and dominates other health workers. The nursing hierarchy is now finding room for men in its upper reaches. But the numerous workers in the health service are to be found lower down the nursing hierarchy and in 'supplementary' professions and 'ancillary' jobs. These are women's work.

Women's health and health care

Physical disability, chronic sickness, and ageing

Women combine the capacity to give life with the capacity to live long lives themselves. From conception it appears that males are more vulnerable to early loss. In childhood, and increasingly with age, male mortality rates outstrip female ones

(Reid 1982: 33–4, 48–9). There is no parallel for women to the heavy male death rate through heart disease. These differences are large.

However, life and health are not synonymous. Mortality statistics may be used as an indicator of health, but they must be used with caution. This may apply particularly to the study of women's health. Government statistics are, in fact, poorly organized to tell us much about women's health, apart from longevity (Macfarlane 1980).

But there are reasons to suppose that women suffer disproportionately from certain forms of ill health. Probably the most important is that longer life in itself exposes women much more than men to the degenerative diseases of old age, and to the handicaps imposed by reduction and loss of ordinary function. Some illnesses, particularly chronic disabling ones which are compatible with life, appear to attack women more than men. Second, reproduction and its control have hazards (Beral 1979). While changes in child-bearing, particularly since the 1930s, must have enormously enhanced women's health, there is evidence (Wynn and Wynn 1979) that many women's health, even in developed countries, is sufficiently poor to damage their capacity to produce healthy children. Finally, there is evidence, particularly from the *General Household Survey* (Office of Population Censuses and Surveys 1984) that women feel less healthy than men. They are more likely to report chronic illness, to visit general practitioners, and to be referred to other health facilities, and much less likely to say that their health during the past year has been good (Reid 1982: 34–45; *General Household Survey 1982*).

At one end of this spectrum, it is clear that disability affects more women, despite a slightly higher incidence of handicap among boys at birth (Reid 1982: 34).

'There are many more women with disabilities than men in this country. For example, of the estimated three million people aged over 16 living in private households who have some physical impairment, over one and three-quarter million are women. This is partly due to the fact that women live longer than men and many of their disabilities are connected with ageing. In the age group over 65 years, there are twice as many handicapped women as men. In addition, some disabilities affect women more often than men. There are nearly 700,000 women with arthritis compared to 200,000 men. Women are much more likely to contract poliomyelitis, have strokes or suffer from multiple sclerosis. They have a higher prevalence of migraine, high blood pressure, varicose veins and rheumatic fever.' (Campling 1981b: 142)

To be a woman and to be disabled is double disadvantage. It is also, as the women in Campling's book tell us, to have a distinct experience of disability (Campling 1981a). Disability may be damaging to self-image, in a world where images of women have special meanings, to sexuality and sexual experience, to marriage, to the ability to care for children, and to the expected role for women as carers of others (Campling 1981a, 1981b). Disabled women are also particularly likely to have low incomes, and to be exposed to the cold winds of the social security system's treatment of women as dependants of men (see Chapter 7).

Disability, then, is on the feminist map. A feminist epidemiology needs to indicate more clearly the experience of chronic and disabling ill health among women (Evers 1985). There is also room for a better understanding of the extent to which a male – dominated medicine and NHS establishment neglect predominantly female maladies.

The misdirection of medical effort towards high technology, acute medicine is well documented, not least by critics from within medicine and in official documents. The other side of the heart transplant coin is the persistently low levels of spending in the chronic sector, in long-stay hospitals and in the community. This misdirection has (among other connections with structuring social variables) particularly damaging effects on women.

One indication comes from hospital in-patient statistics. If those women in hospital for childbirth are excluded, it appears that the average length of stay for women is considerably greater than for men (17 days compared with 12). The gap increases with age, to 47/27 days at 75 years and over. This results partly from men being discharged to women's care, but is also connected to age and causes of admission (Reid 1982: 42–3). The implication is that long-stay beds, which are the most under-financed, are disproportionately occupied by women. This is certainly true for mental hospital beds (see pp. 194–95).

A feature of the low priority given to women's handicapping illness is the under-financing of orthopaedic work in the NHS. Waiting times for operations such as hip-joint replacements are such that people die waiting, or turn to private practice. Limited medical interest in disabling conditions such as rheumatism, arthritis, and incontinence are very damaging to the large numbers of disabled women who suffer from these ailments.

Finally, there is the evidence of the neglect of domiciliary care for those disabled and elderly – the majority – living at home. This issue is more often considered from the perspective of female carers (see Chapter 3). However, one key to the experience of tension between carers and those cared for is total dependence. Women who have spent their lives caring for others may find the experience of being cared for highly distressing. Under current NHS and social services priorities, such intense dependence is scarcely mitigated by statutory help. The pain of the cared-for can only be guessed at, in many cases, from the accounts of their carers.

Mental illness

One in eight women will be admitted to hospital for a mental condition at some time in their lives, and one in twelve men (Grimes 1978, quoted in Reid 1982: 44). All diagnostic categories except alcoholism and alcoholic psychosis have higher admission rates among women. In particular, depression 'perhaps more than any other contemporary illness, is associated with the social condition of women' (Jordanova 1981: 112). Hospitals apart, the Brown and Harris study, described in Chapter 3, showed extremely high rates of depression among young mothers at home with children, particularly working-class mothers (Brown and Harris 1978).

The sex-patterning of mental illness, then, is clear and the differences are large. The meaning of such patterns is disputed. At one extreme, the figures may be said to show more about psychiatry than they do about women. Thus, Busfield argues:

'Far from providing good evidence in itself either of women's greater emotional volatility, irrationality, or vulnerability, or of the greater tension and stressfulness of their lives, the data that suggest higher levels of mental illness among women, are primarily a reflection of psychiatry's differential involvement with the problems and difficulties of men and women and, thereby, of the way in which the category "mental illness" has been constituted.'   (Busfield 1983: 107)

At the other extreme, the 'data' on sex and mental illness may be said to exemplify the sad experience of being a woman in a man's world. Thus, in a rejoinder to Busfield, Williams writes:

'the issues raised by Busfield are important; they concern the definition of mental illness, the way sex-role related processes can affect both "illness behaviour", and the social and professional reactions to mental illness in women and men. These problems are difficult to resolve and currently we are at the stage of having more theories than data to decide between them. However, this should not preclude from consideration the ways that sex-based social differentiation actually affects psychological well-being. Finally, it may be useful to reframe the issue. Given the well documented inequalities between the sexes, why should this not be reflected in the mental health of women?' (Williams 1983: 139–40)

Definitions of mental illness are male definitions; the tendency to describe women as mentally ill may have something to do with the unflattering stereotypes of women that male doctors seem to carry (see, for example, Doyal and Pennell 1979: 219–28; Oakley 1983: 105–6; Scully and Bart 1978); and those figures based on treatment, particularly in hospitals, are the product of an array of social processes. However, there are reasons to believe in women's greater mental suffering. Community studies, such as the Brown and Harris one, are less flawed than evidence based on treatment; and that particular study does seem to reflect women's own accounts of their ambivalent experience of motherhood. A further point is that mental confusion can be part of the ageing process, thus affecting more women for demographic reasons. Finally, if the indications of a heavy incidence of chronic physical illness are accepted, as described above, it would not be fanciful to expect it to go along with a higher incidence of mental illness. A feminist understanding of health must surely include an understanding of the unity of mind and body.

Two points may be made about medicine's treatment of mental illness. The first is that mental illness is an acknowledged 'Cinderella' area, and that institutions for the elderly confused in particular have figured strongly in public scandals and government investigations. The second is that the medicalization of mental health is the subject of a considerable literature. Less often remarked is that medical treatment of mental illness is usually men's treatment of women.

7

Women and Social Security

The family and equality in social security

'Housewives, that is married women of working age.'
(Beveridge 1942: 10, para. 19 ii)

'During marriage most women will not be gainfully occupied.'
(Beveridge 1942: 50, para. 111)

'The attitude of the housewife to gainful employment outside the home is not and should not be the same as the single woman – she has other duties.'
(Beveridge 1942: 51, para. 114)

'In the next thirty years housewives as mothers have vital work to do in ensuring the adequate continuance of the British race and of British ideals in the world.'
(Beveridge 1942: 53, para. 117)

'I am told there is a word for "latchkey kid" in every European language . . . in more and more families mothers are combining earning with home-making. . . . There is now an elaborate machinery to ensure her equal opportunity and equal rights; but I think we ought to stop and ask: where does this leave the family?'
(Patrick Jenkin, as Conservative social services spokesman, 1977, quoted in Coote and Campbell 1982: 84)

'If the good Lord had intended us all having equal rights to go out to work and to behave equally, you know he really wouldn't have created man and woman.'
(Patrick Jenkin, as Secretary of State for Social Services, 1979, quoted in Coote and Campbell 1982: 87)

'A husband and wife who live in the same household form a single assessment unit. Only the husband can normally receive benefit.'

(Supplementary Benefits Handbook, DHSS 1982: 29)

The above quotations span four decades; they take us from the beginning of the post-war 'Welfare State' to recent times; they speak the language of high principle and the language of bitter practice. The ideas conveyed form the continuing underlay of social security policy and practice. Men go out to work and earn money; women stay at home, are housewives, have children, and depend on men for maintenance. This is, and ought to be. Social security should thus focus on interruptions in men's capacity to provide. These themes, brilliantly articulated in the Beveridge report, are more often assumptions and undercurrents.

Despite 'equal treatment reforms' made mainly in deference to the EEC Directive on Social Security, the Beveridge model of family life still underpins social security. One consequence is that women's position in social security is paradoxical. The system is designed around a traditional male working life – its prime concern is with gaps in men's abilities to earn and provide; from the point of view of policy, then, women often appear to be at the margins. But in practice women figure largely among recipients of social security benefits, particularly among the poorest recipients on Supplementary Benefit. This is because women's connections to other forms of income are fragile: the labour market offers low pay and insecurity; marriage – despite some claims to the contrary – is not a meal ticket for life. Thus women turn to social security benefits more often than do men, and social security – like other aspects of the Welfare State – is particularly important to women.

Social security policy and practice depend more explicitly on a notion of the family than do other areas of social policy. In health, housing, and education, legislation has long been overtly egalitarian, unconcerned with whether the individuals it is dealing with are male or female, married, single, or separated; only the more subtle workings of the social services in practice show their ways of connecting to the family. Social security, however, has dealt much more explicitly with men and women, with supporters and dependants, with workers, breadwinners, housewives, and children. As a result it has proved a rich mine for feminists trying to understand the connections between state welfare, women, and the family (see especially Wilson 1977; Land 1978; Land and Parker 1978).

The general themes that occupy feminist writing about social security are that it reflects the family ideology so clearly expressed in the Beveridge report; that it operates on the assumptions: (1) that women are available to do housework and care for children and elderly relatives, without pay; (2) that couples consist of one full-time worker (usually a male breadwinner) and one 'housewife' whose work outside the home is insignificant, being merely for 'pin-money'; and (3) that women can look to men for financial support. All of these assumptions are open to challenge. Where they are factually wrong, they lead to policies which discriminate against women and leave them in poverty. As ideological constructs with which women themselves may disagree, they can lead to policies which push women into unwelcome family forms and unwelcome particular relationships.

The first of these points is most clearly articulated in the Invalid Care Allowance (ICA), paid to those who have given up employment to care for certain disabled dependants. It is available to men and to single women, but not to married women, or to separated women who receive maintenance payments. It is thus assumed that women are available to care, and can depend on their husband or ex-husband. Such assumptions run extensively through social security, though rarely so explicitly as in the ICA. In particular, there is a long history of rules preventing married or cohabiting women from claiming benefit in their own right while they are caring for children or other dependants.

The second general theme of a feminist critique is that social security centres around a male 'breadwinner'. Women may be treated (almost) like men if their working lives follow a male pattern. But, characteristically, women's lives follow a different pattern; and, characteristically, the interruption of female earnings is treated less seriously. Three examples will be given here. First, women in part-time employment are usually not entitled to benefits to cover loss of earnings in sickness or unemployment, or to pensions, except through husbands. Second, maternity – a major 'risk' in terms of women's earning capacity – is sparsely and patchily covered in social security benefits: one instance is that Unemployment Benefit (more often claimed by men) lasts for a year, while Maternity Allowance usually lasts for nineteen weeks, despite the responsibility that maternity brings. Third, women may lose entitlement to Unemployment Benefit if they are thought not to have adequate child-care arrangements. These examples show the loss of a woman's earnings being treated as unimportant; and treated as unimportant because she can turn to a man.

The third theme is the way social security treats women as dependants of men. For example, in National Insurance, men's contributions qualify their wives for widows' benefits and for retirement pensions. Women's contributions do not normally carry the equivalent benefits. Thus social security not only assumes but provides for the dependency of women on men.

Finally, the breadwinner/dependant model makes poor social security where there is no male 'breadwinner'. This leaves several groups of women vulnerable, in particular those such as single mothers with dependants. Single mothers cannot relate to the social security system in the approved way, through a male; but as mothers with total responsibility for children, it is difficult to relate to it as full-time employees. Thus single mothers tend to rely on means-tested benefits, and to be poor.

Poverty among single mothers belongs primarily to the condition of being unconnected to a male 'breadwinner', but the risk is increased by the assumption of a male-style working life. Thus Family Income Supplement (FIS) is designed for those 'at work', while Supplementary Benefit is designed for those 'not at work'. Unfortunately, women who care for dependants usually fit into neither category properly, being partly in paid and partly in unpaid work. They may thus fall into a kind of poverty trap between the two benefits. For example, a single mother who worked part time for fifteen hours a week, being paid £1.90 an hour (average figures for part-time women workers in 1982 (Martin and Roberts 1984: 43–4)) would have worked too few hours to qualify for FIS, and would have her Supplementary Benefit entitlement cut on account of her earnings. Single parenthood thus illuminates the difficulties women have in relating to the social security system.

This, then, is the argument in brief: that social security relates to the family and is designed around a male breadwinner/female carer model of the family. It reflects ideals held about such a model of family life, and protects that model in practice. Feminists have argued that social security's concern with the family is central. In this they differ from those – mainly Marxist analysts – who have put employment at the centre of social security practice. Those who have argued that social security provisions are primarily concerned with enforcing low-paid work, with labour market discipline, have often had men in mind. While the precise incentive effects of benefit rules can be contradictory, it is often the case that for women, their tendency is to discourage work for low pay in favour of work for no pay at all.

If traditional ideas about the family provide the underlay for social security practice, there is overlay, too, about equality and justice. This extends from Beveridge to the present:

> 'The position of housewives is recognized in form and in substance. It is recognized by treating them, not as dependants of their husbands, but as partners sharing benefit and pension when there are no earnings to share. It is recognized in substance in the greatly improved provision made for the real needs of widowhood and separation, for maternity in grant and benefit, for children's allowances and for medical treatment both of the housewife and of the children for whose care she has special responsibility.'   (Beveridge 1942: 52, para. 117)

> 'Article 4 (of the EEC Directive on Equal Treatment in Social Security Benefits) defines equal treatment as "no discrimination whatsoever on the ground of sex either directly or indirectly by reference in particular to marital or family status".'   (Atkins 1978–79:245)

Thus Beveridge claimed the possibility of equality of treatment within the framework of traditional family patterns as he saw them; the EEC Directive reflects feminist criticism in its implication that equality of treatment has to be sought despite such family patterns. (It is perhaps not surprising that the EEC Directive allows exceptions.) British practice has been to make changes on top of the 'Beveridge family' model of social security, to comply in a minimal way with EEC policy. Thus some of the language of social security has become gender-neutral, and some concessions to women's position have been made. The detailed effects of these changes will be discussed in the separate sections below. Some points should be made, however, to keep the changes in perspective. One is that it is possible to go backwards and forwards at the same time – witness the development of some highly discriminatory legislation (in the ICA and other disability benefits) at the same period as the Equal Opportunities and Equal Pay Acts. Another is that these acts do not cover social security. Lastly, change has been imposed on top of a social security system whose basic building blocks included the 'Beveridge family'. Hence, Beveridge's ideas still underpin social security practice and provide a starting point for analysis.

The report on Social Insurance and Allied Services *(Beveridge)*

The Beveridge report was, and is, a key document for social policy practice. It was also one of the clearest statements of a family ideology, reconstructed for post-war purposes.

In the Poor Law tradition women were both present and not present. They figured largely among those subject to the Poor Law's small mercies. 'Throughout the history of the New Poor Law, from its introduction in 1834, women were a majority of adult recipients of Poor Law relief' (Thane 1978: 29). But their needs were not specifically identified. The 1834 Poor Law Amendment Act concerned itself centrally with men's employment and unemployment; women's dependence on men's wages was assumed; if the issue of men's work was confronted, women would be taken care of. The policy-makers of 1834:

'took for granted the universality of the two-parent family, primarily dependent upon the father's wage, and the primacy of the family as a source of welfare. Hence the poverty of women and children was thought to be remediable by the increased earnings of husbands and fathers. These were assumptions quite incompatible with the realities of the 1830s, of industrial low pay and recurrent unemployment, and early or sudden death. Many deserted or abandoned women were left to support children or other dependants on less than subsistence wages.' (Thane 1978: 29)

Neither did this approach take heed of the significance of women's wages for family survival (Thane 1978: 32–3).

Similar assumptions ran through twentieth-century provisions, for example the National Insurance Act of 1911, which scarcely catered at all for women. The situation that Beveridge confronted in 1942 was that failures of family support were among the major causes of poverty and women predominated among the needy; yet the prevailing approaches to social security centred on male unemployment. Women were at the margins.

Beveridge's response was to retain the focus on male employment and unemployment; and to develop a family ideology which elevated women's role as he saw it. The first point may be

202 · *Social Policy*

illustrated through the account given by José Harris of the stages of developing the Beveridge proposals. By January 1942, Beveridge had written two papers which 'outlined many of the assumptions and proposals that were eventually to be embodied in his final report' (Harris 1977: 390). He proposed a unified system of insurance, financed by equal contributions from the worker, the employer, and the state. This implied an 'archetypal insurance contributor' in the form of an adult male worker (p. 392); married women were to form a separate class with special benefits. But at this stage of the plans much remained to be settled, including 'the treatment of groups with special needs – such as married women, "domestic spinsters", unsupported mothers and "unmarried wives"' (p. 395). Thus the basic ideas were developed around the insurance of the adult male worker; women remained to be grafted on. Only the single female could be assimilated directly; all other groups of women formed special categories for special treatments.

Beveridge then made a virtue of the way the scheme related women to men, by recognizing the important work of housework and child-care, and idealizing marriage and motherhood. House-work was work: Beveridge referred to the 'needless exhausting toil for the housewife in struggling with dirt and discomfort' (Harris 1977: 431); he also advocated 'provision of paid help in illness as part of treatment' when housewives were incapable of 'household duties' (Beveridge 1942: 124, para. 311). Desertion was 'like an industrial accident' (quoted in Harris 1977: 406). And raising children was work for the Empire. Thus the Beveridge report helped to weave the fabric of a peculiarly intensive advocacy of family-centred life in post-war Britain.

The Beveridge framework survives. Insurance, based on a notion of a male-style 'working life' remains a central plank of social security provision, despite useful modifications. Large numbers of women still receive benefits as dependants or survivors of men rather than as beneficiaries in their own right. Individual marriages have become less reliable as the foundation of women's 'social security'. And more women than ever are subject to the Supplementary Benefits system, which has as much in common with the Poor Law as with Beveridge's high ideals. Not all the poverty among women today can be attributed to failures in Beveridge's proposals: some were not implemented, and there have been very many changes, both in marriage and in policy, since the 1940s. But the following evidence about the number of women in poverty today owes a lot to the male-centred, female-dependent system promoted in his report.

Women and poverty

'Women are the poorest of all. Women are responsible for family finances but they have none of the power that goes with possession. Having it in their hands never made money their own.'   (Campbell 1984: 57)

'Women's poverty is an increasing part of world poverty. It is a special kind of poverty whose causes are not fully understood, that are in fact still largely invisible to most males engaged in official and unofficial poverty research.'   (Scott 1984: 15)

Whether as single mothers, caught between the labour market, social security, and their children's needs; as the majority among the disabled and elderly and their carers; or as wives without incomes of their own, women predominate among the poor. This assertion can be only partly supported by official evidence, because official evidence relies on the 'household' or 'family' as a measuring device; it shows little concern for the gender of those in the 'household' or 'family'; and displays even less concern for which members benefit from household income.

Thus the *Family Expenditure Survey* (Department of Employ-ment 1982) gives some information about one-parent families, most of which will be women with children, but it does not differentiate by sex; and its other households contain 'adults' or 'head of household, wife and other household members'. We are not told which households rely mainly on female incomes nor who benefits from household spending.

This section uses two sources to give a brief indication that women are the chief recipients of means-tested benefits, and that – as under the Poor Law – they predominate among the most acutely deprived. It is easier to count women's poverty among households without men. One indicator of poverty among such households is the extent of reliance on Supplementary Benefit and Family Income Supplement. There is more general evidence about the gender of those in poverty, though rather old now, from *Poverty in the United Kingdom* (Townsend 1979).

Women are a majority among recipients of regular payments under Supplementary Benefits. At the end of 1982 there were 2,174,000 women and 2,092,000 men receiving regular weekly payments (DHSS, *Social Security Statistics 1984*: 215 and 216, Tables 34.73 and 34.75). This is despite the fact that women who lived with men as wives or cohabitees could not then receive benefit in their own right. There were then a further 1,010,000 women receiving Supplementary Benefits as dependants (p. 217, Table 34.76).

The largest group of women on Supplementary Benefit are elderly. There were 1,280,000 drawing benefit in their own right and 341,000 dependent wives of sixty or over whose husbands were drawing benefit (*Social Security Statistics 1984*: 216 and 217, Table 34.74). There are particularly large numbers of women, aged seventy and above, drawing Supplementary Pensions (p. 216, Table 34.71). As Phillipson remarks: 'Moving into the upper-age range groups the social world becomes almost exclusively female. Among the "old" elderly, for example (those aged 75 and over), women outnumber men by more than two to one' (Phillipson 1982: 72). Many live alone, and are highly restricted in their social activities through both poverty and disability (Phillipson 1982: 71–6). A very high proportion of such elderly women are living on poverty incomes; Townsend's study showed 58 per cent of households of women aged sixty or more living 'on the margins of poverty', and 20 per cent 'In poverty; these were the highest proportions for any household type' (Townsend 1979: 289). Women when they reach sixty may face very low incomes for a very long time.

The second largest group of women on Supplementary Benefits is single mothers. At the end of 1982 there were 417,000 one-parent families headed by a woman who was drawing benefit (DHSS, *Social Security Statistics 1984*: 218, Table 34.80). Single mothers in employment also formed a high proportion of those entitled to Family Income Supplement. There were 77,000 such families in 1984 (p. 182, Table 32.32). One-parent families rely heavily on means-tested benefits rather than on earnings; and there is a 'gross over representation of one parent families among the very poor' (Popay, Rimmer, and Rossiter 1983: 14). Most single parents are women. They too may be on benefit for a long time (DHSS, *Social Security Statistics 1984*: 224, Table 34.90).

To date, married women appear in the Supplementary Benefit statistics only as dependants. Of the 1,591,000 men below pension age drawing Supplementary Benefits in 1982, 702,000 were drawing for wives as well (DHSS, *Social Security Statistics 1984*: 215 and 217, Tables 34.73 and 34.77).

Thus the majority of recipients of Supplementary Benefits, the safety net of social security, are women. This indicates the inadequacy of insurance schemes for women (of which more on pp. 206–13). It also indicates that women predominate among the poorest. Townsend's study confirms that, in the population at large (rather than among benefit recipients only), a higher proportion of women than men are poor (even within age-groups and aggregating household incomes: see *Table 3*).

Table 3 *Percentage of each sex/age group who are:*

age	in poverty		on the margins of poverty	
	m	f	m	f
0–14	8.1	6.5	24.8	28.7
15–29	2.3	4.0	12.5	16.2
30–44	3.4	3.8	20.6	19.8
45–64	2.8	5.2	11.0	16.4
65+	13.8	16.8	36.8	42.9
all ages	5.4	6.7	19.5	23.8

Source: re-presented from Townsend 1979 (285).

Within nearly all categories, then, the proportion of women is higher than that of men; and it must be remembered that the 65+ age-group contains more women.

Households without men are more likely to be poor. But we know very little of what happens within households (see Pahl 1980; David and Land 1983; Burns 1984 for reviews of the evidence). There is, however, a historical tradition, graphically recounted in such books as Pember Reeves's *Round about a Pound a Week* (1913/1979), of women in poverty putting men first, eating bread themselves, giving what meat there was to men. It finds an echo today, in *Wigan Pier Revisited* (Campbell 1984), in accounts given by women in a refuge: 'I bought a steak and kidney pie, heated it up with the peas and some potatoes and put a couple of spoonfuls of peas on my plate to kid him I'd had some'; 'I always tried to buy some kind of meat, mainly for my husband, chops or rabbit, mince, a couple of chicken joints for a casserole. If I got him a chop I'd have a sausage or an egg with the bairns'; 'I'd not eat during the day, then eat the same as him at night'; 'Often I could only afford a small steak and kidney pie and I'd give it to him, or a chop. I'd have potatoes and cabbage and gravy'

(Campbell 1984: 84–90). The author concludes: 'All the women in the refuge are poorer than men, all are allocated less money, distribution of resources, food, drink, clothing, money and time within their own families' (p. 93). Campbell writes of 'widows' liberation'. It is not that widows are well off; rather they are the poorest of the poor, but they can for the first time make decisions about time, friends, and money for themselves (p. 59).

The benefit system

The following detailed account of the benefit system will show the ways in which it is constructed around the lives of men, assumes the dependency of women, and fails to keep women out of poverty. However, other features will emerge. Measures to equalize treatment under the EEC Directive will remove some grosser forms of discrimination. Some women do find in social security, however painfully, an independent income which enlarges choice about relationships with men. And for many women child benefit is a reliable and regular form of income which is their own and possibly only entitlement. Despite the general tendency of social security measures to regard women as dependants of men, it is to benefits that many women must look if they are to live without men; and, however inadequately, social security provides an alternative.

National Insurance

Contributors and dependants

The Beveridge report was called *Social Insurance and Allied Services*. Insurance was to be the centrepiece of the 'way to Freedom from Want' (Beveridge 1942: 7, para. 11). 'The main feature of the Plan for Social Security is a scheme of social insurance against interruption and destruction of earning power and for special expenditure arising at birth, marriage or death' (Beveridge 1942: 9, para. 17). Insurance was to pave the way to the end of the Poor Law, to give people benefits as of right rather than by test of means. Existing insurance schemes had not succeeded, as Beveridge admitted (p. 7, para. 12), but extension and rationalization would be effective.

Insurance meant contributions, and contributions meant people with incomes and employers with employees. 'Housewives' should have policies, too, but since (it was assumed) they had neither incomes nor employers, contributions would come from husbands. Benefits would be paid to husbands on behalf of wives. Hence was built a structure in which men contributed for benefits for themselves and for wives and children. Women appeared mainly as dependants of men; their benefit rights depended on their relationship to a particular man and on his contribution record. Men's contributions covered them against unemployment, sickness, and invalidity, and paid for retirement pensions. They also covered additions for dependants, both wives and children, and pensions for widows of insured men.

Beveridge recognized the insecurities inherent in this arrangement (insecurities subsequently compounded by changes in marriage and divorce), and proposed an analogy between marriage/housewifery and paid work. The end of marriage would be like the end of employment, and so there should be widows' benefits (implemented) and separation benefits (not implemented). Unfortunately, marriage breakdown presented a dilemma that could not easily be solved within an insurance system. It was undeniably a 'risk' to the housewife whose maintenance depended on a husband. But crucial to the insurance notion was that people should not provoke their own need for benefit. Notions of guilty and innocent parties had to be dispensed with, as insurance was to end the need for personal enquiries; so wives, whether deserted or deserting, must be treated alike. The dilemma could not be resolved; separation benefits were abandoned; even the divorce benefits proposed by Beveridge were abandoned in the actual schemes; and single parents remained a 'problem', to be picked up by the 'safety net' (see Harris 1977: 406–07). Here was a major 'loophole'. Women's social security would depend crucially on marriage: but not all women would marry (though some of the unmarried would bear children), and not all marriages would endure. And while Beveridge acknowledged a parallel between the end of employment for men and the end of marriage for women, he centred on the first at the expense of the second. Women's relationship to marriage was to be a key factor in their social security.

While women's position as dependants was central to the plan, they could count as contributors in their own right. Single women would be treated like men. But married women constituted a special category. They would not need the same benefits as men since they could look to husbands for accommodation and maintenance. And their work, and their attitude to it, would be different. A Maternity Allowance would give special recognition to the needs of contributing women; but women's contributions would not cover their husbands, their children, or their housing (Beveridge 1942: 49–53).

Hence was born the Married Woman's Option, an invitation to women to choose individually between the devil and the deep: dependency on the one hand, or independence in a man's world on the other. A woman could either accept the main drift of the scheme, and her position in it as a dependant of her husband. Or she could contribute to a scheme designed around the working lives of men and their dependants; accept the inferior benefits offered; and still possibly find at retirement that she was better off relying on her husband's insurance record than on her own. Since there was no 'married man's option' to reduce his contributions in the event that the married woman paid on her own behalf, making separate contributions as an employee meant effectively paying twice. Not surprisingly 'three quarters of married women chose to opt out of the national insurance scheme, and there was much to encourage them to do so' (Land and Parker 1978: 339).

The Married Woman's Option is being phased out: women now have independence thrust upon them. From 1977 new women workers and women returning to the labour market after two years have been obliged to pay full contributions. However, the conditions in which women have previously opted out of independent contributions have not substantially changed. Women's employment patterns, and social security incorporating benefits for women as men's dependants, remain. Women may well ask whether compulsory contributions to National Insurance are in their own interests.

Any benefits flowing to women from their position as contributors will be long term. Women who had chosen to opt out by 1977 may continue that choice; and many who (willingly or because of breaks in employment) find themselves paying full contributions, will be too late to acquire an adequate record for retirement pensions. One of the many disadvantages of social insurance is the length of time it takes for policy changes to bear fruit. This particular change will bear its (probably meagre) harvest of benefits to elderly women well into the next century.

The end of the Married Woman's Option in 1977 was one of several changes designed to make women into National Insurance contributors on terms nearer to those of men. It coincided with improved rates of Unemployment and Sickness Benefit for contributing women. It was closely followed by provision for protecting pension rights during periods of 'home responsibility'. This means that those staying at home to look after children under sixteen or an elderly or disabled person (themselves in receipt of certain benefits) may continue to qualify for a basic pension (see p. 212). And it acknowledges the way women's caring role interrupts the capacity to contribute. The assumption of male contributor and female dependant is also partially unpicked in some provisions of the Social Security Act 1980, designed to accord with the EEC Directive. These changes mean that women's contributions will be earning dependency increases for their husbands in some cases and not just – as previously – when the husband is 'incapable of self-support'.

Some discriminatory features remain, however, and continue to reflect the notion that the dependency of women upon men is natural and acceptable, while dependency of men upon women is unnatural and to be avoided. Women's contributions are thus still less likely to earn dependency increases than men's. This applies in long-term benefits such as the Invalidity Pension, where detailed rules about earnings of 'dependants' still discriminate between men and women, and means that men with earning wives are more likely to receive dependency increases than women with earning husbands (the tapered earnings rule). It also applies in the major area of retirement pensions: widows' and retirement pensions will still be payable to women as dependants of men, but not vice versa. (A full account of these issues is given in Atkins 1981, and Luckhaus 1983, and retirement pensions are also discussed on pp. 211–13.)

The drift, though, is plain. Employed women will henceforth be included as contributors to National Insurance on quite similar terms to men; they will even receive some additional protection in view of their 'home responsibilities' (protection available to men but mostly relevant to women). The implication is that women, now, can earn their own benefits.

In an equal world this would be an incontestable advance for women. In a world where women work for low pay and often part time to accommodate 'home responsibilities', it will not bring equal social security. National Insurance is still designed round men's working lives; and to the extent that pension entitlements since Beveridge have been more closely linked with pay while at work, the insurance system will be yet less likely to meet women's needs. It will still often be the case that women, particularly in retirement, will be better off as dependants of men than as contributors in their own right. The equalizing of contribution arrangements in National Insurance has been more thoroughly carried through than has equalizing elsewhere in social security (no doubt women's contributions will make useful revenue), but the benefits to women in low-paid and/or part-time work are dubious.

It can be said, then, that National Insurance has undergone a not quite thoroughgoing overhaul, in which the model of woman as dependent wife has partly given way to the model of woman as contributor on her own behalf. It can also be said that some of the key failures of National Insurance today relate to women, especially as single parents, the disabled and the elderly; and that despite changes in the model these failures are unlikely to be remedied in a world in which women number so largely among the low-paid and part-time workers. And it is quite possible that women have gained 'independence' as contributors, without gaining independence as beneficiaries.

Unemployment

The evidence of social security statistics is that far fewer women receive Unemployment Benefit than men. The evidence of the numbers of women 'unemployed' is more contentious. It is certain that women are made redundant, lose jobs, and lose income and identity in the process; and equally certain that women are less likely to be registered as 'unemployed' than are men. Unemployment, though, is a male concept: a concept that implies that without paid work there is only idleness. It is not surprising if women find difficulty applying the concept of unemployment to themselves (deciding not to register or to seek employment) and if benefit officers have similar difficulty (deciding that they are not 'really' unemployed).

The relatively small number of women receiving benefit, then, is not just a reflection of the numbers who have lost paid work. First, women do not fit well with the assumptions of a contributory scheme organized around a male working pattern. Many women fail to qualify for benefit through an inadequate insurance record, because of the Married Woman's Option (affecting older women), because of low pay and part-time work, or because of periods spent caring for dependent relatives.

But, even where the woman has a sufficient contribution record, she may find it more difficult to prove unemployment than a man. A man of working age is assumed to be economically active, unless there is evidence to the contrary. A woman may be thought to be a housewife, and have to prove that she is 'economically active' too. Thus a woman's responsibilities for unpaid care may be held against her when she claims unemployment benefit. If child-care arrangements are thought inadequate she may be held 'not available for work'. Refusing jobs which do not fit with domestic responsibilities may disqualify her from benefit. One study of women made redundant in the clothing trade argues:

> 'men and women seem to restrict their availability for work in different ways. Working women have pressures on their time and are reluctant to work certain hours. They may also limit the distance they are prepared to travel to work, both because of cost and time. . . . Men are fare more likely to restrict their availability because of the wage offered and the skill needed.'
>
> (Coyle 1984: 48–9)

Men's restrictions on availability have some legitimacy within social security practice, and will not necessarily disqualify them from receiving benefit. Women's restrictions call into question the idea that they are unemployed at all.

Retirement pensions

> 'In 1978, major changes in the legislation governing both statutory and occupational retirement provision came into force. These changes incorporated measures designed not only to improve the status of women as beneficiaries in their own right of state and occupational retirement-pension schemes, but also their entitlement, if married, to widows' benefits. Thus, at one and the same time, such measures advanced the position of women as generators of their own financial independence in retirement, while yet confirming them in their traditional role as the financial dependants of their husbands. Herein lies the continuing paradox of retirement-pension provision as it relates to women.'
>
> (Groves 1983: 38)

Dulcie Groves shows that provision for widows and elderly women has been a contentious and problematic feature of insurance-based schemes, since discussions preceding the first state pensions. Such schemes have always included provision for widows and elderly women on the basis of husbands' contributions. This will continue under all current legislation (these benefits are exempted from the EEC Directive). Thus dependency continues to be built in, despite changes which will make more women earn pensions in their own right.

The situation of today's pensioners reflects the assumptions of previous decades; the contribution arrangements of today will – unless there is radical change – be affecting pensions in thirty or forty years time. The most patent conclusion of earlier contributory schemes is the failure of National Insurance to keep elderly women out of poverty. But one curious paradox of Beveridge's National Insurance schemes must still be noted: it is that the most significant benefits are retirement pensions, paid mainly to women; but that payment depends largely on the insurance records of men. It is marriage that provides the connecting link between contributions and benefits. The relationship between contribution and benefit is thus even more tenuous than is usually described, and elderly women's circumstances depend on marriage, separation, and divorce as much as on any direct contributions.

The future hangs on the 1975 Social Security Act – unless its principles are seriously challenged by current social security reviews. This legislation provides that women will in future be independent contributors. Retirement pensions will consist of two elements: a Basic Pension which is the same for everyone with a full contribution record; and an Additional Component, which is earnings related and in which the best twenty years' earnings are those taken into account. Home Responsibility Credits apply to Basic Pension and help women to earn their own Basic Pension. This will be worth somewhat more than the one they could otherwise claim as dependent wives. The Additional Component will be calculated according to the best twenty years of contributions; this aspect will be advantageous to those with gaps in their employment record; most women, again, will qualify for something in their own right (see Joshi and Owen 1983 for a full analysis of these issues).

The detailed arrangements offer concessions to women and seem to make independence possible. The catch is that the earnings-related part of the scheme will reflect women's generally low earnings. This will affect women with uninterrupted employment, because of women's low pay; but it will affect those whose employment is interrupted even more. Home Responsibility Credits offer some compensation for women's caring work, but they are inadequate to the task. One measure is made by Joshi and Owen, who calculate the disadvantage for women – in pension terms – of having children. They conclude that 'for the most common types of family the effect of children on pension rights appears to be around 1.4 times as great as their effect on participation (in the labour market)' (Joshi and Owen 1983: 15). The credits make up in part for the years without earnings, but not for the longer term reduction in earnings. This pension scheme will continue to reflect the idea that women's working lives are worth less reward in retirement than are men's.

It is often remarked that insurance is a means by which those who are poor during working life are kept poor in unemployment, sickness, and old age; it is less often remarked how many of these are women. The disparities are compounded when occupational schemes are included. The Equal Opportunities Commission found that:

> 'While direct discrimination in pension schemes is almost non-existent, the concentration of women in lower-level, lower paid jobs, their probably shorter service and their lower retirement age make it virtually certain that tomorrow's elderly women will be little better off, comparatively speaking, than are the elderly women of today.'
>
> (Equal Opportunities Commission 1981c: 30)

Supplementary Benefits

Failed by National Insurance, by the labour market, and possibly by men, many women must turn to the 'safety net' of Supplementary Benefits (SB). Yet, paradoxically, the majority of women have been ineligible as claimants: married and cohabiting women have been entitled to benefit only through men. This has affected women whether they are inside or outside marriage or other relationships: single women claimants may be suspected of being not really single. The rules within Supplementary Benefit about the dependency of married and cohabiting women thus have wide significance for all women's social security. This section looks at these rules, at the changes made recently in response to the EEC Directive, and at the continuing vulnerability of women to the 'cohabitation rule', whereby benefit may be withdrawn from women who are thought to be living with men. A final part looks at women's special vulnerability under Supplementary Benefit's 'board and lodging' policy.

Breadwinners and dependants/couples and claimants

Until November 1983 a woman who was living with a man as his 'wife' could not claim benefit in her own right. The *Supplementary Benefits Handbook* explained:

> 'in the case of a couple or a single person with dependent children, the family's requirements and resources are taken together ("aggregated"). Each such group is called an "assessment unit". Only one person can be the claimant in each assessment unit. Only the husband can normally receive benefit.'
> (DHSS 1982: 29)

Notoriously, the same rule applied to a man and woman who were thought to be 'living together as husband and wife'; this is still known unofficially as the 'cohabitation rule'. A woman separated from her husband could receive benefits in her own right, but the DHSS could look to the husband for maintenance payments (not very successfully in general). (See Hayes (1978–79: 216–25) for an account of Supplementary Benefits and the liability of men.) If she appeared to be establishing a new relationship, the DHSS would assume she (and her children) could look to the new man for financial support.

The underlying principle was a husband's liability to maintain his wife, and its extension to relationships analogous with marriage. Wherever a woman could be deemed part of a marriage-like relationship, she would be assumed to depend on a man. Thus women who lived with men had no fundamental rights to security from the state. Married women could look to men's legal obligation to maintain their wives (not necessarily successfully); cohabiting women had no fundamental rights to security from the state or from the man they lived with. Men, whatever their condition, were assumed to be breadwinners.

In November 1983 these arrangements were adapted to comply with the EEC Directive. The language is now gender-neutral: we have 'couples', of whom one partner is the 'claimant'. The regulations give considerable flexibility about which partner is to be claimant. Couples may benefit from this where, for example, the woman as claimant might be eligible for the higher long-term rate. But the (exceedingly complicated) regulations seem designed to exclude two groups of women. To be preferred as claiming partner a person has to show some evidence of attachment to the labour market or good reason for absence from it. Disabled women may not be able to demonstrate such attachment, and looking after children full time does not count as good reason for absence. Thus where disabled women and mothers are living with men, they may be unable to establish themselves as the claiming partner (see Luckhaus 1983 for a full account).

Even those women who could be claimants may not become so. They will need to hear about the regulations and understand them; and they may meet opposition from the men they live with. It seems very likely that most couples will continue to consist of a man who is eligible to claim, and a woman treated as dependent.

Thus has the DHSS invented regulations of labyrinthine complexity to meet the EEC's demand that married and cohabiting women should no longer be barred from claiming SB. The effect seems to be that it has met the demand while minimizing disturbance to SB practice.

The choice has been made to continue to pay benefit to 'couples' rather than to individuals. 'Couples' receive less than two individuals separately; and any savings or income are joined together, on the assumption that one partner's income is available to maintain the other. This means that decisions still have to be made about whether people are living as 'couples', and the 'cohabitation rule' still applies. In future it may be applied more frequently to men than in the past, but history and social structure suggest that women will continue to be more vulnerable. So evidence about its operation gathered under the old rules is still pertinent.

The 'cohabitation rule' or 'living together as husband and wife'

'We have again concluded that it is right and necessary for the law to treat unmarried couples in the same way as married couples for the purposes of supplementary benefit. The reason is that it would be unjustifiable for the State to provide an income for the woman who has the support of a man to whom she is not actually married when it is not provided for the married woman.'

(Supplementary Benefits Commission 1976: 29, para. 100)

'The cohabitation ruling only embodies in slightly more glaring form the innermost assumption of marriage which is still that a man should pay for the sexual and housekeeping services of his wife.'

(Wilson 1977: 81)

In principle, the cohabitation rule applies in many areas of social security; in many occupational pension schemes; and to men as well as to women. But it is most vigorously applied in the Supplementary Benefits scheme, and 'the great majority of those affected are women with dependent children' (Supplementary Benefits Commission 1976: 3–4). Women – single, separated, and divorced, and some prisoners' wives – form a growing group of claimants on Supplementary Benefits, particularly as one-parent families. The cohabitation rule puts all these at risk of instant social insecurity.

Among single parents, only widowed mothers usually have rights to benefit under National Insurance, and are thus generally better off (Marsden, in Townsend 1979: 773). Unmarried mothers, and separated and divorced women may be entitled to maintenance from a man, but in practice it will often be insufficient and irregular. Thus these women must depend on their own earnings (possibly in combination with maintenance plus Family Income Supplement) or on Supplementary Benefits. In fact, compared with mothers in marriages, a high proportion of lone mothers are employed (57 per cent of lone mothers compared with 34 per cent of other mothers in the Townsend survey (Townsend 1979: 764)). But lone mothers' access to the labour market and their earnings from it are poor, both as women and as mothers with sole responsibility for children. Thus most single mothers are failed by National Insurance, by the fathers of their children, and by a male-oriented labour market. And their final 'safety net', Supplementary Benefits, may be withdrawn if they are thought to be cohabiting.

Neither are older women exempt from the working of the rule. In a case that went to the High Court, Mrs Butterworth was held by officers of the Supplementary Benefits Commission and the Supplementary Benefits Appeal Tribunal to be not entitled to claim benefit, because she and 'Mr J' were 'living together as husband and wife':

'The claimant had sustained serious injuries in an accident in September 1978 which had resulted in a prolonged period in hospital. On her return home she was unable to cope and needed help around the house. Since her children were not available to assist, an old friend, Mr J, moved in with her in January 1979 in order to look after her. Mr J did this out of feelings of loyalty and not because of any other bond between them. Indeed Mr J had his own bedroom with a lock on the door and there was no suggestion of a sexual relationship. Mr J did however help with the household chores, he did the cooking and a common household was maintained.'

(Journal of Social Welfare Law 1981: 372)

In this case the High Court reversed previous decisions, and allowed Mrs Butterworth's appeal.

Officially, the meaning of 'living together as husband and wife' is determined not by law or regulations, but by a set of criteria originally established by the Supplementary Benefits Commission in 1976. No one of these criteria is supposed to be decisive; rather the case is considered on a combination. They are: (1) members of the same household; (2) stability; (3) financial support; (4) sexual relationship; (5) children; (6) public acknowledgement (DHSS 1982: 31–2). Even if these criteria were applied in a balanced and non-punitive way, there would be uncertainty in applying them to the complex relationships of the real world. In practice it is hard for any woman living a normal life to avoid the hazards entirely. For example, women who take male lodgers, women whose ex-partners visit their children, or women who have any interest in forming new relationships with men are all likely to be suspected of cohabiting. After investigation, they may have benefit summarily withdrawn. They have a right to appeal, of which they should be informed, but in the meantime they are presumed able to turn to a man for support. And even if the DHSS thinks a man should support, the man's view, and practice, may be different.

There are clear indications that the rule is not applied in precisely the way the official documents suggest. 'The reality of the practical interpretations of the concept of cohabitation by the (Supplementary Benefit) Commission's officers appears to be far removed from the theory as presented in the Commission's own publications' (Lister 1973: 8). In her study of women to whom the rule had been applied, Lister found little evidence of financial support, especially for children of other men, or of stable relationships. What did seem to count was sex:

'Taking the evidence of present and past sexual relations together, this factor can be seen to be the most common of all and was probably that which was most obvious to the investigating officers. This casts some doubt on the Commission's frequent assurances that they are not interested in whether women claiming benefit are sleeping with their men friends. It is particularly significant that . . . evidence of sexual relations far outweighs that of financial assistance from the man.'

(Lister 1973: 8)

Enforcement means investigation of women's personal lives, direct and surreptitious, formal investigation, and informal spying by neighbours. The constant threat thus posed may deter women from forming new relationships or may send a man precipitately away. Furthermore, the practice of investigation is particularly likely to be distant from the principles of official documents. Lister published many examples of this in 1973; ten years later (July 1983) the DHSS found it necessary to instruct investigators 'not to press claimants into saying that they no longer wish to receive benefit or to offer amnesties, or stop claimants' benefit by snatching order books' (*Guardian*, July 1983).

The Special Claims Control investigators, employed by the DHSS to root out 'scroungers', pay special attention to single mothers. A woman 'accused' of cohabitation will offer instant savings in benefit. Women may even be driven into cohabitation despite risk of violence (Campbell 1984: 25–30).

Thus women on Supplementary Benefits lead precarious lives, always at risk of being pushed by the 'safety net' into dependence on men; and always at risk that men may decline support. This is the sharp end of a social security practice which is founded on the assumption that women do not need an independent source of income. Thus is the concept of the dependent 'wife' 'alive and kicking women in the teeth' (London Women 1979: 21).

Board and lodging

Present government policy towards the elderly and dependent has another arm in addition to 'community care'. This arm is private enterprise, publicly supported. Supplementary Benefit regulations allowed 'board and lodging' payments on behalf of elderly and infirm residents in private mental and nursing homes. Until April 1985, these were relatively generous; the limits were locally arranged, but could reach £285 per week. Payments may be made to non-profit-making voluntary agencies, or to profit-making concerns attracted by quick and guaranteed returns from a government department. The result has been a growth industry in private homes, financed by the DHSS for some of its most vulnerable clients. The cost of this support has risen dramatically, from £10 million in 1979 to £190 million in 1984.

One aspect is uncontrolled public expenditure and an invitation to those in search of quick profits. Another is discouragement of local authority provision. Recent policy suggests a reversal. New national limits applying to new residents put many establishments out of reach of those on Supplementary Benefit. And further legislation subjects homes to more careful scrutiny. A policy which was never designed to improve conditions for the elderly and frail – especially the very elderly and frail who offer the least profits – may now inflict further hardship, by closing establishments and squeezing places for those in need. Needless to say, the victims must be predominantly elderly women (Hencke 1985; Wolmer 1985).

Supporting children

Child support is a key issue for women. As providers, women are disadvantaged, in the labour market and in social security. Yet their responsibility for children, for caring and maintaining, tends to continue, whether or not men provide. It is not surprising, then, that support for family allowances has a long feminist pedigree. The most famous protagonist, Eleanor Rathbone, published *The Disinherited Family* in 1924. In it, she specified, with admirable lucidity, a programme of feminist analysis:

> 'I doubt whether there is any subject in the world of equal importance that has received so little serious and articulate consideration as the economic status of the family – of its members in relation to each other and of the whole unit in relation to the other units of which the community is made up.'
> (Rathbone 1924/1949: ix)

Her case for family allowances was set firmly within such an analysis. It rested on a discussion of unpaid housework, the legal status of women, the dissatisfaction of housewives, and the vulnerable position of women in bad marriages:

'the securing of provision for the children would take the worst of the sting out of the sufferings of an ill-treated wife. It is their helplessness and the knowledge of her inability to support them that so often obliges her to endure in silence. Their future secured, she would gladly dare all for herself.'

(Rathbone 1924/1949: 81)

Family allowances, then, were for women, as well as to deal with child poverty. The starting point for Eleanor Rathbone's family allowance campaign was 'undoubtedly her interest in feminism' (MacNicol 1980: 20). Family allowances would reduce the dependence of wives upon husbands; and would undermine the principle of the 'family wage', a doctrine that put women at a serious disadvantage in the labour market.

In practical politics it was economic and demographic arguments that finally won the case, rather than feminist ones; and Rathbone had still to press, in 1945, for the money to be paid to women rather than to men (Hall, Land, Parker, and Webb 1975: 157–230). Subsequently, the case for extending and increasing family allowances has been taken up by those concerned more with differences between families than with women's position within the family. Child Benefit, as it is now called, has become the strategy of choice for attacking child poverty.

The issue of family allowances has been capable, in more modern history, of appearing in Rathbone garments rather than in those of Beveridge, Keynes, or the Child Poverty Action Group. The change from Family Allowances + Child Tax Reliefs, to Child Benefit involved a redistribution from 'wallet to purse', and nearly foundered in the process (Land 1977). That battle was won for women, who generally draw Child Benefit. But the low level of award (below subsistence level and the levels paid in Europe) reflects women's poor bargaining position and government reluctance to undermine the male 'breadwinner' principle.

The importance of Child Benefits to women should not be obscured. They reduce women's and children's dependence on men; and they give some secure income to women with young children. Their avoidance of means tests is often remarked; equally important for women is their independence of insurance records, employment, and marital status. Child Benefit has also been used – with the same advantages – to add to single parents' incomes.

An extension of these benefits – of Child Benefit and One

Parent Family Benefit – is the chosen strategy for organizations representing women as parents (see, for example, the National Council for One Parent Families' *Evidence to the Social Security Reviews* (1984)). But current policy is to compensate for inadequate Child Benefits with Family Income Supplement (FIS). This is a means-tested benefit for parents in full-time or nearly full-time employment with low wages.

In practice a very high proportion of payments go to women as single parents. This makes FIS an important benefit for single mothers, but it does not make it a good one. FIS shares the problems of means-tested benefits, of low take-up, and the poverty trap. In two ways single mothers on FIS are peculiarly disadvantaged: they suffer acutely from the poverty trap, because of the way decreasing benefits and increasing tax interact over the typical range of women's earnings (one calculation suggests that it is possible to double gross income without becoming better off (National Council for One Parent Families 1984:1, 13)). Second, FIS carries an employment condition. Although the rules about hours of paid employment are relaxed for single parents, mothers on FIS must be employed for more hours than are mothers in general. Child-care arrangements and costs may therefore make it impossible for a woman to qualify. FIS, then, is a poor substitute for an adequate Child Benefit.

Woman as carer, man as provider, children's emotional needs met by the one, economic needs met by the other: the image has a neat symmetry. Child poverty owes something to the failures of this image in reality. The most obvious instance is the poverty of the children of single mothers; but, as with women themselves, it is likely that more child poverty is hidden in household accounting. The segregation of emotional and economic support between two persons makes a fragile context for children.

The fragility of this basis has long been recognized in one arm of social security provision, and consistently ignored in others. Thus Family Allowances were paid, from the first, to mothers. Other benefits have usually been paid to a man if there was one. The results for some women and children are well described by Beatrix Campbell:

'When a man lives in, a woman's independence – her own name on the weekly giro – is automatically surrendered. The men become the claimants and the women their dependants. They lose control over both the revenue and the expenditure, often with catastrophic results; rent not paid, fuel bills missed, arrears mounting. It is conventional wisdom among advice agencies, local authorities and fuel boards that it's the women who pick up the tab for men's mismanagement.'

(Campbell, 1984: 76)

Child support is still a feminist issue.

Disability

Two groups inadequately served by contributory benefits under National Insurance are the disabled and their carers. Both groups are disproportionately women: more women suffer disability than men (see Chapter 6), and more women stay at home to look after relatives and friends (see Chapter 3). The poor social security of all these is a compound of their positions as women, as disabled, and as carers. All are 'supposed' to be dependent and all may be unable to 'earn' benefits through contributions.

Contributory National Insurance does cover the minority with an adequate insurance record. That minority are mostly men. There are nearly five times as many men receiving the contributory invalidity allowance as women, and as *Table 4* shows, very small numbers of women have any entitlement.

Table 4 *Invalidity benefit: pensions current at 2 April, 1983, analysed by age at 31 May, 1983 (in thousands)*

age at 31 May	males	females
under 30	19	22
30–39	43	24
40–49	83	30
50 and over	449	68
total	593	144

Source: DHSS, *Social Security Statistics 1984*: 45, Table 4.30.

Until November 1984, disabled women who were married or cohabiting were not entitled to claim Supplementary Benefits in their own right; since this date their position has become less clear, but disabled women seem unlikely to be able to establish themselves as 'claimants'. Thus the provision of non-contributory benefits to the disabled should be particularly relevant to the needs of those women who may not be covered either by National Insurance or by Supplementary Benefits.

Pressure groups for the disabled won a number of concessions in the 1970s, including an Invalid Care Allowance (ICA) for those looking after the seriously handicapped, and a Non-contributory Invalidity Pension (NCIP) for those whose disability prevented employment. However, both discriminated against married women – the largest group of disabled and carers. In doing so they also provided an unusually lucid statement of the assumptions underlying social security provision in the 1970s and 1980s (assumptions not so far removed from those of the 1940s): women as wives are expected to care, to do housework, and to find their financial security in the men with whom they live. Furthermore, housework is not really work (*pace* Beveridge), and even quite seriously disabled women may be expected to do it and thus earn their keep from their men.

Overt discrimination now seems likely to disappear. The NCIP and HNCIP have been replaced by the Severe Disablement Allowance, for which you do not have to be single or male. And the ICA is being challenged, so far successfully, in the courts. Discriminatory practice, however, is not yet at an end. These benefits warrant a careful look, for their continued impact on the shape of disablement income, as well as for their unusual lucidity about the dependence and caring role of women.

Invalid Care Allowance (ICA)

It might be thought that an Invalid Care Allowance, for those caring for the disabled at home, would be aimed directly at married women. But married women are excluded from the allowance because they 'might be at home in any event' (HMSO 1974, para. 60, quoted in Lister and Wilson 1976: 14). Land and Parker quote a test case on this issue as follows:

> 'a national insurance commissioner reversed a decision to pay an invalid care allowance to a young married woman who looked after, but neither lived with nor was maintained by, her severely disabled husband. In doing so he explained that married women had been specifically excluded from this benefit on the assumption "that a married woman would not usually work and therefore would not lose wages or rights to national insurance benefit".'

(Land and Parker 1978: 340–41)

The assumption that women are provided for by husbands is often inappropriate but, as the Equal Opportunities Commission point out, 'it is absurd in the case of a wife caring for her disabled husband' (Equal Opportunities Commission 1981a: 20). In practice, women do work for pay, particularly at the ages of most risk for giving up work to care for elderly relatives (Coussins 1981: 18–19). Losing this pay will often add to already critical money problems (Equal Opportunities Commission 1981a: 14–20). Not surprisingly, 'the exclusion of married and cohabiting women from eligibility for an ICA is widely felt to be unjust' (Equal Opportunities Commission 1981a: 15) and very few Invalid Care Allowances are paid. 'Of the 1.25 million people in Britain who have been defined in this report as carers, only 0.5 per cent receive ICA' (Equal Opportunities Commission 1982a: 31). Even those single women who can claim may feel a justified sense of grievance if they have an insurance record. Giving up work to care is primarily a woman's risk, not covered under the contributory scheme; the Invalid Care Allowance, though better than nothing, is paid at a much lower rate than contributory benefits (Campling 1981b: 154).

Housewives' Non-contributory Invalidity Pension (HNCIP)

The HNCIP has been replaced. But it is described here because the pattern of benefits set up with HNCIP will largely continue under its replacement.

The Non-contributory Invalidity Pension was available to a 'person' who was 'incapable of work' and was 'either a man or a woman who is not married or cohabiting with a man' (Social Security Act 1975, Section 36 (1) and (2)). The government gave in to pressure to include married and cohabiting women in the benefit; but such a woman had to satisfy a dual test: 'both that she is incapable of work outside the home, and that she is incapable of performing normal household duties' (Richards 1978–79: 69). Though disability may have forced a woman to give up employment, this was immaterial if she was deemed capable of housework. If deemed incapable of work and housework, she was entitled to the benefit usually known as the Housewives' Non-contributory Invalidity Pension (HNCIP). This amounted to an assumption that all married and cohabiting women were 'housewives'.

The dual test was very stiff. Despite the small proportion of disabled women claiming contributory benefits, compared with men, a very small number actually received HNCIP. There were 63,000 men and 68,000 women on NCIP, but only 45,000 women on HNCIP (DHSS, *Social Security Statistics 1982*: 51, Table 5.44; figures for 31 May, 1980). DHSS policy was to apply the test highly restrictively, so that anyone capable of some household tasks, even with considerable exertion, was likely to be refused. Richards (1978–79: 70–71) describes the DHSS amending the regulation about incapacity for household duties when the National Insurance Commissioners interpreted it too leniently. And many women obliged to leave paid work on account of disability were disqualified from HNCIP because they were deemed capable of housework (Loach and Lister 1978; Glendinning 1981). It was even possible for women to be receiving an Attendance Allowance, which meant that they needed help looking after themselves, and yet be refused HNCIP, presumably on the grounds that they could look after the house and family (Equal Opportunities Commission 1981a: 11). The message that housework is not real work could hardly be clearer. Nor could the message that married women should look to their husbands for support, and do not need earnings, or social security against interruption of earnings.

The 'household duties' test was widely criticized on three counts: its essential unfairness to women, its ambiguity and inconsistency in operation, and the distress it caused women applying for benefit. First, women who become disabled have more often than not been doing paid work. Glendinning reported 'that 65 per cent of all women who applied for the pension during one week in September 1979 had been in paid employment during the previous five years; and that three quarters had had to give up work for reasons connected with their disability' (Glendinning 1981: 15; figures collected by DHSS). The second point, the ambiguity and inconsistency, was well illustrated by the high rate of success on appeal against DHSS decisions, which has stood at over 50 per cent (Richards 1978–79: 75), and by numbers of cases published by the Disability Alliance (Loach and Lister 1978; Glendinning, 1981). The third point, the distress, and sense of injustice among HNCIP applicants, follows from the rest. The EOC record the anguish of many women who wrote to them on the subject: 'It appears to me that they expect you to be both incapable of shuffling around and completely mentally retarded. Unfortunately, I am only crippled with rheumatoid arthritis' (quoted in Equal Opportunities Commission 1981a: 10).

The housework test has a long history in social security practice (Land 1978: 262–65). For women under the 1911 National Insurance scheme: 'Provided they were capable of doing the housework they were not deemed to be ill and therefore women found doing housework when the sick visitor called had their benefit withdrawn in spite of the fact that they were not fit enough to return to the mill or factory' (p. 263). Until 1977 under the sickness benefit scheme, doctors were asked about women's capacity for housework; only after 1977 were such questions asked about men (p. 264). The HNCIP is therefore no aberration.

The government argued that these benefits were outside the scope of the EEC Directive because, conveniently for these purposes, women would be defined as outside the labour market, and thus not covered by it. However, in 1984 the NCIP and HNCIP were replaced with the Severe Disablement Allowance. Here, overt discrimination against married women disappears, but in practice there will be little room for them to receive benefit. The regulations for this benefit have been tightly drawn to prevent much widening of the net. At the same time those already receiving NCIP or HNCIP have been automatically transferred to the new benefit. Thus a few anomalies will disappear, a few more women will become entitled to benefit; but large numbers of married and cohabiting disabled women will continue to be excluded. Changed rules will not mean much change in the pattern of eligibility.

Maternity rights and benefits

The Beveridge scheme treated maternity as an insurable risk. Most maternity provisions are thus connected to women's paid employment. This has contradictory implications. On the one hand, it acknowledges that paid work and babies are both part of women's lives, and that some tensions and needs follow. On the other hand, women's employment and benefit conditions ensure that women must look elsewhere for maintenance. Most women will have to depend on men, as well as, or instead of, on benefits. Thus are the needs arising from childbirth made into a private matter, a family responsibility.

Women without men are at high risk of poverty in general; these maternity provisions put them at particularly high risk in pregnancy and early parenthood; this in turn may contribute to their children's high risk of early death and handicap (see Chapter 6).

The relation of maternity coverage to paid employment has other implications: those with tenuous connection to the labour market lack maternity coverage. This increasingly includes young mothers never in employment, as well as part-time and low-paid workers. In fact, National Insurance Benefits reach just under half of all women in childbirth, and the poorest are least likely to qualify.

To this must be added women's position in Supplementary Benefits, described on pp. 213–18. Married and cohabiting women are more likely to be treated as dependants than as claimants. The SB scheme does not operate as a safety net for maternity, then, except for women alone.

In 1985 it would be strange to write that any social security provision was generous and easy to understand. But maternity provisions do express the idea that coverage of women's incomes is an optional extra, less important than coverage of men's incomes. The fifty-two weeks' duration of Unemployment Benefit (claimed mostly by men) is inadequate at present unemployment levels; the nineteen weeks of Maternity Allowance is more inadequate, and has been so since the 1940s. Perhaps it is not just women's incomes but maternity itself that is seen as an optional extra.

Birth is acknowledged by legislation under the Department of Employment as well as the DHSS, and it is convenient to include all provisions here. But the existence of several sources of support in maternity should not be taken to imply largesse – on the contrary, maternity is covered in a fragmentary and incoherent fashion.

'In the 26th week of her pregnancy she wrote to her employer saying she was taking maternity leave and intended to return to work. She sent the form for free prescriptions, dental treatment and free milk and vitamins. The next week she claimed Maternity Grant and Maternity Allowance. At the end of the 29th week she stopped work and her Maternity Pay started the following week at 90% of her basic pay minus Maternity Allowance. Her Maternity Allowance had not yet arrived. In the 31st week she claimed a tax rebate. At the end of the 32nd week her Maternity Grant arrived and her Maternity

Allowance book of orders. At 36 weeks her Maternity Pay ran out and her only income was Maternity Allowance. She claimed standard housing benefit and there was a 6 week delay in processing her claim, due to a backlog in the housing benefit office.

Her daughter was born in the 41st week. The next week, after she came out of hospital, she claimed Child Benefit and One Parent Benefit. She contacted the housing benefit office for a reassessment of her claim. At 48 weeks her Maternity Allowance ended. She claimed Supplementary Benefit on the next Tuesday and had to wait for four hours in the office. Her first Supplementary Benefit payment was received for the next Monday. She claimed a single payment for items for the baby that week. The same week her employer wrote asking if she still intended returning to work. She started looking for a childminder. . . . At 70 weeks she returned to work. She stopped claiming Supplementary Benefit. She claimed Family Income Supplement after she received her first payslip and applied to the Inland Revenue for the Additional Personal Allowance.'

(National Council for One Parent Families 1984: 4.4)

The endowment of motherhood by the Welfare State amounts to the sum of £25 per baby. This Maternity Grant is the only sum to which every mother is entitled without condition. In addition, there are three ways in which women may receive benefits to compensate for loss of earnings and meet confinement costs. Through the Department of Employment's Maternity Fund, mothers may qualify for Maternity Pay. Through National Insurance contribution records, some mothers qualify for Maternity Allowance, a regular weekly payment, supposed by Beveridge to compensate those who paid full contributions for some of the disadvantageous elements in the scheme. Finally, through poverty, some mothers qualify for Supplementary Benefits – though not, in general, if they are living with men in paid work.

Maternity Allowance and Maternity Pay do not guarantee security to employed women for two main reasons. First, many do not have the kind of employment record needed to qualify for these benefits. Ironically enough, maternity provision shares with National Insurance in general the assumption of a male working pattern. The predominance of women in low-paid and part-time work, together with a child-care pattern that persuades most women to leave full-time work on the birth of a first baby, mean that many women do not have adequate employment or insurance records. Thus, in 1981, there were 654,000 Maternity Grant awards (for which most mothers – but not all – would have qualified in that year) but only 365,000 Maternity Allowances (dependent on contributions). Maternity Pay is yet more restrictive, depending on two years' continuous employment with the same employer, as well as excluding part-time workers (under sixteen hours a week). Only about one-fifth of women are entitled to it. Employers may fill the breach, but they do so in a very unequal way. Again, the majority, especially the low paid, will be left without (see Daniel 1980, for a full account).

The second issue concerns the duration and amount of benefits. There is some official sanction for a period of absence from employment, starting eleven weeks before birth and lasting until twenty-nine weeks after it. The first date is part of National Insurance legislation, under which women are entitled to full National Insurance benefits only if they stop work at this time. The second is part of Employment Protection legislation which provides that, under certain circumstances, a woman's job must be kept for her up to that date. In practice, women take quite varied patterns of leave, though the first date is fairly widely followed (Daniel 1980). In so far, though, as government policies suggest, and encourage, a pattern of leave, it amounts to forty weeks, starting eleven weeks before birth.

However, absence from work and payment during absence from work are quite different matters. Maternity Pay, amounting to 90 per cent of normal pay (minus Maternity Allowance), is the most significant weekly sum within state provision for covering loss of income; but it lasts for only six weeks, which means that women leaving work early enough to collect full National Insurance will have used their entitlement five weeks before their babies are due. Maternity Allowance lasts a bit longer – until eight weeks after the birth – but is below subsistence level. Eight weeks after the birth all statutory financial provision ends, except for women on Supplementary Benefit.

The implication is that women who have babies must depend on men. A woman who takes forty weeks away from paid employment will find that benefits cover her, inadequately, for less than half the period.

Another aspect of maternity provision concerns protection of employment. This includes the rights not to be dismissed on account of pregnancy, and to return after giving birth. These may seem rather primitive entitlements, given the universality and necessity of reproduction. But the Protection of Employment Act produced considerable controversy, and more restrictive legislation followed in 1980. In practice, the rights are limited to women with unusually consistent employment patterns. More important, perhaps, they are perceived by most concerned as irrelevant.

According to Daniel, the right to reinstatement 'contained the three main ingredients necessary to make it attractive to a government committed to social reform. It made a powerful symbolic impact. It changed very little in practice. It cost nothing to the public purse' (Daniel 1981: 75). His studies suggest that most employers are willing to accept women back after birth, regardless of legal entitlement. Most women, however, find it impossible or undesirable to return to their previous employment. The world of paid work in general makes too few concessions to the existence and needs of small children; and mothers' sole responsibility for them is entrenched in practice and social policy. Thus women returning to employment tend to go back to 'women's jobs'. For a small minority, in such occupations as teaching and nursing, this may be the same job as before. For the majority of those wishing to return it will be to jobs which have shorter hours, more flexibility, and lower pay.

> 'When women went back to different employers their net hourly rates of pay tended to fall dramatically, they tended to do lower grade work and they tended to drift towards the private small firm sector. While that sector may have been able to provide the flexibility of working arrangements they were seeking, the quality of jobs tended to be lower on most other dimensions that we were able to measure in the survey.'
>
> (Daniel 1980: 106)

The women surveyed were more interested in child-care and work patterns than in maternity rights:

> 'By far the largest general demand was for more or improved nurseries, creches or play groups. Very many linked that demand specifically to the need for such facilities to be provided at the place of work. Other particular points concerned the dearth of facilities for infants under three years old, the lack of approved, registered childminders and the need for specific

provision to be made during school holidays. The second general area of concern related essentially to the rigidity of working hours. There were demands for arrangements that would enable mothers to cope with children's holidays, illnesses and so on; for more and better part-time working opportunities; for increased and improved scope to work at home; and for a better deal for the part-time, self-employed and homeworkers.' (Daniel 1980: 106–7)

None of this is to suggest that maternity rights might as well be withdrawn. They have a real value for a minority, and even their symbolic value is not negligible. But the structures of public and private life ensure that their use is to a minority. While employment continues to be organized around male workers without a significant domestic role, and child-care is mothers' undivided responsibility, most women will not be able to use their rights.

There is then little effective independent security for women having babies, either of income, or of employment. While provisions acknowledge the tensions between paid and unpaid work for women, in practice they reaffirm women's place in the home, and their dependence on male incomes. The most tangible, though not the only important consequence, is the very high risk of poverty for those women who have no male incomes, and for their babies.

Conclusion

Egalitarian changes are superficial. At the very foundation of social security policy and practice is a model of family life in which women are wageless and dependent, and a model of work as paid employment carried out mainly by men. Women's incomes, women's paid and unpaid work, and women themselves are marginalized.

At the same time women's security is more fragile than men's. The labour market, responsibilities for children and other dependants, and increasingly, marriage itself conspire to make women insecure. Women thus figure largely among claimants for means-tested social security benefits.

Yet there is another side to this coin. The existence of social security, however inadequate, does make it possible for women to live without men. Women can choose a kind of independence. As Beatrix Campbell puts it:

'The dole-queue mothers aren't just victims, suffering women. . . . If respectability was undermined after the Second World War by married women refusing dependence, and returning to waged work while also having children, it is being undermined again by the new wave of dole-queue mothers who find a measure of independence in motherhood. Both disrupt the rules and regulations of respectability, which was about nothing if it was not about controlling the social status of women. These single parents care about being mothers but they don't care so much about being married and they care even less for being rendered dependent. Unemployment steals from them the economic conditions which supported the new wave of feminism in the sixties and early seventies, but the welfare state, the provision of child benefit, minimal as it is, and supplementary benefit, mean they can survive in the absence of jobs and wages of their own. At least they can get out when the going gets rough, as their grandmothers couldn't.'
(Campbell 1984: 78)

Postscript – the Social Security Reviews

The present government has committed itself to substantial reform of the social security system. The consequent review process has reached the Bill stage. We thus have reviews of current practice and detailed proposals for change; but at the time of going to press it is not clear to what extent the proposals will be put into effect. This section, then, will give a very brief review of the way these reforms might affect women. A fuller analysis will be found in the Social Security Advisory Committee's response to the Green Paper (Social Security Advisory Committee 1985).

Some general conclusions may be drawn about the nature of this review process. First, it is clear that the male breadwinner model of social security is not open to review; second, it seems that some of the ground made by women within that system will be lost.

The first point can be illustrated from the section of the Green Paper on retirement. In arguing the case for a pension system based around occupational and private provision, the Green Paper acknowledges some difficulties:

'The Government believe that the new arrangements should apply to as wide a range of employees as possible but recognize that, as with national insurance, there must be exceptions. It would not be reasonable to expect the pension arrangements to apply to casual workers or those with very low earnings from part-time work. . . . The Government will consider further how those who are employed for only short periods should be dealt with.'   (HMSO 1985: 6)

Thus, as at present, provision for retirement will be predicated on a male working life, with those who do not fit the pattern left for later consideration.

Indeed, pensions is one area where some limited ground gained by women will be lost. Pensions within the present State Earnings Related Pension Scheme (SERPS) are based on the best twenty years of earnings – a provision that can benefit women who take periods out of employment. This will no longer apply in SERPS or in private sector schemes which are to take a larger role. And if women will be worse placed than at present to earn their own pensions, they will also be worse off as widows in both SERPS and occupational schemes.

Another area where ground will be lost is in the Family Credit scheme which replaces Family Income Supplement. Family Credits are to be paid as part of the wage packet rather than as a benefit. This must involve some transfer of resources away from women who care for children. In addition, there appears to be a longer term intention to develop selective Family Credit through the wage packet at the expense of universal Child Benefit. This would further reduce the sole guaranteed income of many mothers who are out of the labour market.

The response of the proposals to the inadequacy of maternity coverage is to abandon universal maternity coverage altogether. In future mothers will qualify only through means test or through NI contributions. Grants will be available from the new Social Fund – but payments will be lower than those now made to people on Supplementary Benefit, and they seem likely to miss many of those most in need – in particular, the young-est mothers may not qualify, and take-up will certainly be incomplete.

The Social Security Review is not a plot against women. Some gains to single mothers seem likely as well as to those entitled to the Maternity Allowance. It is, however, clear that there is nothing fundamental about the review in relation to women's position as dependants and low wage-earners. The Social Secur-ity Advisory Committee conclude that the balance of change is to women's detriment; and that the current failure to analyse and respond to changes in women's position will make it harder to develop a more responsive system in the future. Further:

'We do not think the present proposals have taken adequate account of women's non-financial contribution to the economy, and we believe a further review is required to ensure that the benefit system applies fairly both to men and to women.'
(Social Security Advisory Committee 1985: 80)

Conclusion

Explanatory approaches to social policy: Marxism and socialist feminism

Explanation of the nature of the Welfare State and of its real relationship to 'welfare' has usually been couched in Marxist terms. Such analysis focuses on social policy's services to capital – its meeting of social expenses and its function of social control, for example (O'Connor 1973; Gough 1979; Ginsburg 1979). Or social welfare may be seen as a site of conflict between labour and capital, where workers can wrest some advantages by political action. Such analyses tend to understand the Welfare State in terms of productive relations, the needs of capital being paramount.

Socialist feminists, unhappy with the restriction to productive relations, extended the analysis into the family. The Welfare State's role in supporting capital could be carried into the family. Women, in their domestic work, reproduced labour; on a daily basis they serviced their husbands as labourers, and in raising children they created the new generation of workers. The Welfare State could be seen as protecting the family system within which this work fell to women, and controlling the way the work was done. The family and the Welfare State were seen both as the material site within which women were oppressed and as carrying the load of social control through ideological processes (see especially, Wilson 1977).

Such analyses have been crucial in their task of connecting social policies to wider social processes; they provide an obvious starting point. But they do pose difficulties. One is a tendency to understand reproduction only in a secondary way, as an adjunct to production. Another is a tendency to a deterministic emphasis on structures, and a portrayal of people as victims of those structures.

Here it has been argued that the family and reproduction are not merely adjuncts of productive relations. The family form which is fostered by social policies is not just the form 'necessary' to or consequent upon capitalism; it has roots of its own and, indeed, is not obviously the most efficient model for capitalist exploitation. If this is so, then relations between state and family will be illuminated by a direct analysis, instead of one that begins from their service to capitalist exploitation.

This is not to argue, however, that analysis of relations between state and family should be wholly independent of the productive sphere. Here, the difficulties of building theories which can encompass capitalism and patriarchy are evident. And this book's emphasis on feminist analysis has meant some neglect of production. However, following the work of the Centre for Contemporary Cultural Studies in relation to education, the position taken here is that social policies bridge production and reproduction (CCCS 1981). They span the gulf that was created when capitalist production took 'work' out of the 'family'.

Connecting production and reproduction

The conception of social policies as connecting production and reproduction means that neither realm is prioritized in theory – it is a matter of empirical investigation to discover their relations in practice. This framework makes it possible to begin to understand issues of disability, child-care, and community care which have been obscured by assuming productive relations were paramount. Neither are the results of social policies for women predetermined. The oddity of analysing the Welfare State merely as a structure of control while women fight against cuts may be avoided.

Social policies may bring the resources of the public world to reproduction, and may thus enhance women's work and improve women's lives. Thus women's activity in the politics of family allowances, disability support and health, education and so on can be seen as an effort to increase resources for women and women's work. And education may provide a route out of a domestic future for some girls and women.

But another aspect of social policies is public control of private life. Control of reproductive biology is a key feminist issue: abortion, childbirth, contraception and so on provide examples of the limits to women's control over their reproductive biology, and of the extent to which that control has passed to medicine. This analysis should not be reduced to the notion that 'the state' controls women's bodies. Medicine is authorized through the state, and the apparatus of medicine's dominance over other health professions has legal sanction and practical force in the

NHS. But the connections between the state, medicine, and reproductive biology are not so tight as to leave women no control over their reproductive lives or without the possibility of altering medical practice.

Reproductive biology may be the foundation upon which reproductive relations are built. Moving on to study the building itself opens other ways of analysing social policies as aspects of state control over women's reproductive work. The professionalized structures of health and education may be seen as taking over aspects of reproduction. Some work in this area has stressed the way control and decision-making have passed to men. But other work emphasizes the work still done by women, both in direct care and in mobilizing professional resources (Graham 1985). Such work also emphasizes the need to understand the nature of caring work, its difference in different contexts and its difference from productive work.

If social policies are seen as taking control over reproductive work, they may also be seen as reproducing gender relations. The family remains a prime site for developing children's identity as male and female. But education and health institutions may also be seen as structures for perpetuating gender divisions. Socialist feminist writing on education has elaborated the 'family-education couple' as the key ideological structure for making women into wives, mothers, and low-paid workers (David 1980). Women's health writing has focused on the importance of medicine in mediating between biology and culture, and thus in defining the cultural meaning of female biology (Oakley 1980).

If social policies can be seen as one kind of bridge between production and reproduction, there is another kind. The model of family life in which male breadwinners 'support' female dependants connects the two worlds. The 'family wage' brings resources to the family, while women provide the basis on which men can devote themselves to employment. Such a model of family life maintains the public/private divide, with women as dependants in the home. Feminists have identified social policy's support of this family form as playing an important role in the continuing sexual division of labour. Social security and housing policy, and policy for dependent adults and children constitute part of the material framework within which it is difficult for women to 'choose' any other form of relationship than dependence, or to 'choose' not to do unpaid caring work as the price of that dependence. Social policies which promote this model of the family may thus be seen both as minimizing state activity in reproductive work, and as promoting women's dependence and privacy in the home.

Women's political action

One difficulty with such arguments is the danger of portraying women merely as victims of outside structures – whether of capitalism or of patriarchy. Socialist feminist accounts of education as 'reproducing' gender relations and social policies as the agents of capitalist exploitation of women's work appear to leave no room for contest. The same may apply to the notion of patriarchy as used by some radical feminists in the sense of a universal and overarching system of male domination.

The salience of capitalist production and of male domination of the public sphere to social policies, and their impact on women, does not mean that women are merely victims. There are cultural sources of identity, which mean that women do not simply take over the identity offered through education and medicine. Even looking after others as a source of a distinctive identity for women may lend special strengths. Women's place as paid workers in health, social work, and education gives room for them to be not simply instruments of domination. And women's place in public politics is small but not negligible.

Here it seems appropriate to refer to less formal types of political action. Women play a larger role in community politics than in the bureaucratic structures of national politics (Randall 1982), and much of this activity centres around health, education, and housing. Protest and campaigning groups, around abortion, social service cuts, peace, merge into innovatory groups providing services for women in Rape Crisis Centres, Outwork Campaigns, health groups and refuges. Some of these organizations challenge traditional, bureaucratic forms of service delivery as well as their dominant ideologies.

Analysis of concrete instances shows a variety of ways in which social policy contains and constrains women. But it also shows that there are ambiguities. Any analysis must leave room to understand women's promotion and defence of welfare institutions, and cultural and political sources of identity and change.

References

Note: In general, the reference given is to the first edition. Where a more recent edition has been used, two dates are given, one for the original publication and one for the edition used. In this case publication details refer to the second of these.

Abbott, E. and Bompas, K. (1943) *The Woman Citizen and Social Security*. London: Mrs Bompass.

Abel-Smith, B. (1960) *A History of the Nursing Profession*. London: Heinemann.

Aitken-Swan, J. (1977) *Fertility Control and the Medical Profession*. London: Croom Helm.

Alexander, S. (1979) Introduction to the new edition of M. Pember Reeves *Round about a Pound a Week*. London: Virago.

Allen, I. (1981) *Family Planning Sterilisation and Abortion Services*. London: Policy Studies Institute, no. 595.

Aries, P. (1960/1973) *Centuries of Childhood: A Social History of Family Life*. Harmondsworth: Penguin.

Arnot, M. (1983a) *Educating Girls*. Unit 13 of *The Changing Experience of Women*. Milton Keynes: Open University.

—— (1983b) A Cloud over Co-education. In S. Walker and L. Barton (eds) *Gender, Class and Education*. Basingstoke: The Falmer Press.

Atkins, S. (1978–79) The EEC Directive on Equal Treatment in Social Security Benefits. *Journal of Social Welfare Law* 1: 244–50.

—— (1981) Social Security Act 1980 and the EEC Directive on Equal Treatment in Social Security Benefits. *Journal of Social Welfare Law* 3: 16–20.

Austerberry, H. and Watson, S. (1981) A Woman's Place: A Feminist Approach to Housing in Britain. *Feminist Review* Summer 1981: 49–62.

—— (1983) *Women on the Margins: A Study of Single Women's Housing Problems*. London: Housing Research Group, City University.

Aveling, J. H. (1872/1967) *English Midwives*. London: Hugh K. Elliott.

Banta, D. (1980) Benefits and Risks of Electronic Fetal Monitoring. In H. Holmes, B. Hoskins, and M. Gross (eds) *Birth Control and Controlling Birth*. New Jersey: Humana Press.

Barrett, M. and McIntosh, M. (1982) *The Anti-Social Family*. London: Verso.

Barron, R. D. and Norris, G. M. (1976) Sexual Divisions and the Dual Labour Market. In D. L. Barker and S. Allen (eds) *Dependence and Exploitation in Work and Marriage*. London: Longman, 47–69.

Bart, P. (1981) Seizing the Means of Reproduction: An Illegal Feminist Abortion Collective – How and Why it Worked. In H. Roberts (ed.)

Women, Health and Reproduction. London: Routledge & Kegan Paul, 109–28.

Beechey, V. (1978) Women and Production: A Critical Analysis of Some Sociological Theories of Women's Work. In A. Kuhn and A. Wolpe (eds) *Feminism and Materialism*. London: Routledge & Kegan Paul, 155–97.

—— (1982/1983) The Sexual Division of Labour and the Labour Process: A Critical Assessment of Braverman. In S. Wood (ed.) *The Degradation of Work? Skill, deskilling and the labour process*. London: Hutchinson.

Benett, Y. and Carter, D. (1983) *Day Release for Girls: An investigation of why so few girls receive time off work for part-time study*. Manchester: Equal Opportunities Commission.

Beral, V. (1979) Reproductive Mortality. *British Medical Journal* 15 September: 632–34.

Beveridge, W. (1942) *Social Insurance and Allied Services*. London: HMSO, Cmnd 6404.

Binney, V. (1981) Domestic Violence: Battered Women in Britain in the 1970s. In Cambridge Women's Study Group, *Women in Society*. London: Virago, 115–26.

Binney, V., Harkell, G., and Nixon, J. (1981) *Leaving Violent Men: A Study of Refuges and Housing for Battered Women* (WAF/DE Research Team). Manchester: Women's Aid Federation.

Bland, L., McCabe T., and Mort, F. (1979) Sexuality and Reproduction: Three 'official' instances. In M. Barrett (ed.) *Ideology and Cultural Production*. London: Croom Helm, 78–111.

Board of Education (1923) *Report of the Consultative Committee on Differentiation of the Curriculum for Boys and Girls Respectively in Secondary Schools* (Hadow Committee) London: HMSO.

Bone, A. (1980) Education and Manpower. *Equal Opportunities Commission Research Bulletin* 4: 86:98.

Bone, M. (1977) *Pre-school Children and Their Need for Day Care*. London: OPCS.

Borkowski, M., Murch, M., and Walker, V. (1983) *Marital Violence: The Community Response*. London: Tavistock.

Boston Women's Health Collective (1971/1978) *Our Bodies Ourselves*. British edition by Angela Phillips and Jill Rakusen. Harmondsworth: Penguin.

Boulton, M. G. (1983) *On Being a Mother: a study of women with pre-school children*. London: Tavistock.

Bowlby, J. (1951/1965) *Maternal Care and Mental Health*. Geneva: World Health Organisation. Revised version published in 1953 as *Child Care and the Growth of Love*. Harmondsworth: Penguin.

Bowles, G. and Klein, R. D. (1983) *Theories of Women's Studies*. London: Routledge & Kegan Paul.

Braverman, H. (1974) *Labor and Monopoly Capital: The degradation of work in the twentieth century*. New York: Monthly Review Press.

Breugel, I (1983) Women's Employment, Legislation and the Labour Market. In J. Lewis (ed.) *Women's Welfare Women's Rights*. London: Croom Helm, 130–69.

Brion, M. and Tinker, A. (1980) *Women in Housing: Access and Influence*. London: Housing Centre Trust.

Brown, G. W. and Harris, T. (1978) *The Social Origins of Depression: A Study of Psychiatric Disorder in Women*. London: Tavistock.

Burns, R. (1984) Financial Management and the Allocation of Resources within Households: a research review. *Equal Opportunities Commission Research Bulletin* 8: 17–36.

Busfield, J. (1983) Gender, Mental Illness, and Psychiatry. In M. Evans and C. Ungerson (eds) *Sexual Divisions: Patterns and Processes*. London: Tavistock.

Byrne, E. (1978) *Women and Education*. London: Tavistock.

Campbell, B. (1984) *Wigan Pier Revisited: Poverty and Politics in the 80s*. London: Virago.

Campling, J. (1981a) *Images of Ourselves: Women with Disabilities Talking*. London: Routledge & Kegan Paul.

—— (1981b) Women and Disability. In A. Walker and P. Townsend (eds) *Disability in Britain: A Manifesto of Rights*. Oxford: Martin Robertson.

Carpenter, M. (1977) The New Managerialism and Professionalism in Nursing. In M. Stacey, M. Reid, C. Heath, and R. Dingwall (eds) *Health and the Division of Labour*. London: Croom Helm.

Cartwright, A. and Bowling, A. (1982) *Life after a Death*. London: Tavistock.

Catholic Housing Aid Society (1974) *What Chance a Home?* London: Catholic Housing Aid Society.

Cawson, A. (1982) *Corporatism and Welfare – Social Policy and State Intervention in Britain*. London: Heinemann Educational.

Central Policy Review Staff (1978) *Services for Young Children with Working Mothers*. London: HMSO.

Centre for Contemporary Cultural Studies (1981) *Unpopular Education: Schooling and Social Democracy in England since 1944*. London: Hutchinson.

Chalmers, I., Oakley, A., and Macfarlane, A. (1980) Perinatal Health Services: An Immodest Proposal. *British Medical Journal* 22 March: 842–45.

Chard, T. and Richards, M. (eds) (1977) *The Benefits and Hazards of the New Obstetrics*. London: Heinemann Medical.

Chisholm, L. and Woodward, D. (1980) The Experiences of Women Graduates in the Labour Market. In R. Deem (ed.), *Schooling for Women's Work*. London: Routledge & Kegan Paul.

Chodorow, N. (1978) *The Reproduction of Mothering: Psychoanalysis and the Sociology of Gender*. Berkeley: University of California Press.

Clarke-Stewart, A. (1982) *Day Care*. London: Fontana.

242 · *Social Policy*

Cochrane, A. L. (1972) *Effectiveness and Efficiency: Random Reflections on Health Services*. London: Nuffield Provincial Hospitals Trust.

Cockburn, C. (1977) *The Local State: Management of Cities and People*. London: Pluto.

Coote, A. and Campbell, B. (1982) *Sweet Freedom: the struggle for women's liberation*. London: Picador/Pan.

Coote, A. and Gill, T. (1977/1979) *Battered Women and the New Law*. London: Inter-action Imprint/National Council for Civil Liberties.

Coussins, J. (1981) Invalid Care Allowance. *Poverty* 48: 18–19.

Coussins, J. and Coote, A. (1981) *The Family in the Firing Line*. London: NCCL/CPAG.

Coyle, A. (1984) *Redundant Women*. London: The Women's Press.

Daniel, W. W. (1980) *Maternity Rights: The Experiences of Women*. London: Policy Studies Institute, no. 588.

—— (1981) A Clash of Symbols: the case of maternity legislation. *Policy Studies* 2 (2): 74–85.

David, M. (1980) *The State, the Family and Education*. London: Routledge & Kegan Paul.

—— (1983) The New Right, Sex, Education and Social Policy: Towards a New Moral Economy in Britain and the USA. In J. Lewis (ed.): *Women's Welfare; Women's Rights*. London: Croom Helm, 193–218.

David, M. and Land, H. (1983) Sex and Social Policy. In H. Glennerster (ed.) *The Future of the Welfare State*. London: Heinemann, 138–57.

Davidoff, L. (1979) The Separation of Home and Work? In S. Burman (ed.) *Fit Work for Women*. London: Croom Helm.

Davidoff, L., L'Esperance, J., and Newby, H. (1976) Landscape with Figures. In J. Mitchell and A. Oakley (eds) *The Rights and Wrongs of Women*. Harmondsworth: Penguin.

Davin, A. (1979) 'Mind that you do as you are told': Reading Books for Board School Girls, 1870–1902. *Feminist Review* 3: 80–98.

Deem, R. (1978) *Women and Schooling*. London: Routledge & Kegan Paul.

—— (1980) (ed.) *Schooling for Women's Work*. London: Routledge & Kegan Paul.

—— (1981) State Policy and Ideology in the Education of Women, 1944–1980. *British Journal of Sociology of Education* 2(2): 131–43.

Delamont, S. (1980) *Sex Roles and the School*. London: Methuen.

Delphy, C. (1981) Women in Stratification Studies. In H. Roberts (ed.) *Doing Feminist Research*. London: Routledge & Kegan Paul, 114–28.

Department of Education and Science (1979) *Aspects of Secondary Education in England*. A survey by HM Inspectors of Schools. London: HMSO.

Department of Health and Social Security (1974) *Report of the Committee on One-Parent Families* (Finer Committee). London: HMSO, Cmnd 5629.

—— (1978) *Social Assistance, a Review of the Supplementary Benefits Scheme in Great Britain*. London: HMSO.

—— (1981a) *Growing Older*. London: HMSO, Cmnd 8173.

—— (1981b) *Report of a Study on Community Care*. London: Department of Health and Social Security.

—— (1982) *Supplementary Benefits Handbook*. London: HMSO.

Dinnerstein, D. (1976/1978) *The Rocking of the Cradle and the Ruling of the World*. London: Souvenir Press.

Donnison, J. (1977) *Midwives and Medical Men*. London: Heinemann.

Douglas, J. W. B. (1964) *The Home and the School: A Study of Ability and Attainment in the Primary School*. London: McGibbon & Kee.

Doyal, L. (1983) Women, Health and the Sexual Division of Labour: A Case Study of the Women's Health Movement in Britain. *Critical Social Policy* 7: 21–33.

Doyal, L., Hunt, G., and Mellor, J. (1981) Your Life in their Hands: Migrant Workers in the National Health Service. *Critical Social Policy* 1(2): 54–71.

Doyal, L. and Pennell, I. (1979) *The Political Economy of Health*. London: Pluto.

Dubos, R. (1968/1970) *Man, Medicine and Environment*. London: Pall Mall; Harmondsworth: Penguin.

Dunn, P. M. (1976) Obstetric Delivery Today: For Better or for Worse? *The Lancet* 10 April: 790–93.

Ehrenreich, B. and English, D. (1978/1979) *For Her Own Good: 150 Years of the Experts' Advice to Women*. London: Pluto.

Eide, W. (1979) *Women in Food Production, Food Handling and Nutrition*. FAO Food and nutrition paper. Rome: FAO (UN).

Eisenstein, Z. (1981) Reform and/or Revolution: Towards a United Women's Movement. In L. Sargent, *Women and Revolution*. London: Pluto, 339–62.

Elbourne, D. (1981) *Is the Baby All Right? Current Trends in British Perinatal Health*. London: Junction Books.

Elston, M. A. and Doyal, L. (1983) *Health and Medicine*. Unit 14 of *The Changing Experience of Women*. Milton Keynes: Open University.

Equal Opportunities Commission (1978) *It's not your Business, it's how the Society Works: The Experience of Married Applicants for Joint Mortgages*. Manchester: Equal Opportunities Commission.

—— (1979) *Health and Safety Legislation: should we distinguish between men and women?* Manchester: Equal Opportunities Commission.

—— (1980) *The Experience of Caring for Elderly and Handicapped Dependants: A Survey Report*. Manchester: Equal Opportunities Commission.

—— (1981a) *Behind Closed Doors: A Report on the Public Response to an Advertising Campaign about Discrimination in Certain Social Security Benefits*. Manchester: Equal Opportunities Commission.

—— (1981b) *Education of Girls: A Statistical Analysis*. Manchester: Equal Opportunities Commission.

Equal Opportunities Commission (1981c) *Women and Underachievement at Work*. Research Bulletin no. 5.

—— (1982a) *Caring for the Elderly and Handicapped: Community Care Policies and Women's Lives*. Manchester: Equal Opportunities Commission.

—— (1982b) *Reduction in University Numbers and the Effects upon Women*. Manchester: Equal Opportunities Commission.

—— (1982c) *Who Cares for the Carers? Opportunities for those Caring for the Elderly and Handicapped*. Manchester: Equal Opportunities Commission.

—— (1984) *Carers and Services: A Comparison of Men and Women Caring for Dependent Elderly People*. Manchester: Equal Opportunities Commission.

Evers, H. (1985) The Frail Elderly Woman: Emergent Questions in Aging and Women's Health. In E. Lewin and V. Olesen (eds) *Women, Health and Healing: Toward a New Perspective*. London and New York: Tavistock, 86–112.

Field, F. (1977) *To Him Who Hath: A Study of Poverty and Taxation*. Harmondsworth: Penguin.

—— (1985) *What price a child? A Historical Review of the Relative Cost of Dependants*. London: Policy Studies Institute, no. 637.

Finch, J. (1984) *Education as Social Policy*. Harlow: Longman.

Finch, J. and Groves, D. (1980) Community Care and the Family: A Case for Equal Opportunities. *Journal of Social Policy* 9(4): 487–511.

—— (1982) By Women for Women: Caring for the Frail Elderly. *Women's Studies International Forum* 5(5): 427–37.

Finch, J. and Groves, D. (eds) (1983) *A Labour of Love: Women, Work and Caring*. London: Routledge & Kegan Paul.

Flax, J. (1983) The Family in Contemporary Feminist Thought: A Critical Review. In J. B. Elshtain (ed.) *The Family in Political Thought*. Brighton: Harvester.

Fonda, N. (1980) Statutory Maternity Leave in the United Kingdom: A Case Study. In P. Moss and N. Fonda (eds) *Work and the Family*. London: Temple Smith, 110–34.

Fowkes, F. G. R., Catford, J. C., and Logan, R. F. L. (1979) Abortion and the NHS: The First Decades. *British Medical Journal* 27 January: 217–19.

Fuller, M. (1980) Black Girls in a London Comprehensive School. In R. Deem (ed.) *Schooling for Women's Work*. London: Routledge & Kegan Paul, 166–90.

—— (1983) Qualified Criticism, Critical Qualifications. In L. Barton and S. Walker (eds) *Race, Class and Education*. London: Croom Helm.

Gamarnikow, E. (1978) Sexual Division of Labour: The Case of Nursing. In A. Kuhn and A. Wolpe (eds) *Feminism and Materialism*. London: Routledge & Kegan Paul.

Ginsburg, N. (1979) *Class, Capital and Social Policy*. London: Macmillan.

Glendinning, C. (1981) Married Women and Disability: The Long Campaign for Equal Treatment. *Poverty* 48: 13–18.
―――― (1983) *Unshared Care: Parents and their Disabled Child*. London: Routledge & Kegan Paul.
Gough, I. (1979) *The Political Economy of the Welfare State*. London: Macmillan.
Graham, H. (1983) Caring: A Labour of Love. In J. Finch and D. Groves (eds) *A Labour of Love: Women, Work and Caring*. London: Routledge & Kegan Paul, 13–30.
―――― (1984) *Women, Health and the Family*. Brighton: Wheatsheaf.
―――― (1985) Providers, Negotiators, and Mediators: Women as the Hidden Carers. In E. Lewin and V. Olesen (eds) *Women, Health, and Healing: Toward a New Perspective*. New York and London: Tavistock, 25–52.
Graham, H. and Oakley, A. (1981) Competing Ideologies of Reproduction: Medical and Maternal Perspectives on Pregnancy. In H. Roberts (ed.) *Women, Health and Reproduction*. London: Routledge & Kegan Paul.
Greenwood, K. and King, L. (1981) Contraception and Abortion. In Cambridge Women's Studies Group (eds) *Women in Society: Interdisciplinary Essays*. London: Virago, 168–84.
Griffiths, M. (1980) Women in Higher Education: A Case Study of the Open University, In R. Deem (ed.) *Schooling for Women's Work*. London: Routledge & Kegan Paul.
Groves, D. (1983) Members and Survivors: Women and Retirement Pensions Legislation. In J. Lewis (ed.) *Women's Welfare, Women's Rights*. London: Croom Helm, 38–63.
Groves, D. and Finch, J. (1983) Perspectives on the Invalid Care Allowance. In *A Labour of Love: Women, Work and Caring*. London: Routledge & Kegan Paul, 148–66.

Hakim, C. (1978) Sexual Divisions within the Labour Force: Occupational Segregation. *Department of Employment Gazette:* 1,264–268, 1,278.
Hall, P., Land, H., Parker, R., and Webb, A. (1975) *Change, Choice and Conflict in Social Policy*. London: Heinemann.
Hamilton, R. (1978) *The Liberation of Women*. London: George Allen & Unwin.
Harding, J. (1980) Sex Differences in Performance in Science Examinations. In R. Deem (ed.) *Schooling for Women's Work*. London: Routledge & Kegan Paul.
Hardyment, C. (1983) *Dream Babies: Child Care from Locke to Spock*. London: Cape.
Harris, C. C. (1983) *The Family in Industrial Society*. London: George Allen & Unwin.
Harris, J. (1977) *William Beveridge: A Biography*. Oxford: Clarendon Press.

Hartmann, H. (1981a) The Family as the Locus of Gender, Glass, and Political Struggle: The Example of Housework. *Signs* 6(3): 366–94.

—— (1981b) The Unhappy Marriage of Marxism and Feminism: Towards a more Progressive Union. In L. Sargent (ed.) *Women and Revolution*. London: Pluto, 1–41.

Hayek, F. A. (1944/1976) *Road to Serfdom*. London: Routledge & Kegan Paul.

—— (1949) *Individualism and the Economic Order*. London: Routledge & Kegan Paul.

—— (1960) *The Constitution of Liberty*. London: Routledge & Kegan Paul.

Hayes, M. (1978–79) Supplementary Benefit and Financial Provision Orders. *Journal of Social Welfare Law* 1: 216–25.

Hazelgrove, R. (1979) Homelessness Legislation and Experiences in Bradford. In Issues Occasional Paper no. 4, *Battered Women and Abused Children*. University of Bradford Issues Publications: 42–9.

Hencke, D. (1985) Homing Instincts. *Guardian*: 8 and 15 May.

HMSO (1977) *Housing Policy: A Consultative Document*. London: HMSO, Cmnd 6851.

—— (1974–75) *Report from the Select Committee on Violence in Marriage*. London: HMSO, HC 553.

——(1985) *Reform of Social Security*, Volume 2. London: HMSO, Cmnd 9518.

Hobson, D. (1981) 'Now that I'm Married . . .'. In A. McRobbie and T. McCabe (eds) *Feminism for Girls: An Adventure Story*. London: Routledge & Kegan Paul.

Holland, R. and McKenna, J. (1984) Regaining Trust. In R. Arditti, R. Duelli Klein, and S. Minden (eds) *Test-Tube Women*. London, Boston, Melbourne: Pandora Press.

Housing Services Advisory Group (1978) *The Housing of One-Parent Families*. London: Department of the Environment.

Hughes, M., Mayall, B., Moss, P., Perry, J., Petrie, P., and Pinkerton, G. (1980) *Nurseries Now: A Fair Deal for Parents and Children*. Harmondsworth: Penguin.

Humphries, J. (1977) Class Struggle and the Persistence of the Working Class Family. *Cambridge Journal of Economics* 1: 241–58.

Hunt, A. (1970) *The Home-Help Service in England and Wales*. London: HMSO.

—— (1980) Some Gaps and Problems arising from Government Statistics on Women at Work. *Equal Opportunities Research Bulletin* 4: 29–42.

Hunt, P. (1980/1983) *Gender and Class Consciousness*. London: Macmillan.

Huntingford, P. (1978) Obstetric Practice: Past, Present and Future. In S. Kitzinger and J. A. Davis (eds) *The Place of Birth*. Oxford: Oxford University Press.

Jackson, B. and Jackson, S. (1979) *Childminder: A Study in Action Research*. London: Routledge & Kegan Paul.

Jolly, H. (1975/1977) *Book of Child Care*. London: Sphere.

Jones, K., Brown, J., and Bradshaw, J. (1978) *Issues in Social Policy*. London: Routledge & Kegan Paul.

Jones, K. and Fowles, A. J. (1983) People in Institutions: Rhetoric and Reality. *Yearbook of Social Policy in Britain 1983*. London: Routledge & Kegan Paul.

Jordan, B. (1980) *Birth in Four Cultures*. Montreal: Eden Press.

Jordanova, L. J. (1981) Mental Illness, Mental Health: Changing Norms and Expectations. In Cambridge Women's Studies Group *Women in Society*. London: Virago.

Joseph, Sir K. (1972) The Cycle of Deprivation. In E. Butterworth and R. Holman (eds) *Social Welfare in Modern Britain*. London: Fontana (1975): 387–93.

Joshi, H. and Owen, S. (1983) *How Many Pensionable Years? The Lifetime Earning History of Men and Women*. Government Economic Service Working Paper, no. 65. London: Economic Advisers' Office, Department of Health and Social Security.

Journal of Social Welfare Law (1981) Recent Cases: Butterworth *v* Supplementary Benefits Commission 3: 372–74.

Kamm, J. (1958) *How Different from Us: A Biography of Miss Buss and Miss Beale*. London: Bodley Head.

—— (1965) *Hope Deferred: Girls' Education in English History*. London: Methuen.

Kelly, A. (ed.) (1981) *The Missing Half*. Manchester: Manchester University Press.

King, R. (1971) Unequal Access in Education – Sex and Social Class. *Social and Economic Administration* 5(3): 167–75.

Kitzinger, S. and Davis, J. A. (1978) *The Place of Birth*. Oxford: Oxford University Press.

Knight, I. (1981) *Family Finances*. London: Office of Population Censuses and Surveys, Occasional Paper no. 26.

Land, H. (1976) Women: Supporters or Supported? In S. Allen and D. L. Barker (eds) *Sexual Divisions and Society*. London: Tavistock.

—— (1977) The Child Benefit Fiasco. In K. Jones (ed.) *Yearbook of Social Policy in Britain 1977*. London: Routledge & Kegan Paul.

—— (1978) Who Cares for the Family? *Journal of Social Policy* 7 (3): 257–84.

—— (1979) The Boundaries between the State and the Family. In C. C. Harris (ed.) *The Sociology of the Family: New Directions for Britain*. University of Keele: Sociological Review Monograph 28, 141–59.

—— (1981) *Parity Begins at Home: Women's and Men's Work in the Home and its Effects on their Paid Employment*. Manchester: EOC/SSRC.

—— (1982) The Family Wage. In M. Evans (ed.) *The Woman Question*. London: Fontana.

—— (1983) Who Still Cares for the Family? Recent Developments in

248 · *Social Policy*

Income Maintenance, Taxation and Family Law. In J. Lewis (ed.) *Women's Welfare, Women's Rights*. London: Croom Helm, 64–85.

Land, H. and Parker, R. (1978) Family Policies in Britain: The Hidden Dimensions. In S. B. Kammerman and A. J. Kahn (eds) *Family Policy: Government and Families in Fourteen Countries*. New York: Columbia University Press.

Lavigueur, J. (1980) Co-education and the Tradition of Separate Needs. In D. Spender and E. Sarah (eds) *Learning to Lose*. London: The Women's Press.

Leeson, J. and Gray, J. (1978) *Women and Medicine*. London: Tavistock.

Leevers, M. and Thynne, P. (1979) *A Woman's Place: Family Break-up and Housing Rights*. London: SHAC (The London Housing Aid Centre).

Lewin, E. and Olesen, V. (eds) (1985) *Women, Health and Healing: Toward a New Perspective*. New York, London: Tavistock.

Lewis, J. (1980) *The Politics of Motherhood: Child and Maternal Welfare in England 1900–1939*. London: Croom Helm.

Lister, R. (1973) *As Man and Wife?: A Study of the Cohabitation Rule*. London: Child Poverty Action Group.

Lister, R. and Wilson, L. (1976) *The Unequal Breadwinner: A New Perspective on Women and Social Security*. London: National Council for Civil Liberties.

Llewelyn Davies, M. (ed.) (1915/1978) *Maternity: Letters from Working Women*. London: Virago.

—— (ed.) (1931/1977) *Life as We Have Known It: By Co-operative Working Women*. London: Virago.

Loach, I. and Lister, R. (1978) *Second Class Disabled*. London: Disability Alliance.

Lobban, G. (1978) The Influence of the School on Sex-Role Stereotyping. In J. Chetwynd and O. Hartnett (eds) *The Sex Role System*. London: Routledge & Kegan Paul.

London Women's Liberation Campaign for Legal and Financial Independence and Rights of Women (1979) Disagreggation Now!: Another Battle for Women's Independence. *Feminist Review* 2: 19–31.

Luckhaus (1983) Social Security: The Equal Treatment Reforms. *Journal of Social Welfare Law* 5: 325–34.

McDowell, L. (1983) City and Home: Urban Housing and the Sexual Division of Space. In M. Evans and C. Ungerson (eds) *Sexual Divisions: Patterns and Processes*. London: Tavistock, 142–63.

Macfarlane, A. (1977) *The Psychology of Childbirth*. London: Fontana/ Open Books.

—— (1979) Social Class Variations in Perinatal Mortality. *Journal of Maternal and Child Health*: 337–40.

—— (1980) Official Statistics and Women's Health and Illness. *EOC Research Bulletin* 4.

McIntosh, M. (1979) The Welfare State and the Needs of the Dependant

Family. In S. Burman (ed.) *Fit Work for Women*. London: Croom Helm, 153–72.

McKeown, T. (1976/1979) *Role of Medicine: Dream, Mirage, or Nemesis?*. London: Raven Press; Oxford: Blackwell.

MacLennan, E. (1980) Women, Employment and Low Incomes: Official Statistics as Sources of Secondary Analysis. *Equal Opportunities Commission Research Bulletin* 4: 99–106.

MacNicol, J. (1980) *The Movement for Family Allowances 1918–1943*. London: Heinemann.

McRobbie, A. (1978a) *Jackie: An Ideology of Adolescent Femininity*. Birmingham: Centre for Contemporary Cultural Studies Stencilled Occasional Paper, Women Series SP no. 53.

—— (1978b) Working Class Girls and the Culture of Femininity. In Women's Studies Group *Women Take Issue*. London: Hutchinson, with Centre for Contemporary Cultural Studies, Birmingham.

—— (1980) Settling Accounts with Sub-cultures – A Feminist Critique. *Screen Education* 34: 37–49.

—— (1981) Just like a Jackie Story. In A. McRobbie and T. McCabe (eds) *Feminism for Girls: An Adventure Story*. London: Routledge & Kegan Paul.

Marks, P. (1976) Femininity in the Classroom: An Account of Changing Attitudes. In J. Mitchell and A. Oakley (eds) *The Rights and Wrongs of Women*. Harmondsworth: Penguin.

Marsden, D. (1969) *Mothers Alone*. London: Penguin.

Marshall, T. H. (1949/1963) Citizenship and Social Class. Republished in *Sociology at the Crossroads*. London: Heinemann.

Martin, J. and Roberts, C. (1984) *Women and Employment*. London: Department of Employment/Office of Population Censuses and Surveys.

Merrett, S. (1979) *State Housing in Britain*. London: Routledge & Kegan Paul.

Ministry of Education (1954) *Early Leaving*: A Report of the Central Advisory Council for Education. London: HMSO.

—— (1959) *15 to 18*: A Report of the Central Advisory Council for Education (England) (Crowther). London: HMSO.

—— (1963a) *Half Our Future*: A Report of the Central Advisory Council for Education (Newsom). London: HMSO.

—— (1963b) *Report of the Committee on Higher Education* (Robbins). London: HMSO.

Mishra, R. (1977) *Society and Social Policy: Theoretical Perspectives on Welfare*. London: Macmillan.

Moroney, R. M. (1976) *The Family and the State: Considerations for Social Policy*. London: Longman.

National Council for Civil Liberties (1981) *Positive Action for Women*. London: NCCL.

250 · *Social Policy*

National Council for Civil Liberties (1983) *Amending the Equality Laws: The Next Step*. London: NCCL.

National Council for One Parent Families (1984) *Survival or Security? Evidence to the Social Security Reviews*. London: National Council for One Parent Families.

Newsom, J. (1948) *The Education of Girls*. London: Faber & Faber.

Nissel, M. and Bonnerjea, L. (1982) *Family Care of the Handicapped Elderly: Who Pays?* London: Policy Studies Institute, no. 602.

Nixon, J. (1979) *Fatherless Families on FIS*. London: Department of Health and Social Security, Research Report no. 4.

Oakley, A. (1974a) *Housewife*. Harmondsworth: Allen Lane.

—— (1974b) *The Sociology of Housework*. Oxford: Martin Robertson.

—— (1976) Wisewoman and Medicine Man: Changes in the Management of Childbirth. In J. Mitchell and A. Oakley (eds) *The Rights and Wrongs of Women*. Harmondsworth: Penguin.

—— (1979) *Becoming a Mother*. Oxford: Martin Robertson.

—— (1980) *Women Confined: Towards a Sociology of Childbirth*. Oxford: Martin Robertson.

—— (1981a) Interviewing Women: A Contradiction in Terms. In H. Roberts (ed.) *Doing Feminist Research*. London: Routledge & Kegan Paul.

—— (1981b) *Subject Women*. Oxford: Martin Robertson.

—— (1983) Women and Health Policy. In J. Lewis (ed.) *Women's Welfare/ Women's Rights*. London: Croom Helm, 103–29.

O'Brien, M. (1981) *The Politics of Reproduction*. London, Boston: Routledge & Kegan Paul.

O'Connor, J. (1973) *The Fiscal Crisis of the State*. London: St James Press.

Oren, L. (1974) The Welfare of Women in Labouring Families: England, 1860–1950. *Feminist Studies* 1(3–4): 107–25.

Osborn, A. F., Butler, N. R., and Morris, A. C. (1984) *The Social Life of Britain's Five-Year-Olds: A Report of the Child Health and Education Study*. London: Routledge & Kegal Paul.

Pahl, J. (1978) *Battered Women: A Study of the Role of a Women's Centre*. London: Department of Health and Social Security/HMSO.

—— (1980) Patterns of Money Management within Marriage. *Journal of Social Policy* 313–35.

Pahl, R. E. (1981) Employment, Work and the Domestic Division of Labour. In M. Harloe and E. Lebas (eds) *City, Class, and Capital*. London: Edward Arnold.

—— (1984) *Divisions of Labour*. Oxford: Blackwell.

Parker, R. A. (1981) Tending and Social Policy. In E. M. Goldberg and S. Hatch (eds) *A New Look at the Personal Social Services*. London: Policy Studies Institute, Discussion Paper no. 4: 17–34.

Parsons, T. (1955) *Family, Socialisation and Interaction Process*. Illinois: The Free Press.

Pember Reeves, M. (1913/1979) *Round about a Pound a Week*. London: Virago.

Perkins, T. (1983) A New Form of Employment: A Case Study of Women's Part-Time Work in Coventry. In M. Evans and C. Ungerson (eds) *Sexual Divisions: Patterns and Processes*. London, New York: Tavistock, 15–53.

Pfeffer, N. and Woollett, A. (1983) *The Experience of Infertility*. London: Virago.

Phillipson, C. (1982) *Capitalism and the Construction of Old Age*. London: Macmillan.

Piachaud, D. (1984) *Round about Fifty Hours a Week*. London: Child Poverty Action Group.

Pocock, K. (1983) *The Menopause: A Woman's 'Change of Life'?* University of Nottingham: Dissertation (BA Hons), Social Administration.

Pollert, A. (1981) *Girls, Wives, Factory Lives*. London: Macmillan.

Popay, J., Rimmer, L., and Rossiter, C. (1983) *One Parent Families: Parents, Children and Public Policy*. London: Study Commission on the Family.

Porter, M. (1982) Standing on the edge: Working Class Housewives and the World of Work. In J. West (ed.) *Work, Women and the Labour Market*. London: Routledge & Kegan Paul, 117–34.

Price, S. (1979) Ideologies of Female Dependence in the Welfare State – Women's Response to the Beveridge Report. British Sociological Association Conference, mimeo.

Rakusen, J. (1981) Depo-Provera: The Extent of the Problem. A Case-study in the Politics of Birth Control. In H. Roberts (ed.) *Women, Health and Reproduction*. London: Routledge & Kegan Paul, 75–108.

Randall, V. (1982) *Women and Politics*. London: Macmillan.

Rathbone, E. (1924/1949) *The Disinherited Family*. Enlarged edition printed in 1949 as *Family Allowances*. London: George Allen & Unwin.

Reid, I. (1982) Vital Statistics. In I. Reid and E.Wormald (eds) *Sex Differences in Britain*. London: Grant McIntyre, 29–58.

Rendel, M. (1980) How Many Women Academics 1912–76? In R. Deem (ed.) *Schooling for Women's Work*. London: Routledge & Kegan Paul.

Richards, M. (1978–79) A Study of the Non-contributory Invalidity Pension for Married Women. *Journal of Social Welfare Law* 66–75.

Ridley, A. (1895) *Frances Mary Buss and her Work for Education*. London: Longman.

Riley, D. (1979) War in the Nursery. *Feminist Review* 2: 82–108.

—— (1983) *War in the Nursery: Theories of the Child and Mother*. London: Virago.

Roberts, H. (1981) *Doing Feminist Research*. London: Routledge & Kegan Paul.

Robson, P. W. and Watchman, P. (1981) The Homeless Persons' Obstacle Race. *Journal of Social Welfare Law* 3: Part 1: 1–15, Part 2: 65–82.

Rogers, B. (1983) *52%: Getting Women's Power into Politics*. London: The Women's Press.

Room, G. (1979) *The Sociology of Welfare: Social Policy, Stratification and Political Order*. Oxford: Blackwell.

Rose, H. (1978) In Practice Supported, in Theory Denied: An Account of an Invisible Social Movement. *International Journal of Urban and Regional Research* 2(3): 521–38.

—— (1981) Rereading Titmuss: The Sexual Division of Welfare. *Journal of Social Policy* 10(4): 477–502.

Rutter, M. (1972/1981) *Maternal Deprivation Reassessed*. Harmondsworth: Penguin.

Sarah, E., Scott, M., and Spender, D. (1980) The Education of Feminists: The case for Single Sex Schools. In D. Spender and E. Sarah (eds) *Learning to Lose*. London: Women's Press.

Sargent, L. (1981) *Women and Revolution*. London: Pluto Press.

Savage, W. (1981) Abortion, Sterilization and Contraception. In *Medicine in Society* 7(1): 6–12.

—— (1983–84) Have We Gone Too Far? Technology versus Nature in the Management of Pregnancy. In *Medicine in Society* 9(4): 15–16, 40.

—— (1985) *Trust the Midwives*. Observer, 7 July.

Scott, H. (1984) *Working your Way to the Bottom: The Feminisation of Poverty*. London: Pandora Press.

Scully, D. and Bart, P. (1978) A Funny Thing Happened on the Way to the Orifice: Women in Gynecology Textbooks. In *The Cultural Crisis of Modern Medicine*. New York, London: Monthly Review Press, 212–28.

Secondary Schools Examinations Council (1943) *Curriculum and Examinations in Secondary Schools*. London: HMSO.

Sharpe, S. (1976) *Just Like A Girl: How Girls Learn to be Women*. Harmondsworth: Penguin.

—— (1984) *Double Identity: The Lives of Working Mothers*. Harmondsworth: Penguin.

Shaw, J. (1980) Education and the Individual. In R. Deem (ed.) *Schooling for Women's Work*. London: Routledge & Kegan Paul.

Siltanen, J. and Stanworth, M. (eds) (1984) *Women and the Public Sphere: A Critique of Sociology and Politics*. London: Hutchinson.

Simms, M. (1981) Abortion: The Myth of the Golden Age. In B. Hutter and G. Williams (eds) *Controlling Women: The Normal and the Deviant*. London: Croom Helm, 168–84.

Smart, C. (1984) *The Ties that Bind: Law, Marriage and the Reproduction of Patriarchal Relations*. London: Routledge and Kegan Paul.

Snell, M. (1979) The Equal Pay and Sex Discrimination Acts: Their Impact in the Workplace. *Feminist Review* 1:37–58.

Snell, M. W., Glucklich, P., and Powall, M. (1981) *Equal Pay and Oppor-*

tunities: A Study of the Implementation and Effects of the Equal Pay and Sex Discrimination Acts in 26 Organizations. London: Department of Employment, Research Paper no. 20.

Social Security Advisory Committee (1985) *Fourth Report of the Social Security Advisory Committee*. London: HMSO.

Spender, D. (ed.) (1981) *Men's Studies Modified: The Impact of Feminism on the Academic Disciplines*. Oxford: Pergamon.

Spender, D. (1982) *Invisible Women*. London: Writers and Readers Publishing Cooperative Society.

Spender, D. and Sarah, E. (1980) *Learning to Lose: Essays on Sexism and Education*. London: The Women's Press.

Spinks, J. (1982) Radical Midwives. In M. Rowe (ed.) *Spare Rib Reader 1982*. Harmondsworth: Penguin, 375–83.

Spring Rice, M. (1939/1981) *Working-class Wives: Their Health and Conditions*. London: Virago.

Stacey, M. (1981) The Division of Labour Revisited or Overcoming the Two Adams. In P. Abrams, R. Deem, J. Finch, and P. Rock (eds) *Practice and Progress: British Sociology 1950–1980*. London: George Allen & Unwin.

Stacey, M. and Price, M. (1981) *Women, Power and Politics*. London: Tavistock.

Stanworth, M. (1981/1983) *Gender and Schooling: A Study of Sexual Divisions in the Classroom*. London: Hutchinson.

Supplementary Benefits Commission (1976) *Living Together as Husband and Wife*. London: HMSO.

Tawney, R. H. (1952/1964) Epilogue to *Equality*. London: George Allen & Unwin.

Taylor-Gooby, P. and Dale, J. (1981) *Social Theory and Social Welfare*. London: Edward Arnold.

Thane, P. (1978) Women and the Poor Law in Victorian and Edwardian England. *History Workshop Journal* 6: 29–51.

Titmuss, R. M. (1938) *Poverty and Population*. London: Macmillan.

—— (1943) *Birth, Poverty and Wealth: A Study of Infant Mortality*. London: Hamilton Medical Books.

—— (1950) *Problems of Social Policy*. London: HMSO.

—— (1958) *Essays on the Welfare State*. London: George Allen & Unwin.

—— (1968) *Commitment to Welfare*. London: George Allen & Unwin.

Titmuss, R. M. and Titmuss, K. (1942) *Parents Revolt: A Study of the Declining Birth-rate in Acquisitive Societies*. London: Secker & Warburg.

Tizard, J., Moss, P., and Perry, J. (1976) *All our Children: Pre-School Services in a Changing Society*. London: Temple Smith.

Townsend, P. (1957) *The Family Life of Old People: An Inquiry in East London*. London: Routledge & Kegan Paul.

—— (1979) *Poverty in the United Kingdom: A Study of Household Resources and Standards of Living*. Harmondsworth: Penguin.

Townsend, P. and Davidson, N. (eds) (1982) Inequalities in Health: The Black Report. Harmondsworth: Penguin.

Tunnard, J. (1976a) Marriage Breakdown and the Loss of the Owner-occupied Home. Roof March 1976: 40–43.

—— (1976b) No Father No Home? London: Child Poverty Action Group, Poverty Pamphlet no. 28.

Versluysen, M. C. (1980) Old Wives' Tales? Women Healers in English History. In C. Davies (ed.) Rewriting Nursing History. London: Croom Helm.

—— (1981) Lying-in Hospitals in Eighteenth-century London. In H. Roberts (ed.) Women, Health and Reproduction. London: Routledge & Kegan Paul, 18–49.

Walker, A. (ed.) (1982) Community Care: The Family, the State and Social Policy. Oxford: Blackwell.

Walker, A. (1983) A Caring Community. In H. Glennerster (ed.) The Future of the Welfare State: Remaking Social Policy. London: Heinemann, 157–72.

Webb, J. (1983) Housing for Battered Women? University of Nottingham: Dissertation (BA Hons), Social Administration.

Westwood, S. (1984) All Day, Every Day: Factory and Family in the Making of Women's Lives. London: Pluto Press.

Wickham, A. (1982) The State and Training Programmes for Women. In Open University Reader The Changing Experience of Women. Oxford: Martin Robertson.

Wilkin, M. (1982) Educational Opportunity and Achievement. In I. Reid and E. Wormald (eds) Sex Differences in Britain. London: Grant McIntyre.

Wilkins, N. (1983) The Women's Health Movement. In J. McEwen, C. Martini, and N. Wilkins (eds) Participation in Health. London: Croom Helm, 124–36.

Williams, J. (1983) Rejoinder to Joan Busfield. In M. Evans and C. Ungerson (eds) Sexual Divisions: Patterns and Processes. London: Tavistock.

Willis, P. (1983) Cultural Production and Theories of Reproduction. In L. Barton and S. Walker (eds) Race, Class and Education. London: Croom Helm.

Wilson, E. (1977) Women and the Welfare State. London: Tavistock.

—— (1980) Only Halfway to Paradise: Women in Postwar Britain, 1945–1968. London: Tavistock.

—— (1983) What is to be Done about Violence against Women? Harmondsworth: Penguin.

Wollstonecraft, M. (1792/1975) A Vindication of the Rights of Women. New York: Norton.

Wolmer, C. (1985) Homes may Close as Cuts in Benefit Hit the Elderly. *Observer*, 30 June.

Wolpe, A. (1974) The Official Ideology of Education for Girls. In M. Flude and J. Ahier (eds) *Educability, Schools and Ideology*. London: Croom Helm.

Wright, F. (1983) Single Carers: Employment, Housework and Caring. In J. Finch and D. Groves (eds) *A Labour of Love*. London: Routledge & Kegan Paul, 89–105.

Wynn, M. and Wynn, A. (1979) *Prevention of Handicap and the Health of Women*. London: Routledge & Kegan Paul.

Zaretsky, E. (1976) *Capitalism, the Family and Personal Life*. London: Pluto Press.

—— (1982) The Place of the Family in the Origins of the Welfare State. In B. Thorne and M. Yalom (eds) *Rethinking the Family: Some Feminist Questions*. New York: Longman.

Statistical sources

Central Statistical Office *Social Trends 1 1970*. London: HMSO.

Central Statistical Office *Social Trends 15 1985*. London: HMSO.

Department of Education and Science (1983) *Digest of Statistics*, England edition. London: HMSO.

Department of Employment (1982) *The Family Expenditure Survey*. London: HMSO.

Department of Health and Social Security *Health and Personal Social Service Statistics for England 1982*. London: HMSO.

Department of Health and Social Security *Social Security Statistics 1984*. London: HMSO.

Office of Population Censuses and Surveys (1984) *General Household Survey 1982*. London: HMSO.

Office of Population Censuses and Surveys (1985) *Abortion Statistics 1983*. London: HMSO.

University Grants Commission (1984) *University Statistics 1983–84*. Cheltenham: Universities' Statistical Record.

Name Index

O'Brien, M. 21, 23, 25, 26, 68, 168
O'Connor, J. 235
Oleson, V. 166
Oren, L. 26, 46
Osborn, A. F. 99
Owen, S. 212–13

Pahl, J. 154, 205
Pahl, R. E. 54
Parker, R. A. 45, 89, 92–3, 133, 198, 208, 220, 223
Parsons, T. 12
Pember Reeves 16, 46, 205
Pennell, I. 165, 195
Perkins, T. 49
Perry, J. 78–9, 80, 82
Petrie, P. 78–9, 80, 82
Pfeffer, N. 181
Phillipson, C. 204
Piachaud, D. 42, 96
Pinkerton, G. 78–9, 80, 82
Pocock, K. 165
Pollert, A. 56, 58, 59, 128–29
Popay, J. 204
Powall, M. 50
Porter, M. 56
Price, M. 9, 24, 25, 31–2
Price, S. 8, 18

Rakusen, J. 180
Randall, V. 25, 238
Rathbone, E. 6, 16, 17–18, 45, 46, 47, 219–20
Reid, I. 192–93, 194
Rendel, M. 131
Richards, M. 172, 224–25
Ridley, A. 105
Riley, D. 73, 79, 80
Roberts, C. 43, 48–50, 51, 56, 81, 94, 97, 99, 199
Roberts, H. 3
Robson, P. W. 157, 158–61
Rogers, B. 141
Room, G. 2
Rose, H. 10, 13, 153
Rossiter, C. 204
Rutter, M. 76–8

Sarah, E. 121–22, 127, 131
Sargent, L. 13
Savage, W. 174, 176, 188
Scott, H. 203
Scott, M. 131

Scully, D. 195
Sharpe, S. 56, 57, 60, 128, 130
Shaw, J. 124
Siltanen, J. 25
Simms, M. 175–76
Smart, C. 20
Snell, M. 32, 50
Spender, D. 3, 121–22, 124, 127, 131
Spinks, J. 167, 188
Spring Rice, M. 16, 17, 168
Stacey, M. 9, 24, 25, 30, 31–2, 53, 70–1, 182
Stanworth, M. 25, 125–27

Tawney, R. H. 10
Taylor-Gooby, P. 2, 7
Thane, P. 201
Thynne, P. 144
Tinker, A. 136, 145, 152
Titmuss, R. M. 9–13, 28, 86
Tizard, J. 80
Townsend, P. 2, 37–8, 186, 203, 204, 205, 216
Tunnard, J. 144–45

Versluysen, M. C. 182, 183, 186–87, 188

Walker, A. 88–9, 90
Walker, V. 155
Watchman, P. 157, 158–61
Watson, S. 134, 139, 143, 144, 145, 151–52
Webb, A. 45, 220
Westwood, S. 43–4, 53–4, 56, 58, 59
Wickham, A. 117
Wilkin, M. 114
Wilkins, N. 167
Williams, J. 195
Willis, P. 113
Wilson, E. 12, 22, 25, 34, 37, 53, 198, 235
Wilson, L. 223
Wollstonecraft, M. 104
Wolmer, C. 219
Wolpe, A. 108
Woodward, D. 118
Woollett, 181
Wright, F. 94
Wynn, A. 169, 170, 192
Wynn, M. 169, 170, 192

Zaretsky, E. 7, 26

Subject Index